Oh My Goddess!

ああっ女神さまっ

32

STORY AND ART BY
Kosuke Fujishima

TRANSLATION BY
Christopher Lewis AND Dana Lewis

LETTERING AND TOUCH-UP BY
Susie Lee AND Betty Dong
WITH Tom2K

W9-BJB-633

DARK HORSE MANGA™

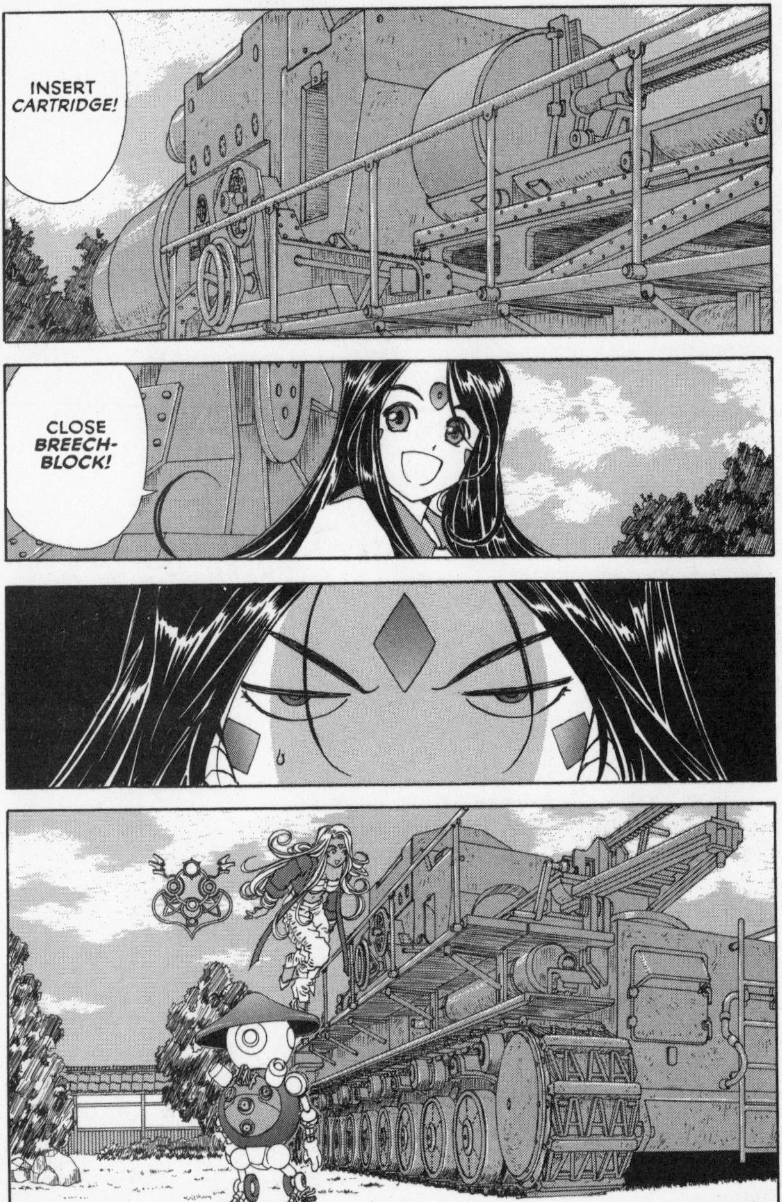
INSERT CARTRIDGE!
CLOSE BREECH-BLOCK!

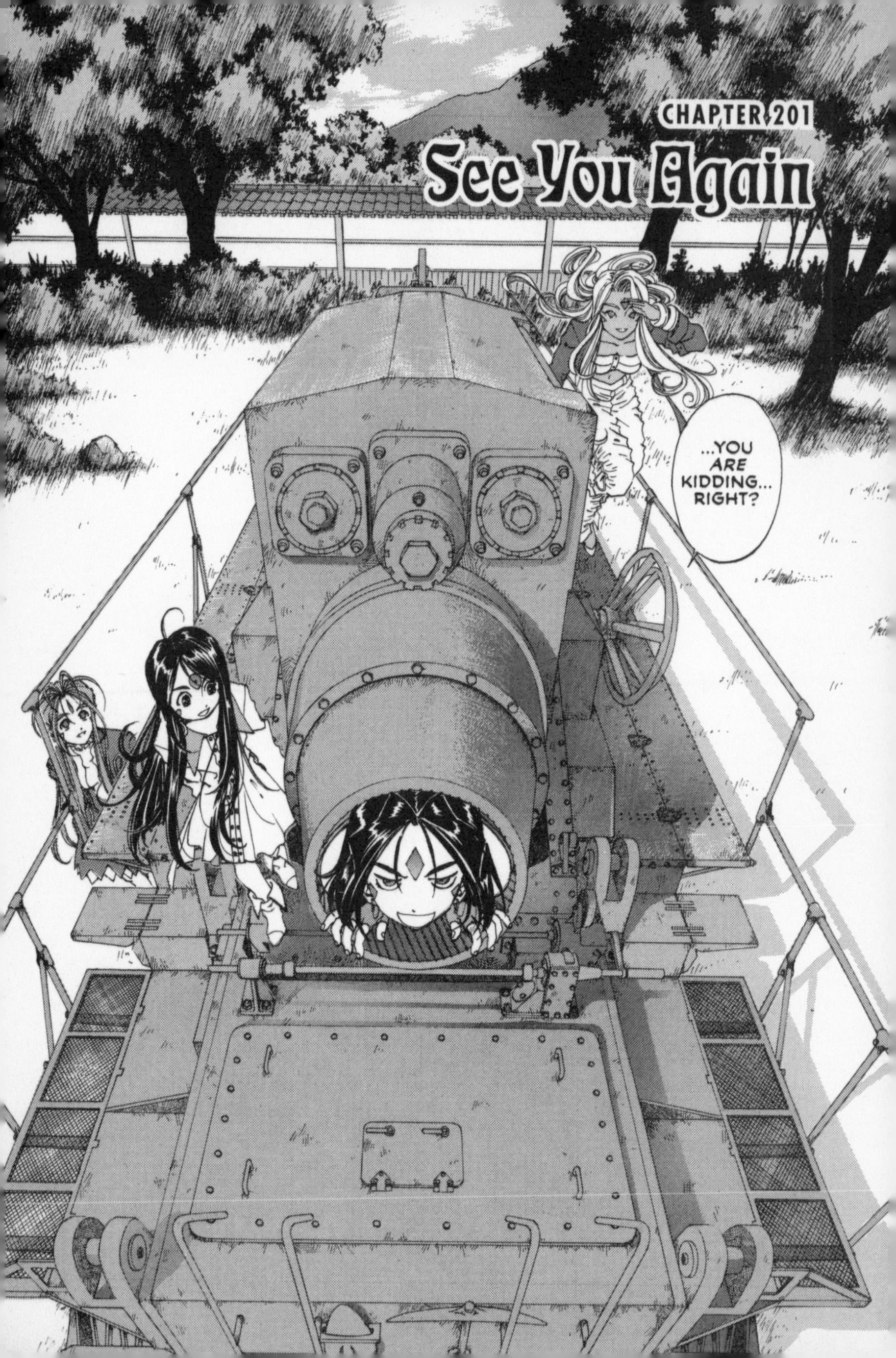
CHAPTER 201
See You Again
...YOU ARE KIDDING... RIGHT?

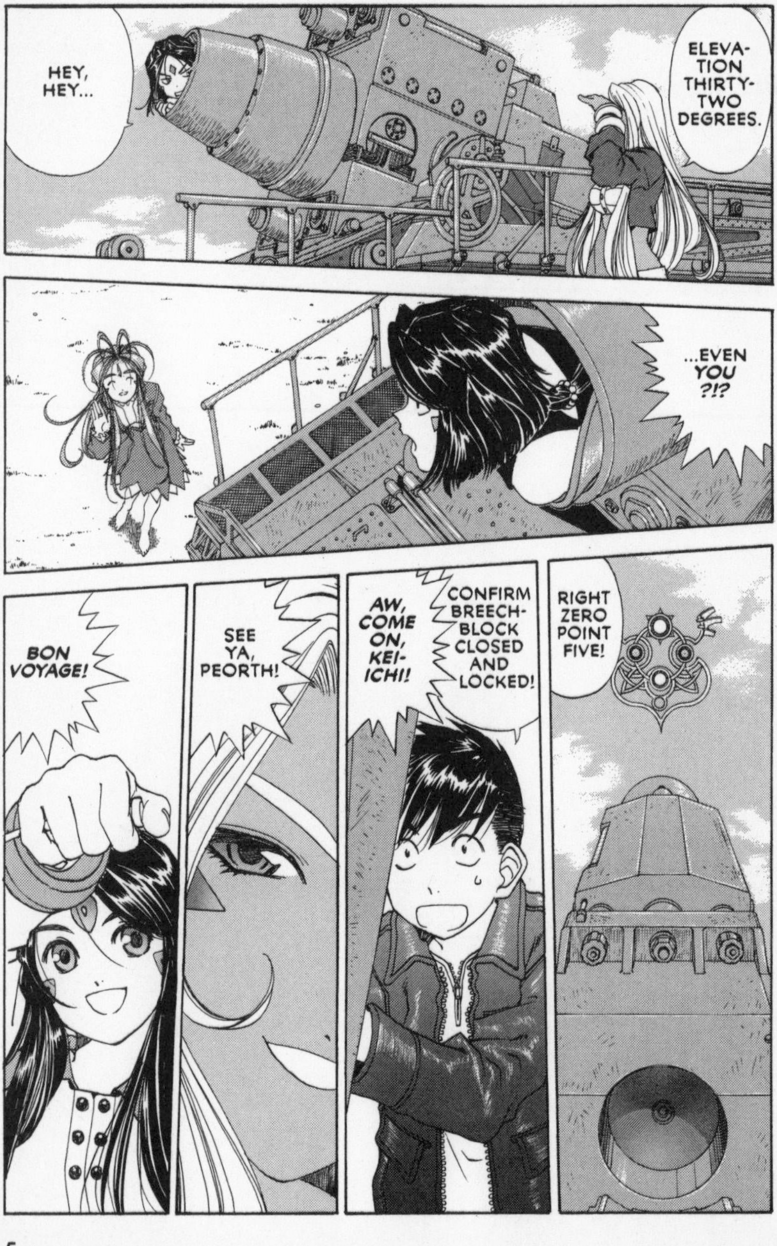
ELEVATION THIRTY-TWO DEGREES.
HEY, HEY...
...EVEN YOU?!?
RIGHT ZERO POINT FIVE!
CONFIRM BREECH-BLOCK CLOSED AND LOCKED!
AW, COME ON, KEI-ICHI!
SEE YA, PEORTH!
BON VOYAGE!

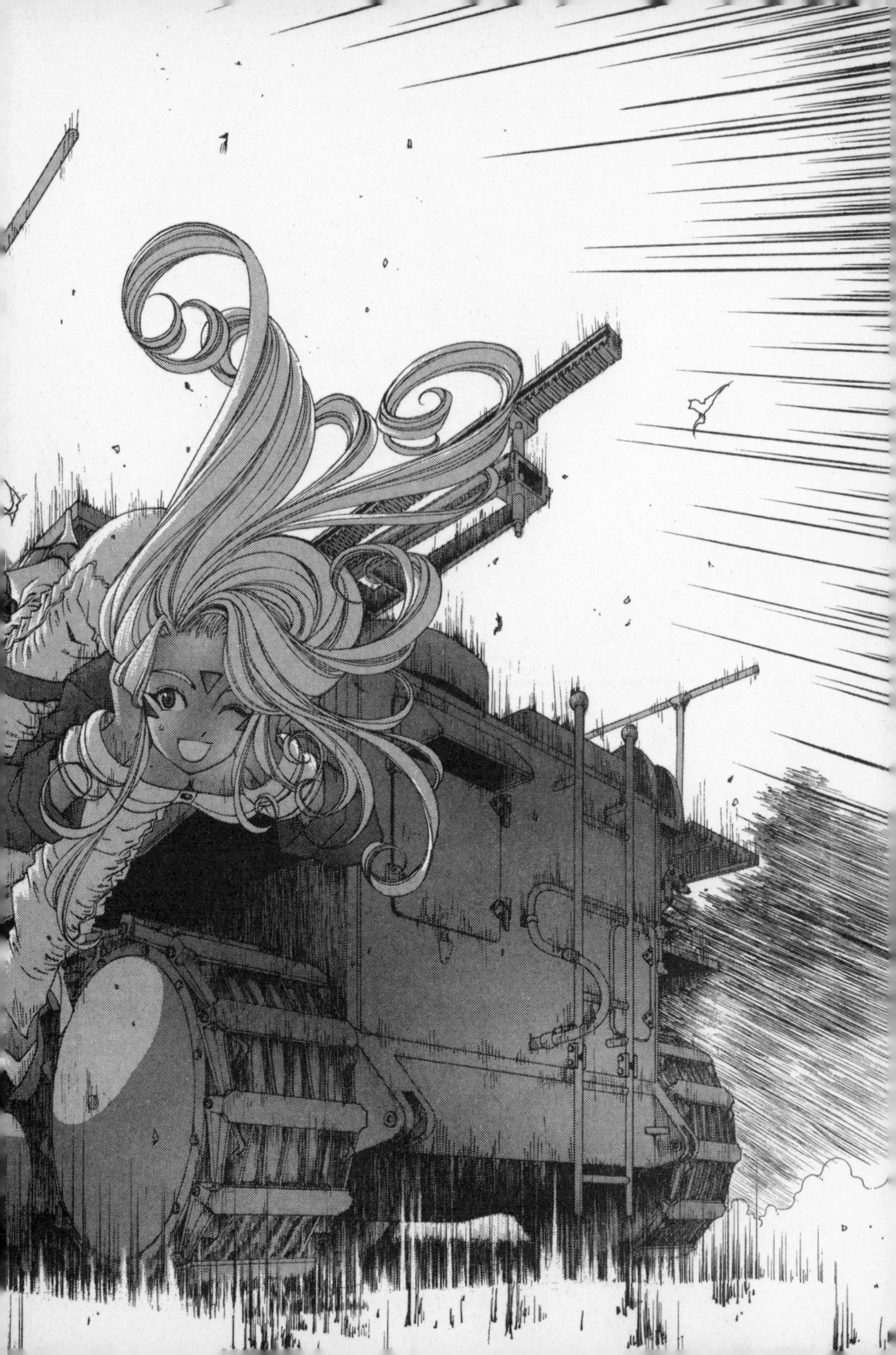

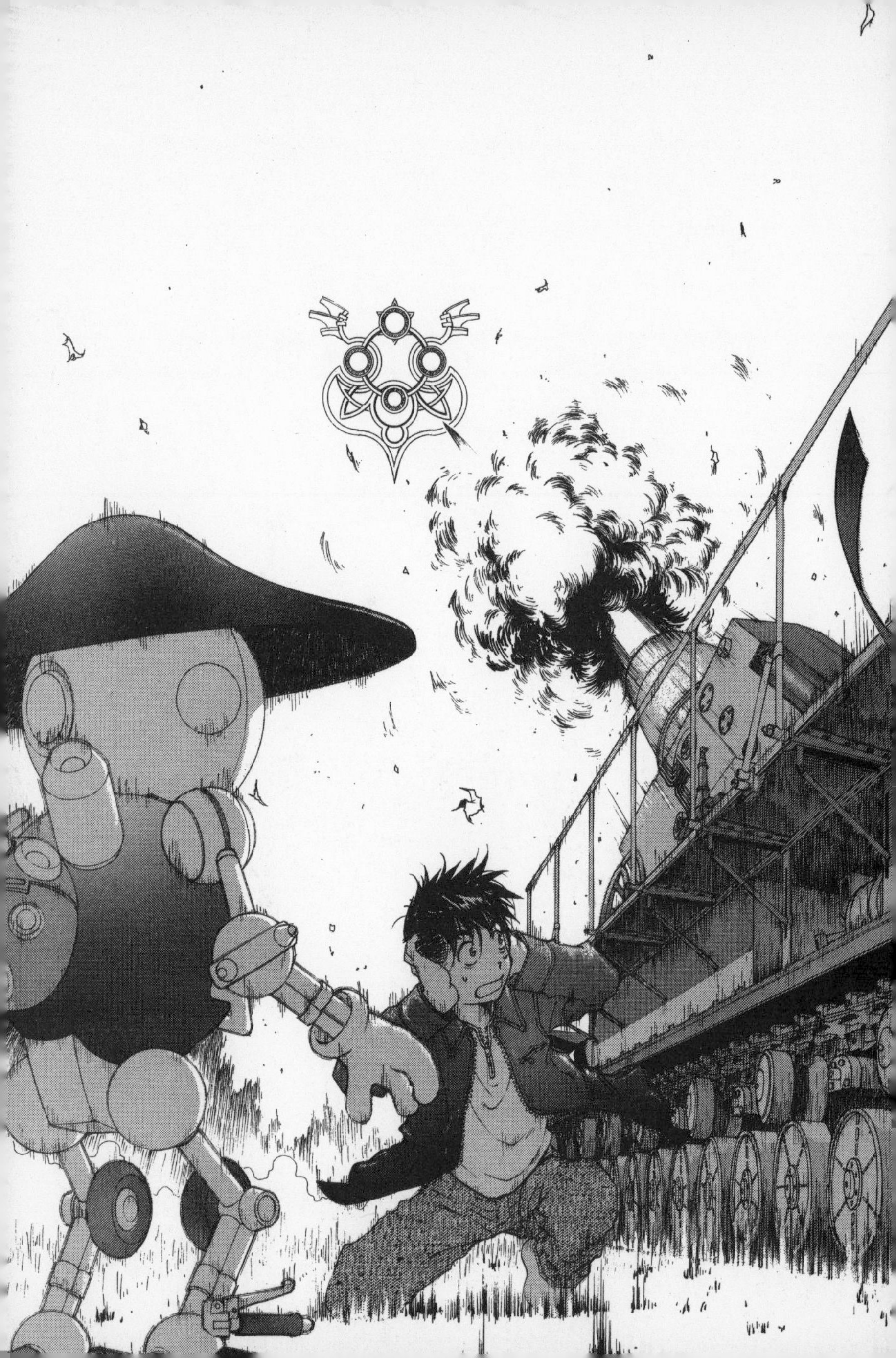

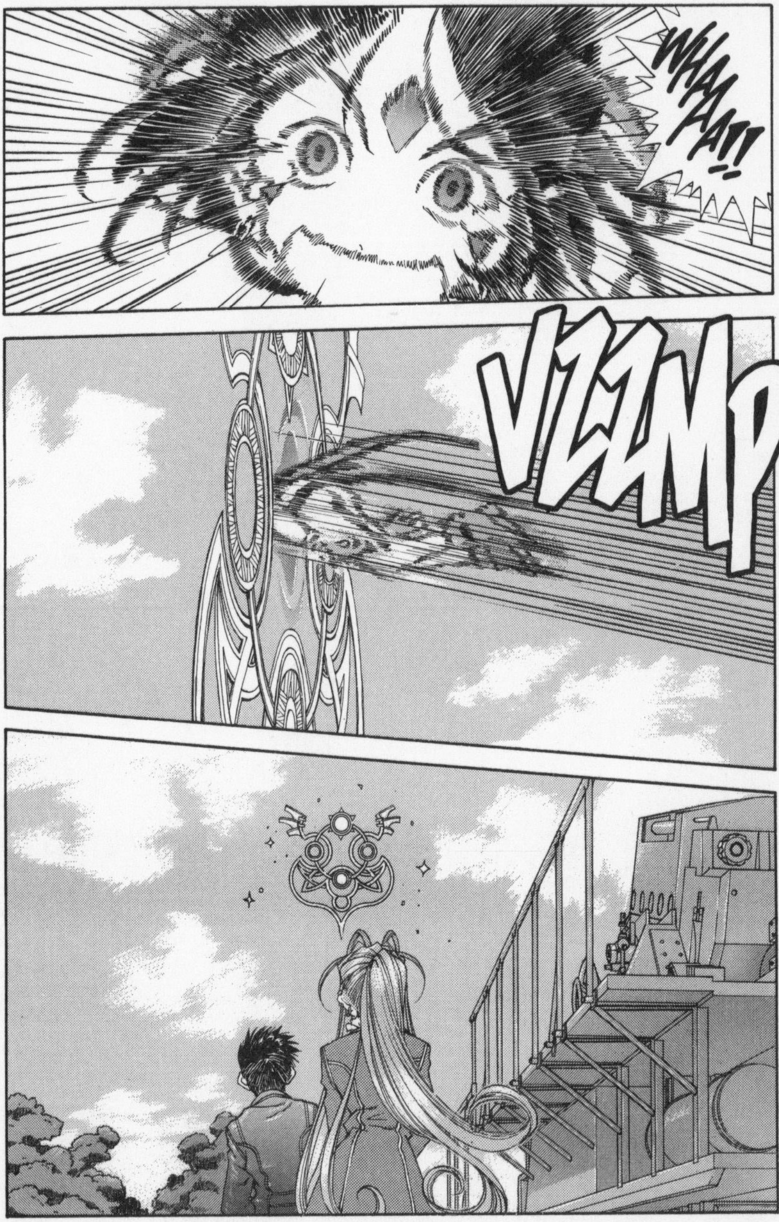
WHAAAA!!
VZZMP

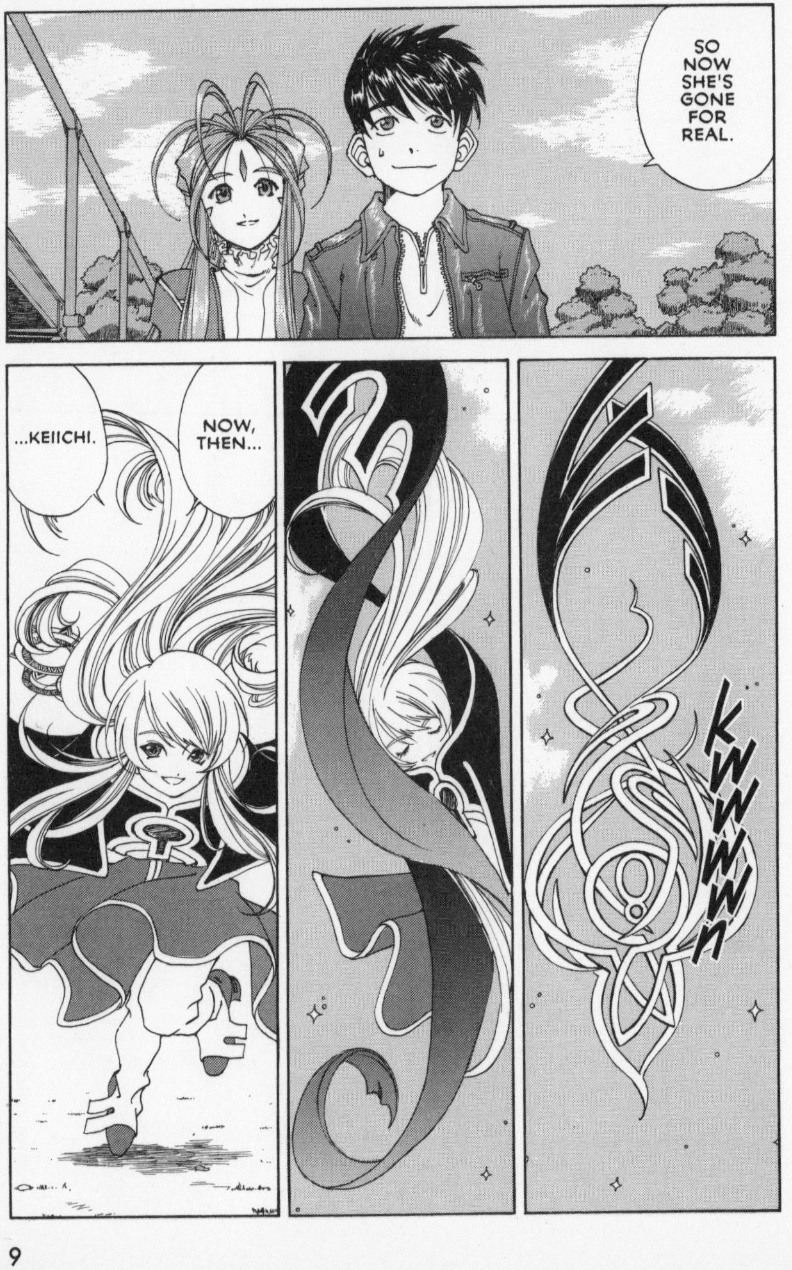
SO NOW SHE'S GONE FOR REAL.
KWWWWN
NOW, THEN...
...KEIICHI.

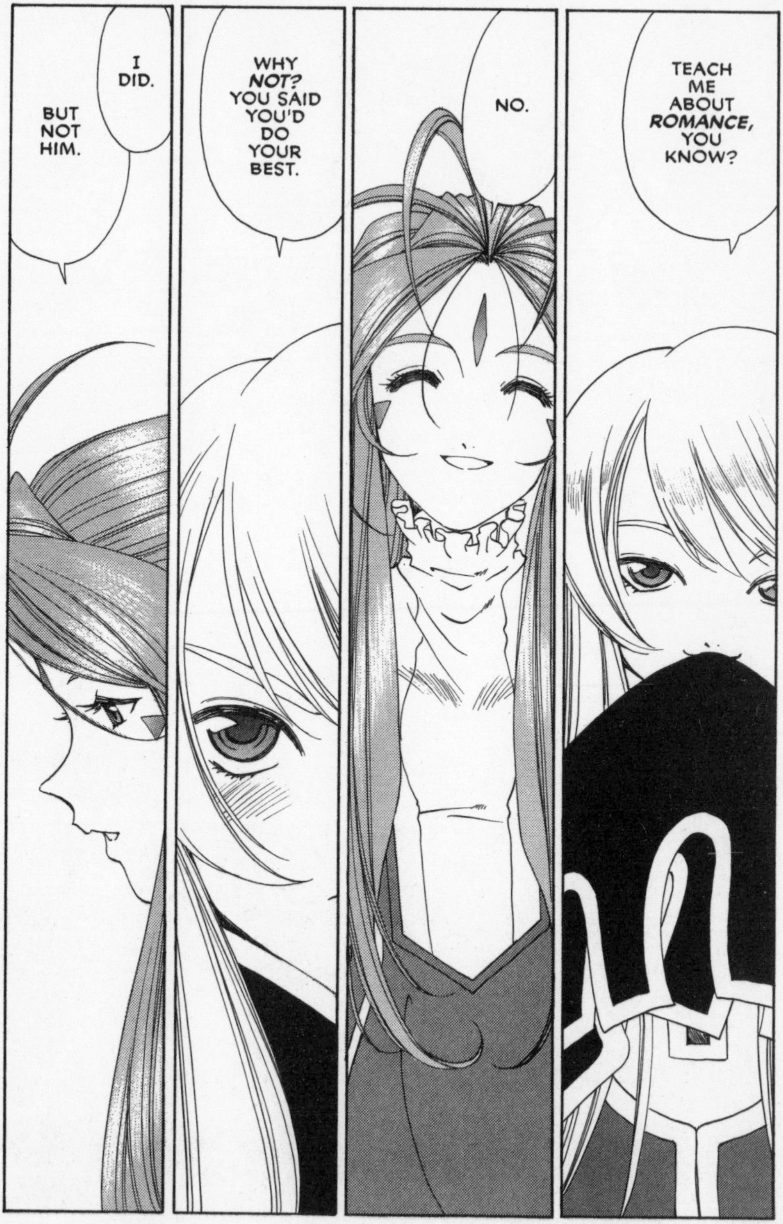
TEACH ME ABOUT ROMANCE, YOU KNOW?
NO.
WHY NOT? YOU SAID YOU'D DO YOUR BEST.
I DID.
BUT NOT HIM.

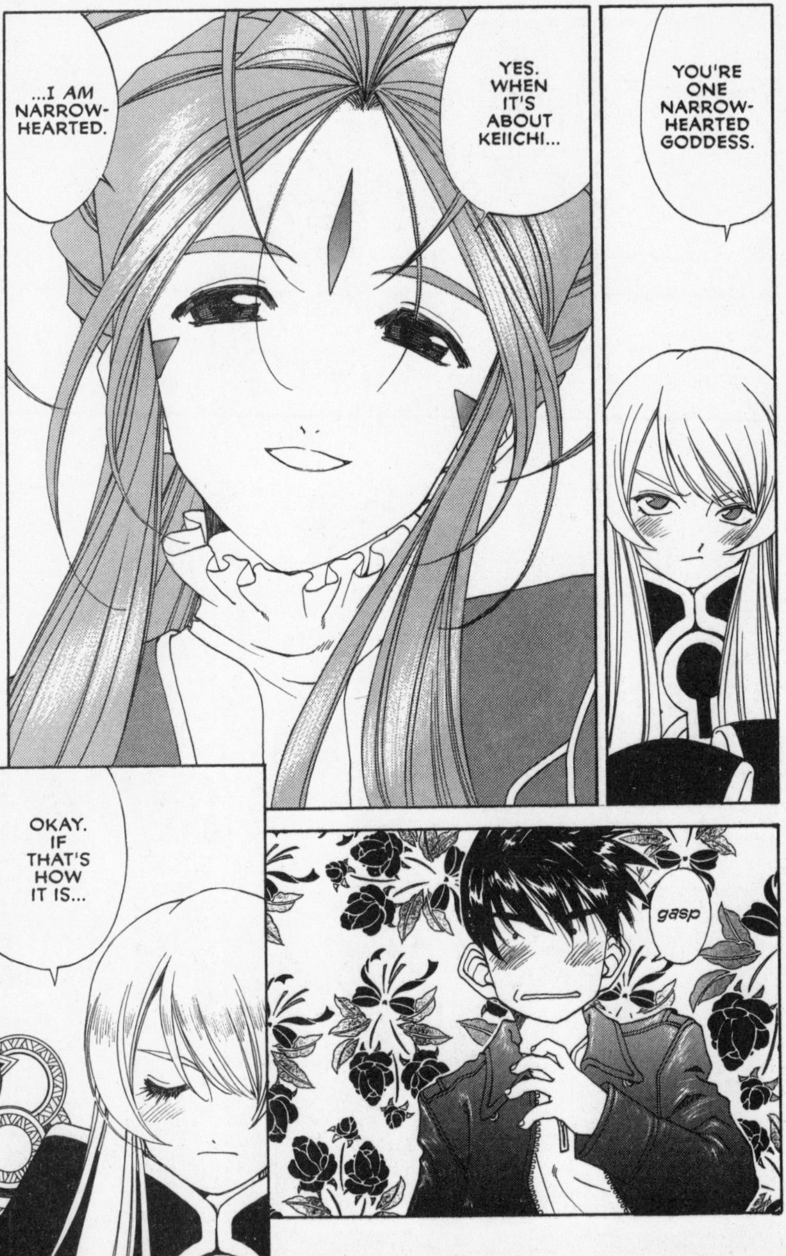
YOU'RE ONE NARROW-HEARTED GODDESS.
YES. WHEN IT'S ABOUT KEIICHI...
...I *AM* NARROW-HEARTED.
gasp
OKAY. IF THAT'S HOW IT IS...

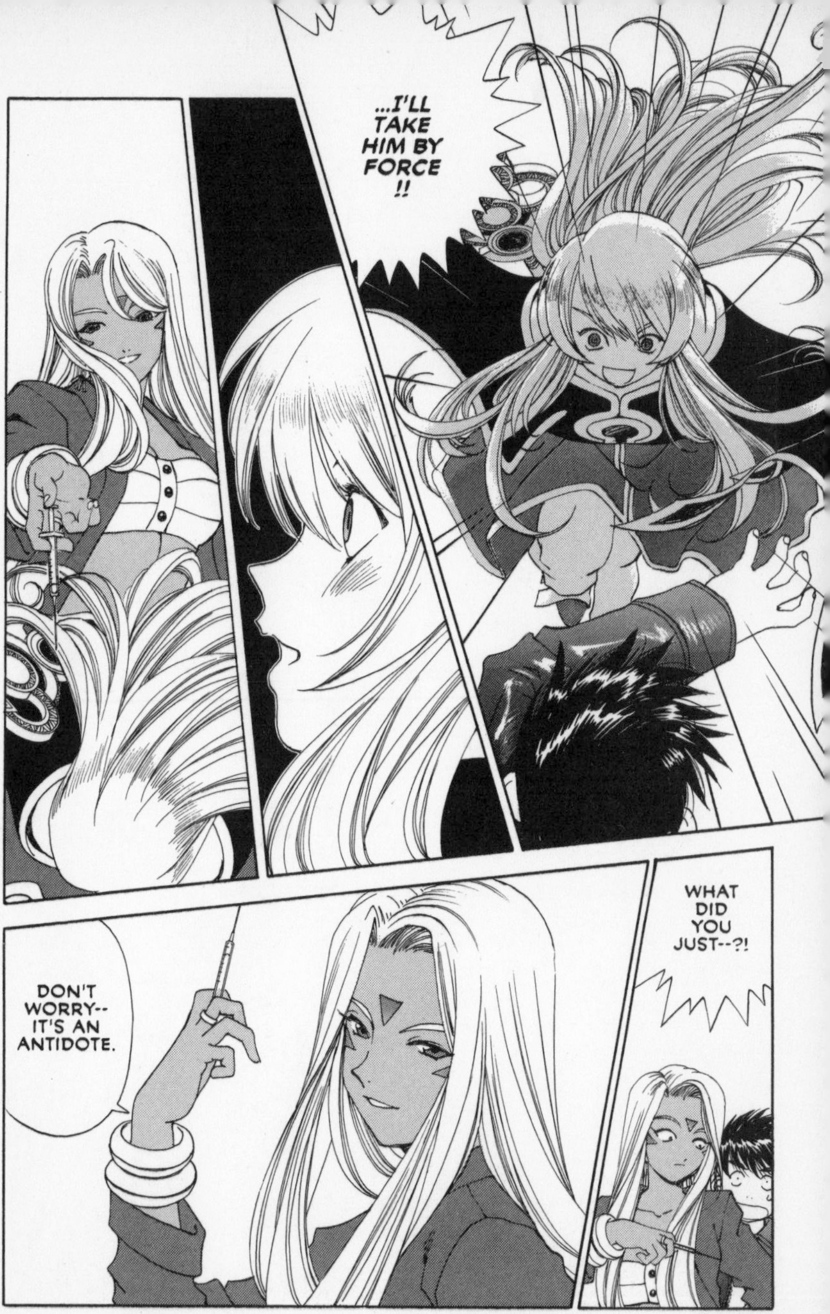

...I'LL TAKE HIM BY FORCE !!
WHAT DID YOU JUST--?!
DON'T WORRY-- IT'S AN ANTIDOTE.

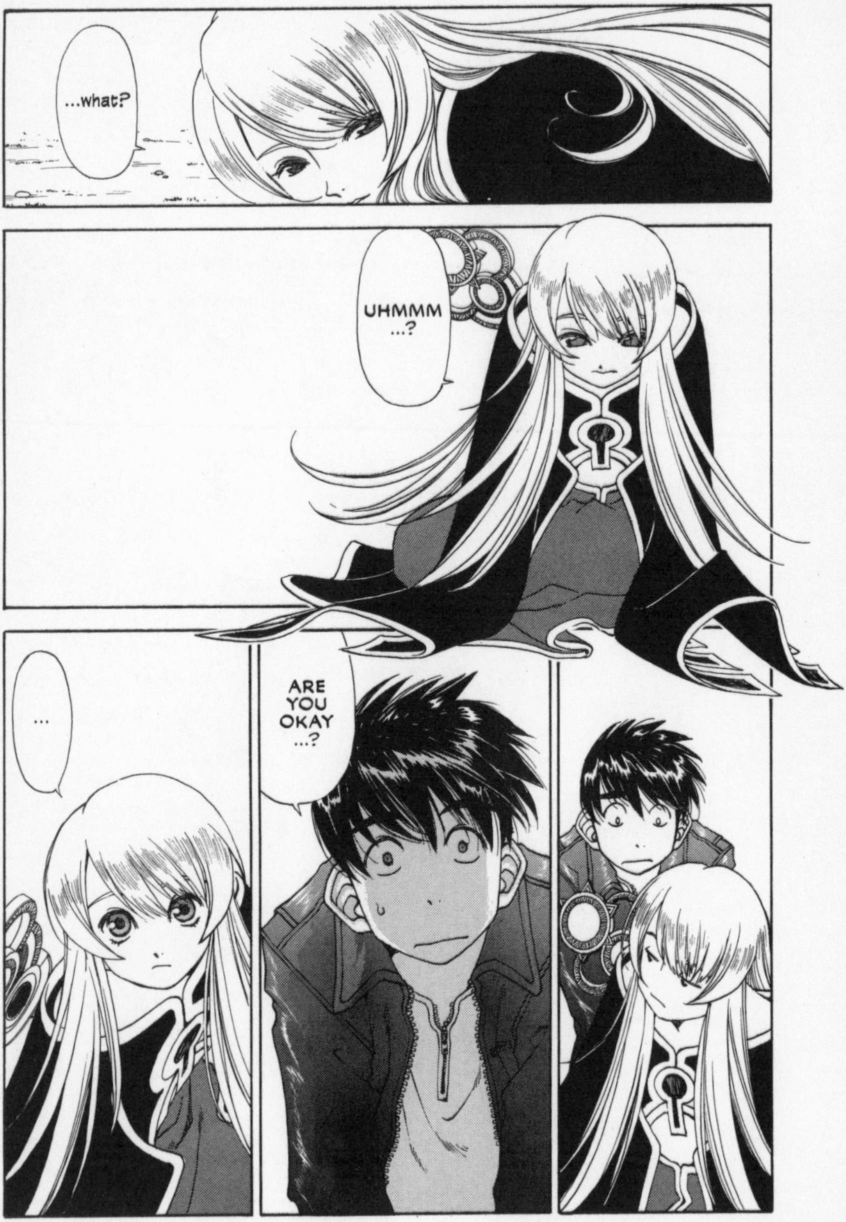
...what?
UHMMM ...?
ARE YOU OKAY ...?
...

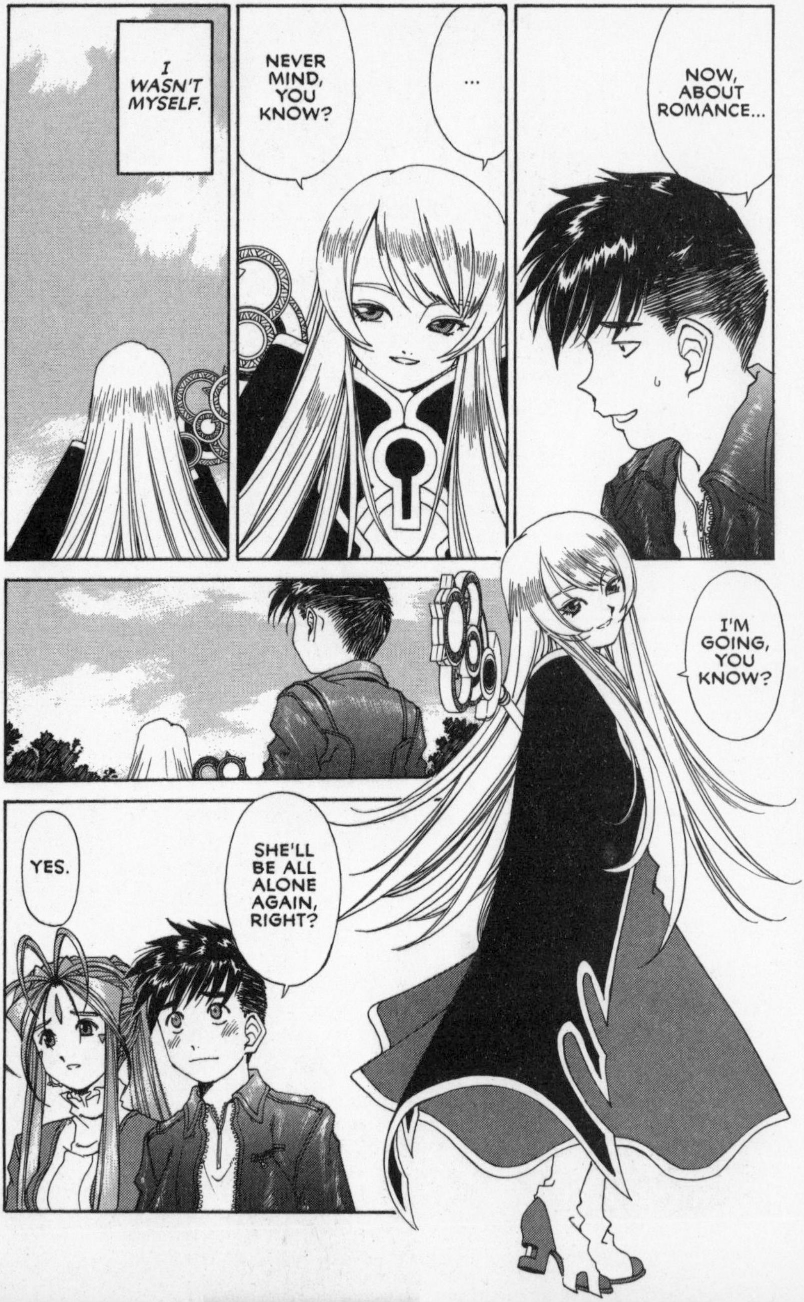
NOW, ABOUT ROMANCE...
...
NEVER MIND, YOU KNOW?
I WASN'T MYSELF.
I'M GOING, YOU KNOW?
SHE'LL BE ALL ALONE AGAIN, RIGHT?
YES.

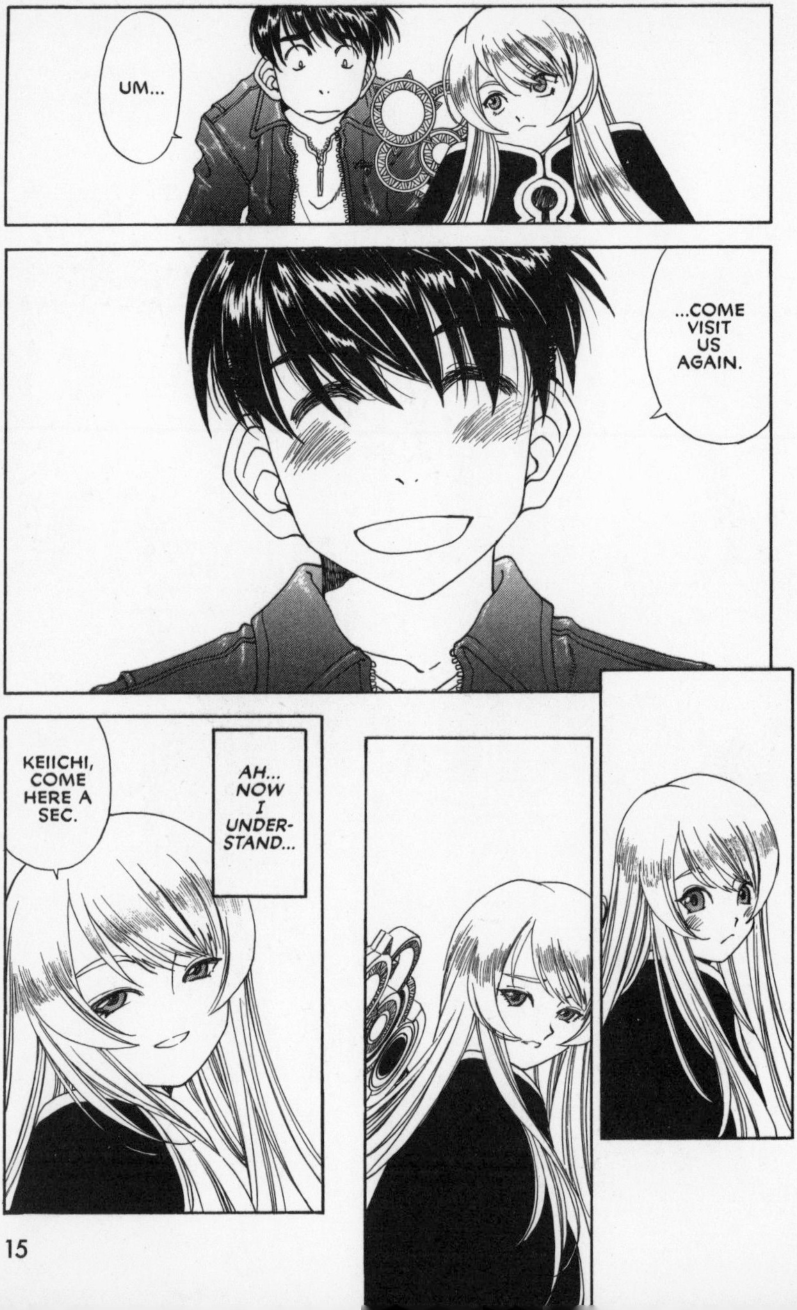
UM...
...COME VISIT US AGAIN.
AH... NOW I UNDER-STAND...
KEIICHI, COME HERE A SEC.

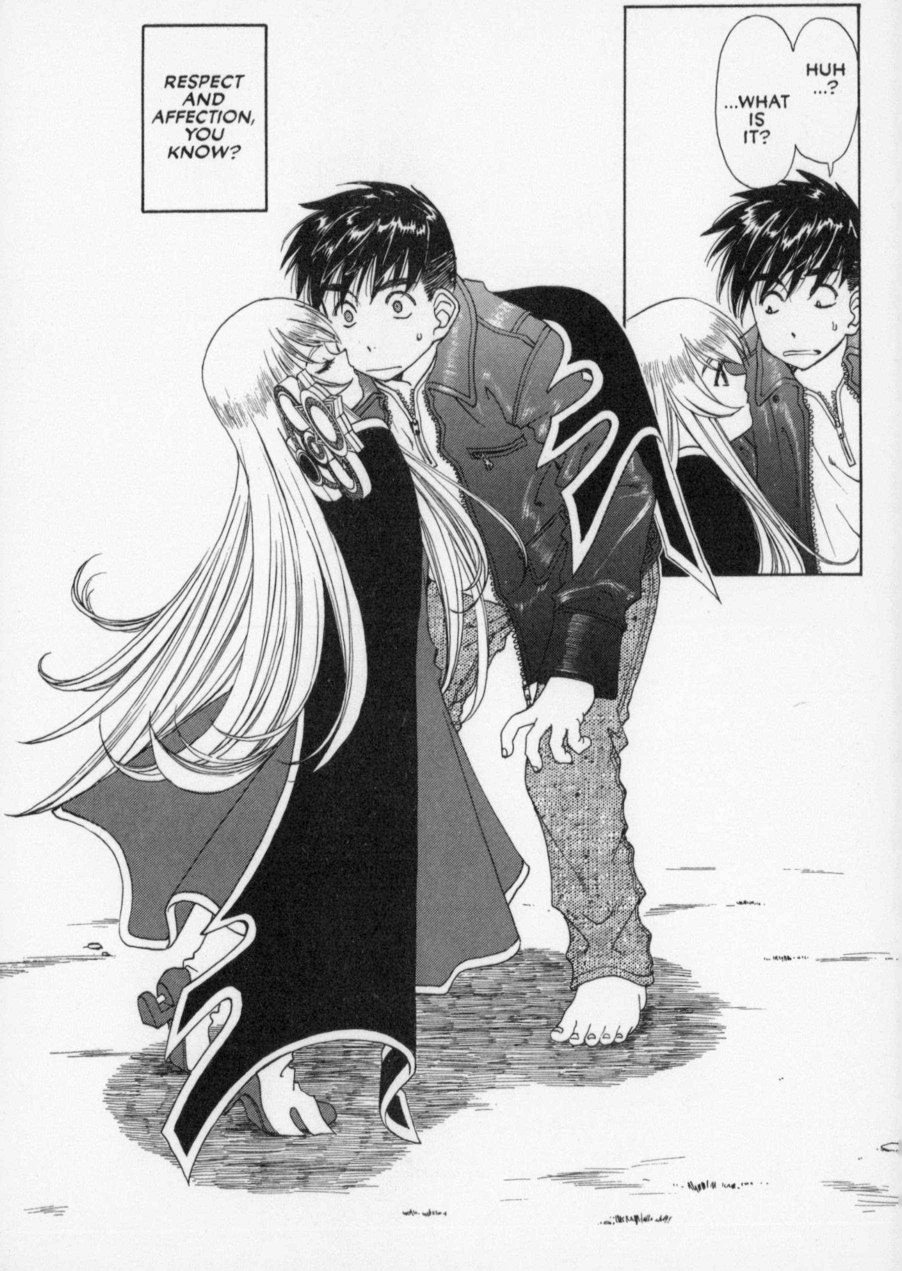
HUH ...?
...WHAT IS IT?
RESPECT AND AFFECTION, YOU KNOW?

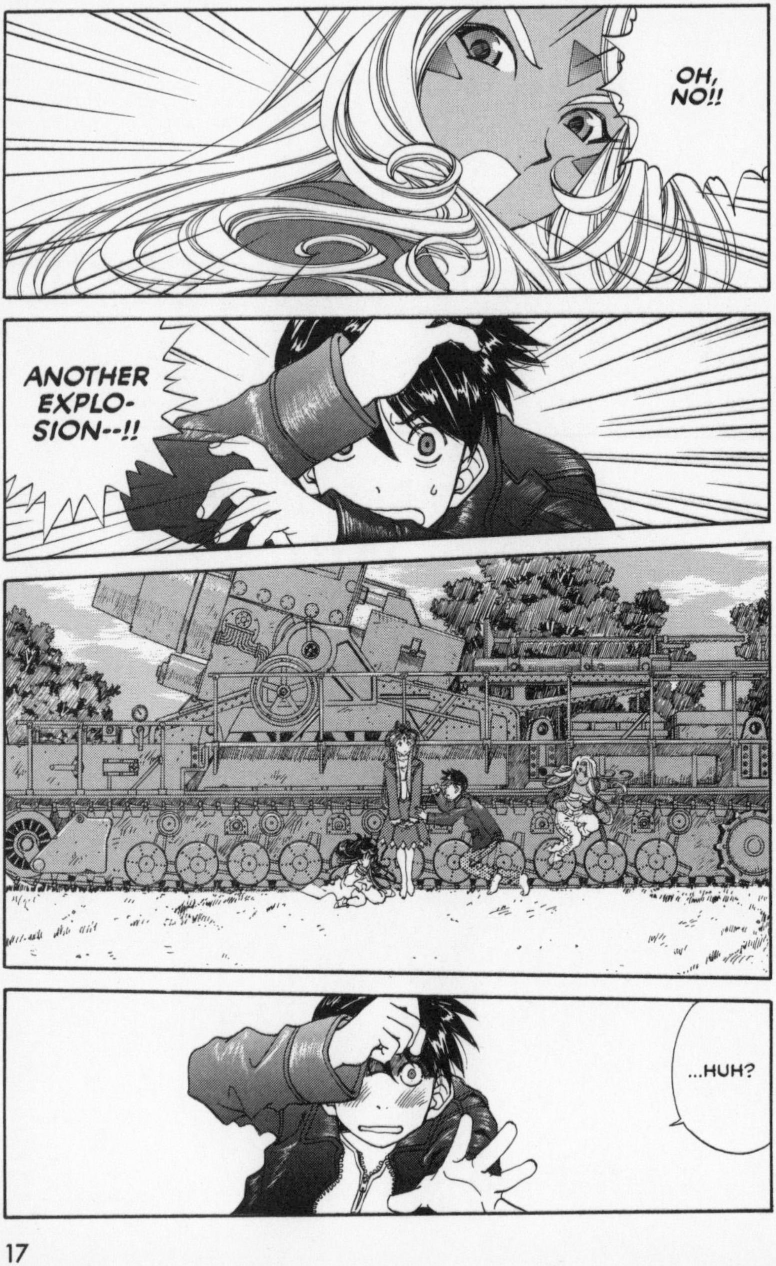
OH, NO!!
ANOTHER EXPLO-SION--!!
...HUH?

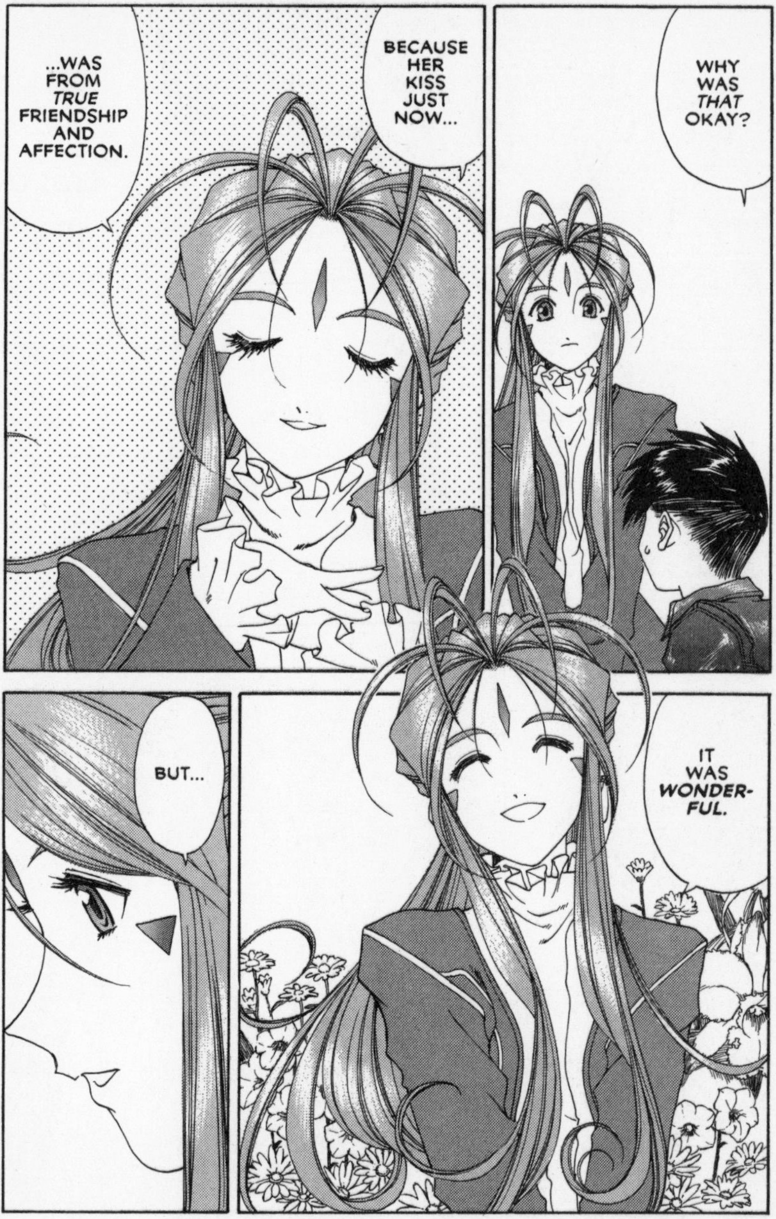
WHY WAS *THAT* OKAY?
BECAUSE HER KISS JUST NOW...
...WAS FROM *TRUE* FRIENDSHIP AND AFFECTION.
IT WAS ***WONDER-FUL.***
BUT...

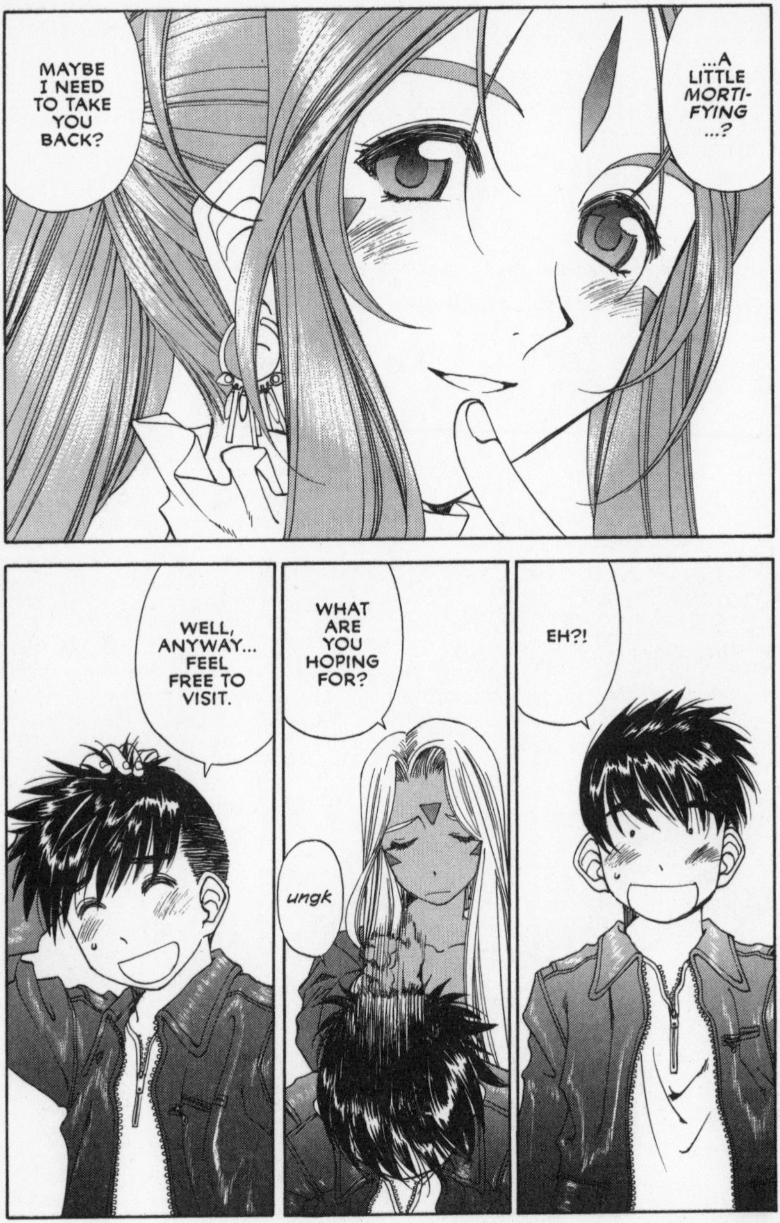
...A LITTLE MORTIFYING ...?
MAYBE I NEED TO TAKE YOU BACK?
EH?!
WHAT ARE YOU HOPING FOR?
ungk
WELL, ANYWAY... FEEL FREE TO VISIT.

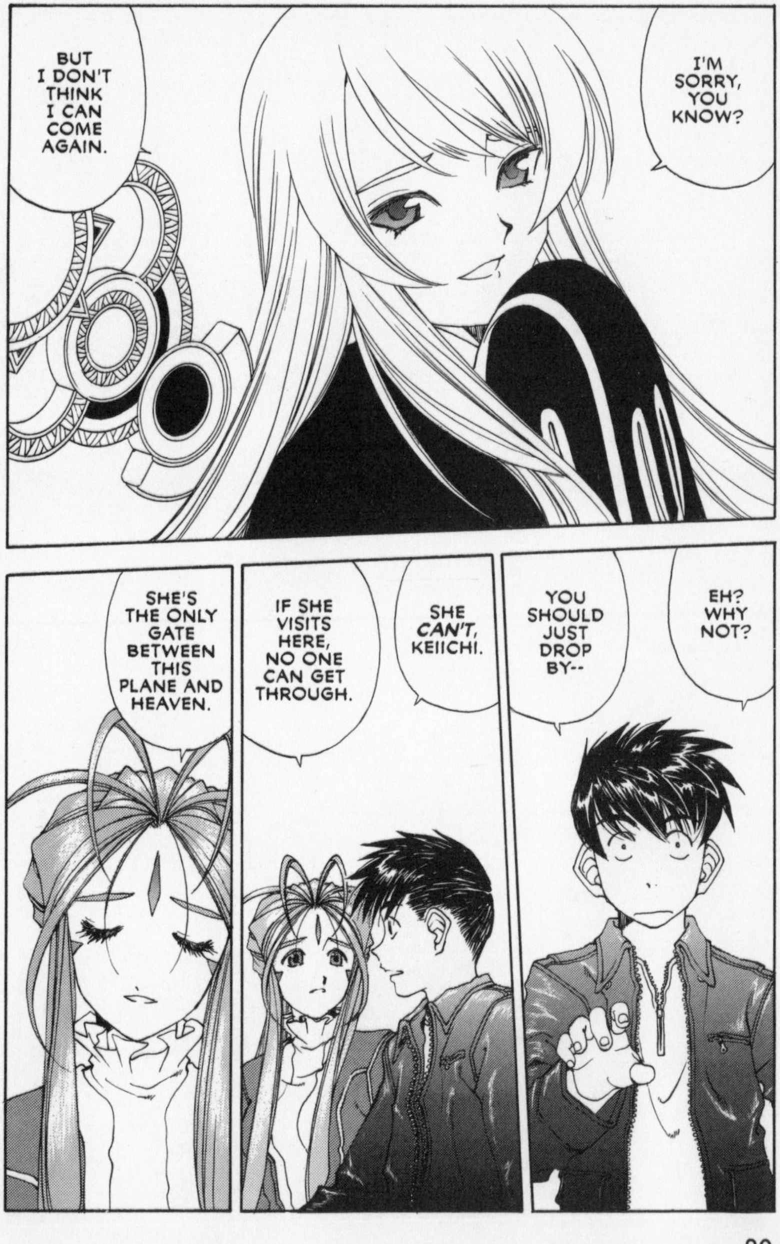
I'M SORRY, YOU KNOW?
BUT I DON'T THINK I CAN COME AGAIN.
EH? WHY NOT?
YOU SHOULD JUST DROP BY--
SHE *CAN'T*, KEIICHI.
IF SHE VISITS HERE, NO ONE CAN GET THROUGH.
SHE'S THE ONLY GATE BETWEEN THIS PLANE AND HEAVEN.

OH...

IN... OTHER...

...WORDS...

HUH?

COME ON. THERE'S *SUCH* A SIMPLE SOLUTION.

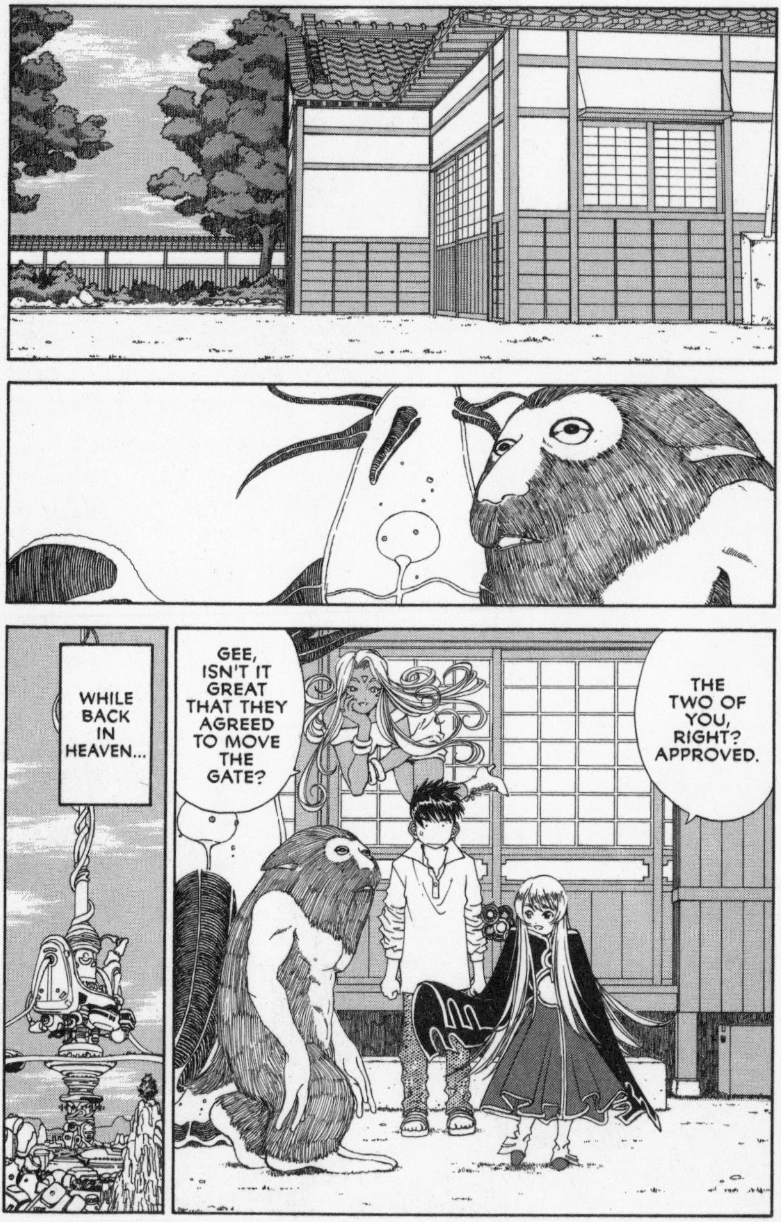
THE TWO OF YOU, RIGHT? APPROVED.
GEE, ISN'T IT GREAT THAT THEY AGREED TO MOVE THE GATE?
WHILE BACK IN HEAVEN...

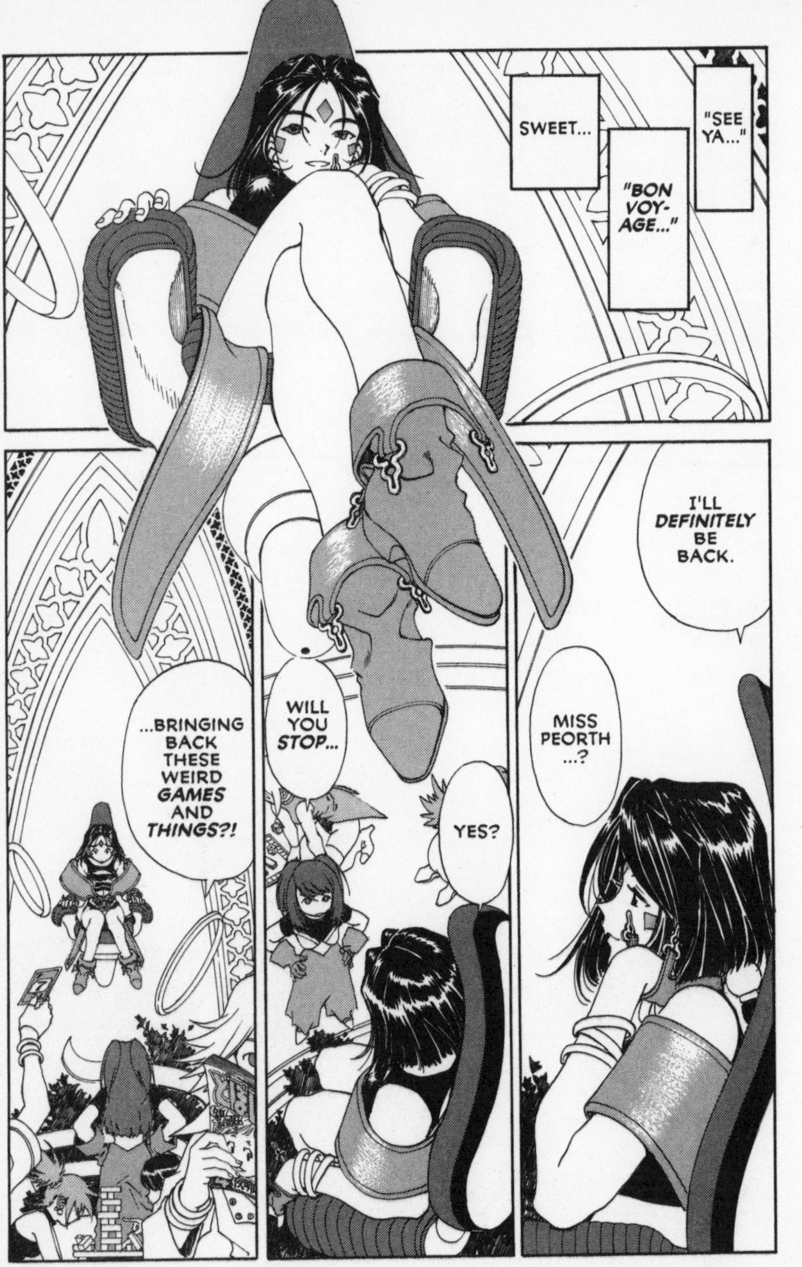
"SEE YA..."
"BON VOY-AGE..."
SWEET...
I'LL DEFINITELY BE BACK.
MISS PEORTH ...?
YES?
WILL YOU STOP...
...BRINGING BACK THESE WEIRD GAMES AND THINGS?!

OH MY GODDESS!
GATE

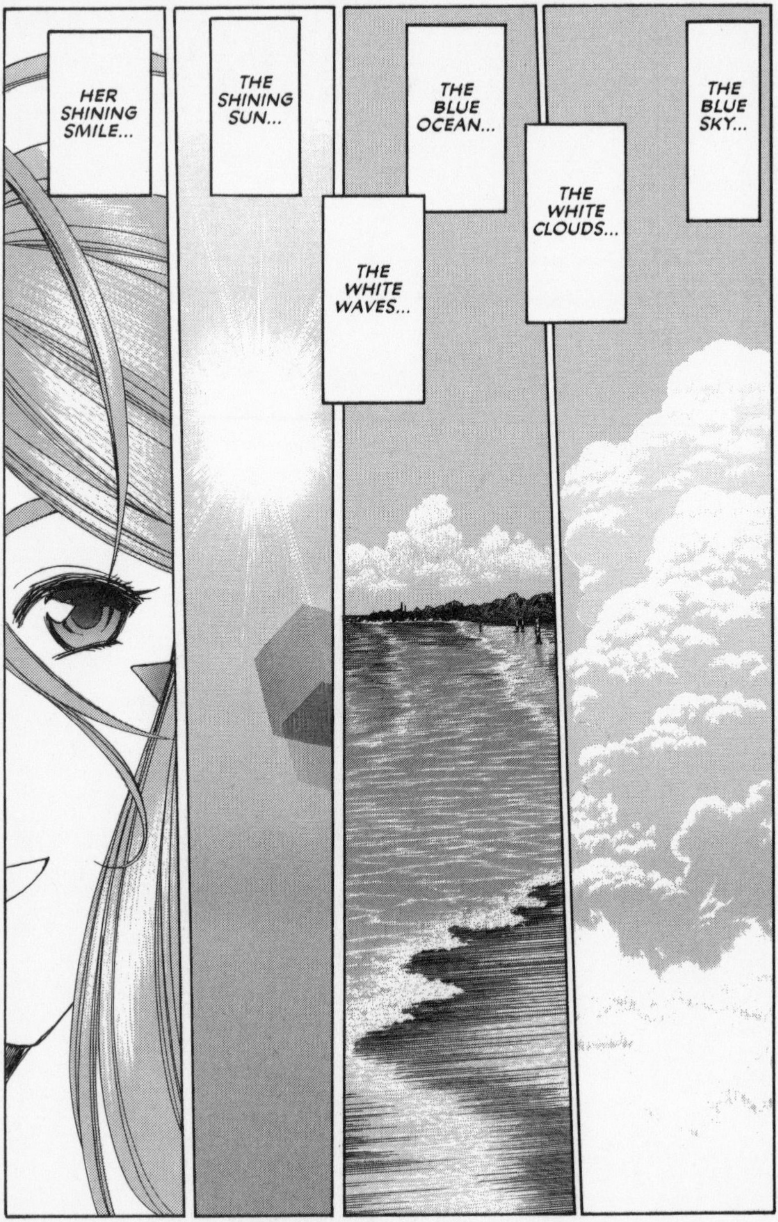

THE BLUE SKY...
THE WHITE CLOUDS...
THE BLUE OCEAN...
THE WHITE WAVES...
THE SHINING SUN...
HER SHINING SMILE...

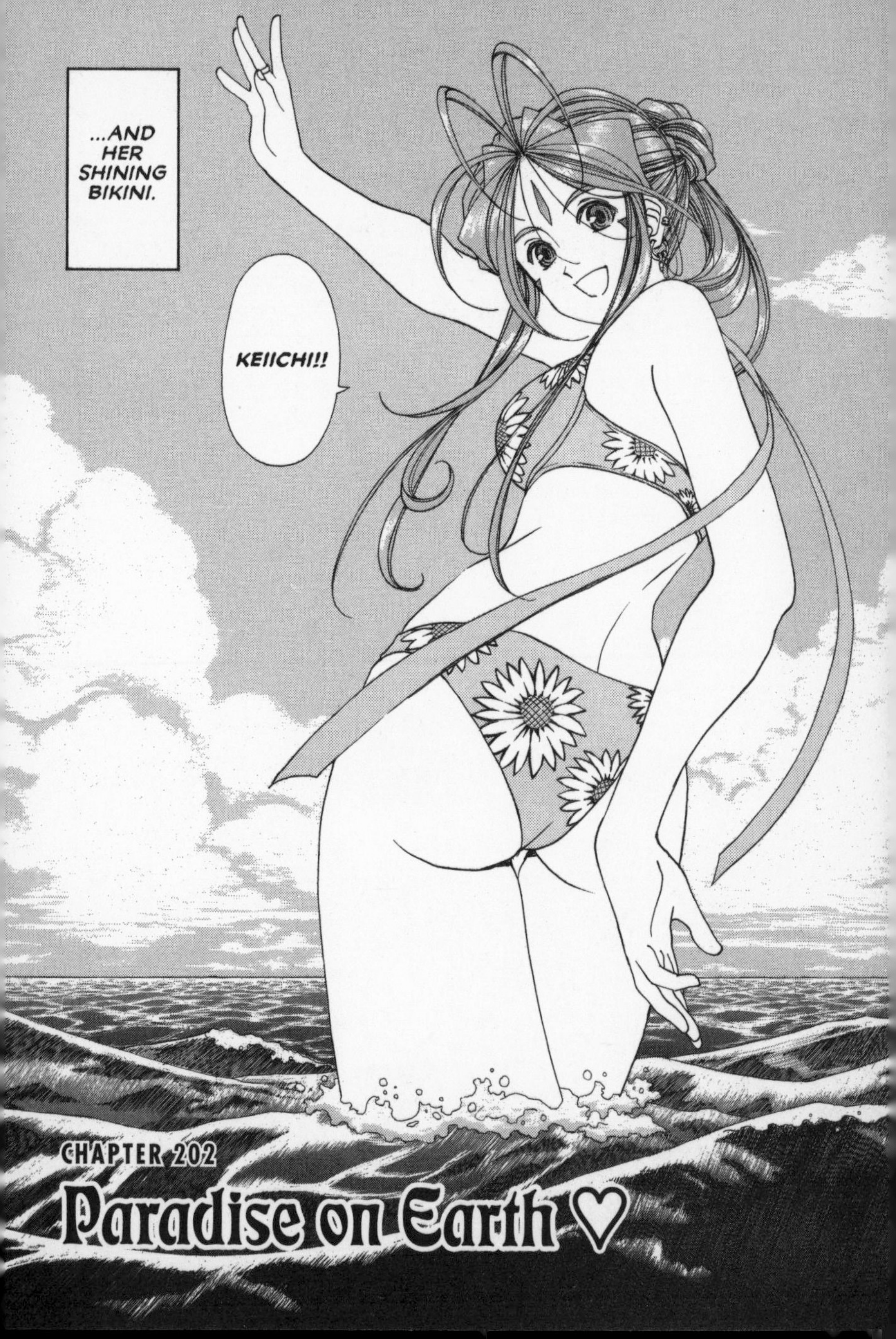
...AND HER SHINING BIKINI.
KEIICHI!!

CHAPTER 202

Paradise on Earth ♡

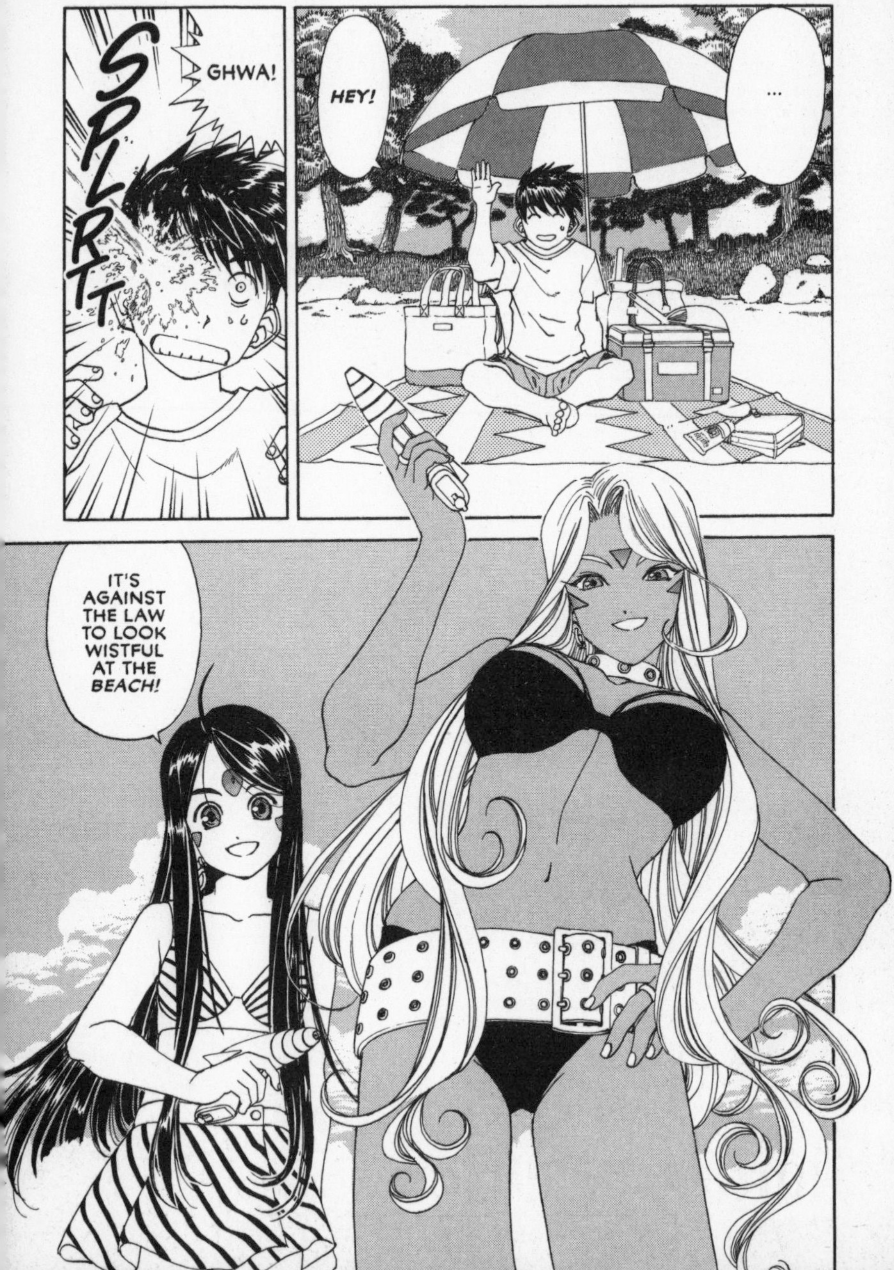
...
HEY!
SPLRTT
GHWA!
IT'S AGAINST THE LAW TO LOOK WISTFUL AT THE *BEACH!*

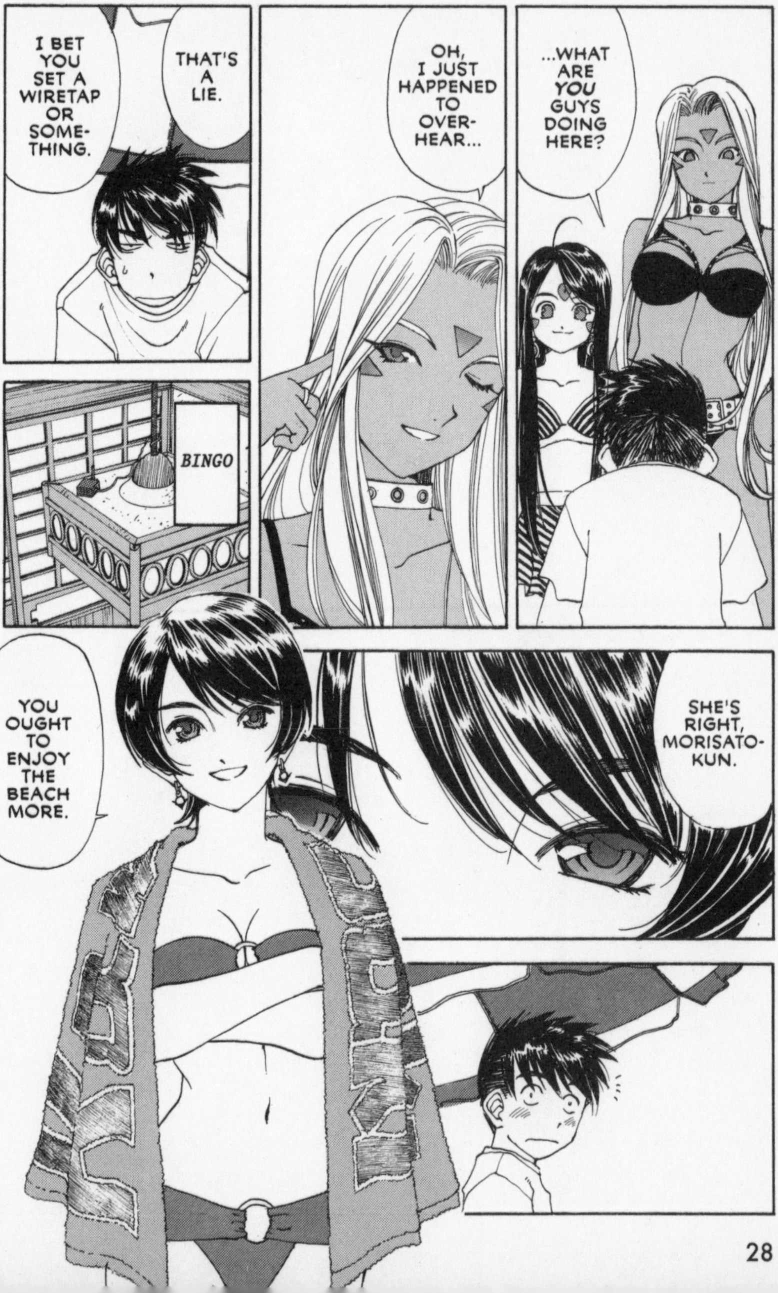

...WHAT ARE *YOU* GUYS DOING HERE?
OH, I JUST HAPPENED TO OVER-HEAR...
THAT'S A LIE.
I BET YOU SET A WIRETAP OR SOME-THING.
BINGO
SHE'S RIGHT, MORISATO-KUN.
YOU OUGHT TO ENJOY THE BEACH MORE.

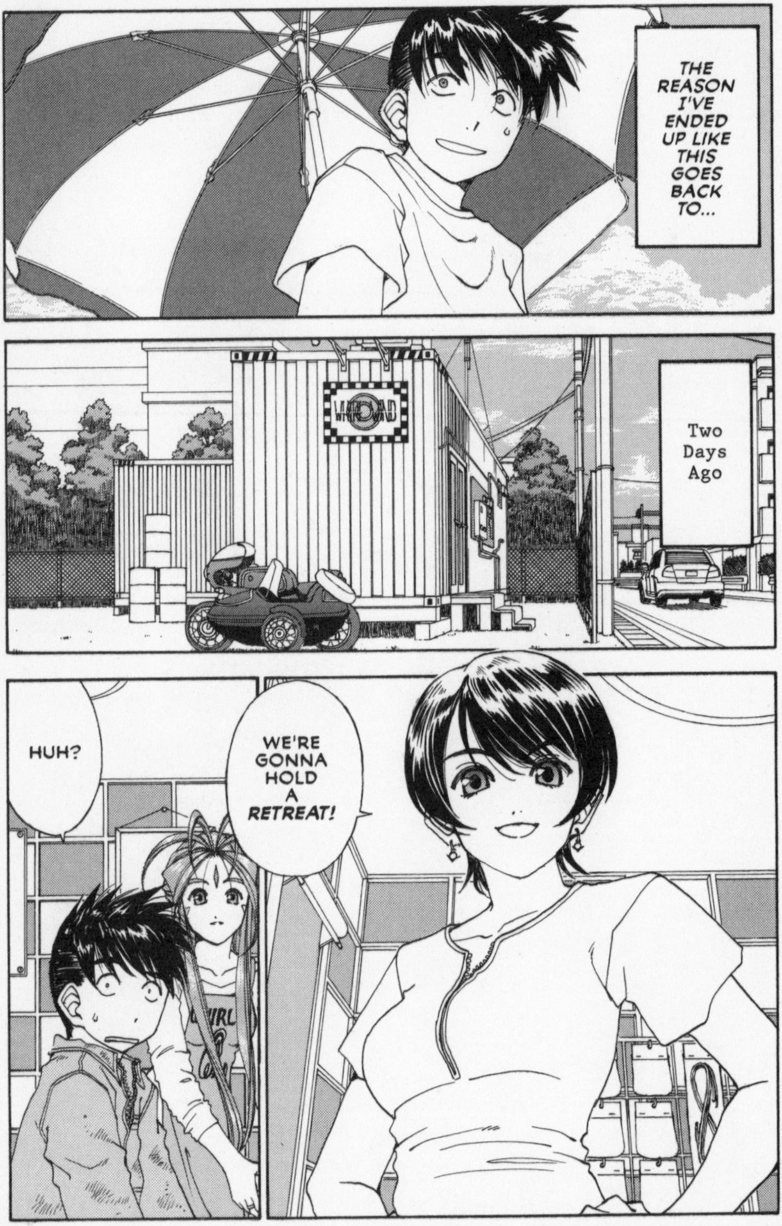
THE REASON I'VE ENDED UP LIKE THIS GOES BACK TO...
Two Days Ago
WE'RE GONNA HOLD A *RETREAT!*
HUH?

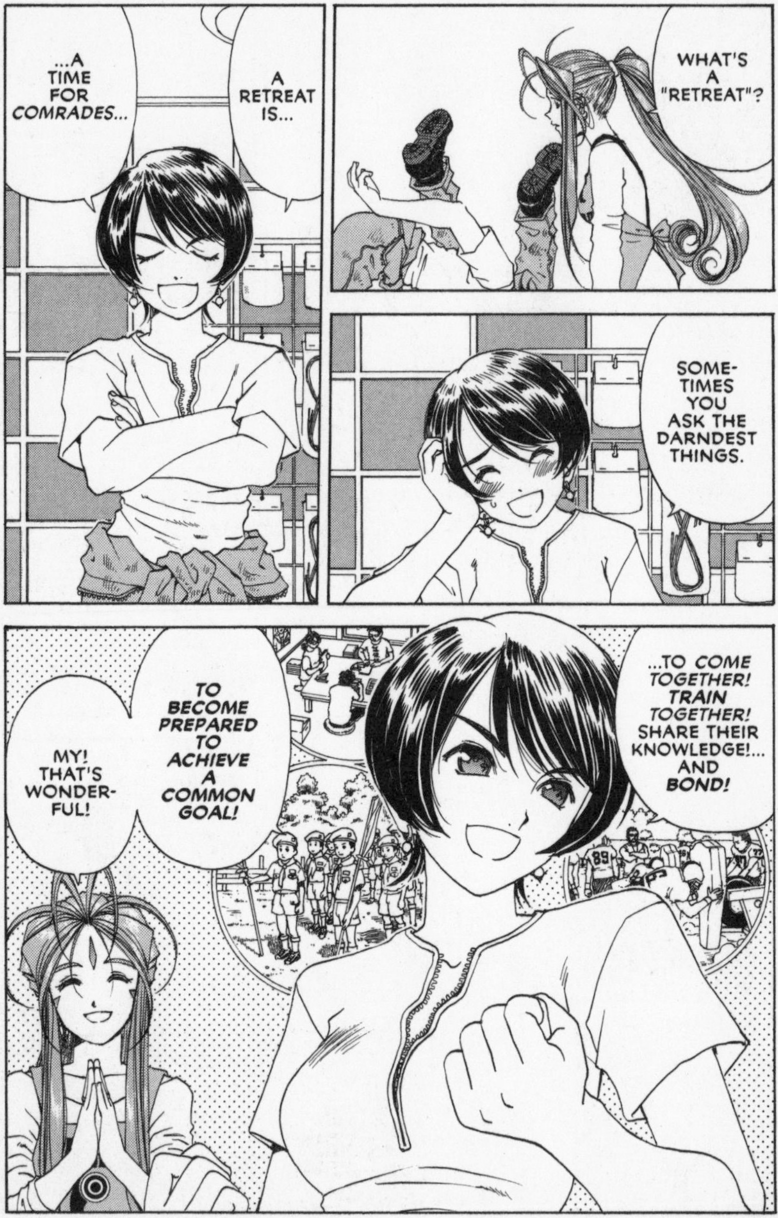
WHAT'S A "RETREAT"?
SOMETIMES YOU ASK THE DARNDEST THINGS.
A RETREAT IS...
...A TIME FOR *COMRADES*...
...TO *COME TOGETHER! TRAIN TOGETHER!* SHARE THEIR KNOWLEDGE!... AND *BOND!*
TO BECOME PREPARED TO ACHIEVE A COMMON GOAL!
MY! THAT'S WONDERFUL!

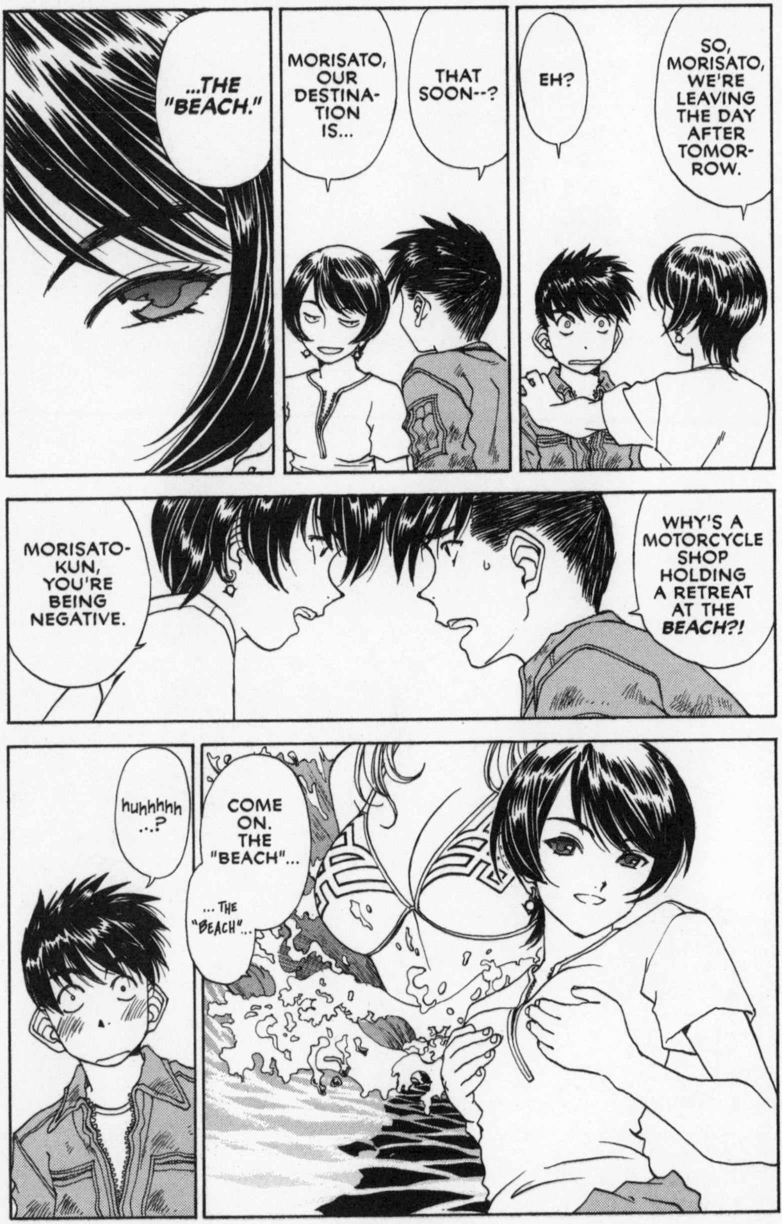
SO, MORISATO, WE'RE LEAVING THE DAY AFTER TOMORROW.
EH?
THAT SOON--?
MORISATO, OUR DESTINATION IS...
...THE "BEACH."
WHY'S A MOTORCYCLE SHOP HOLDING A RETREAT AT THE BEACH?!
MORISATO-KUN, YOU'RE BEING NEGATIVE.
COME ON. THE "BEACH"...
... THE "BEACH"...
huhhhhh ...?

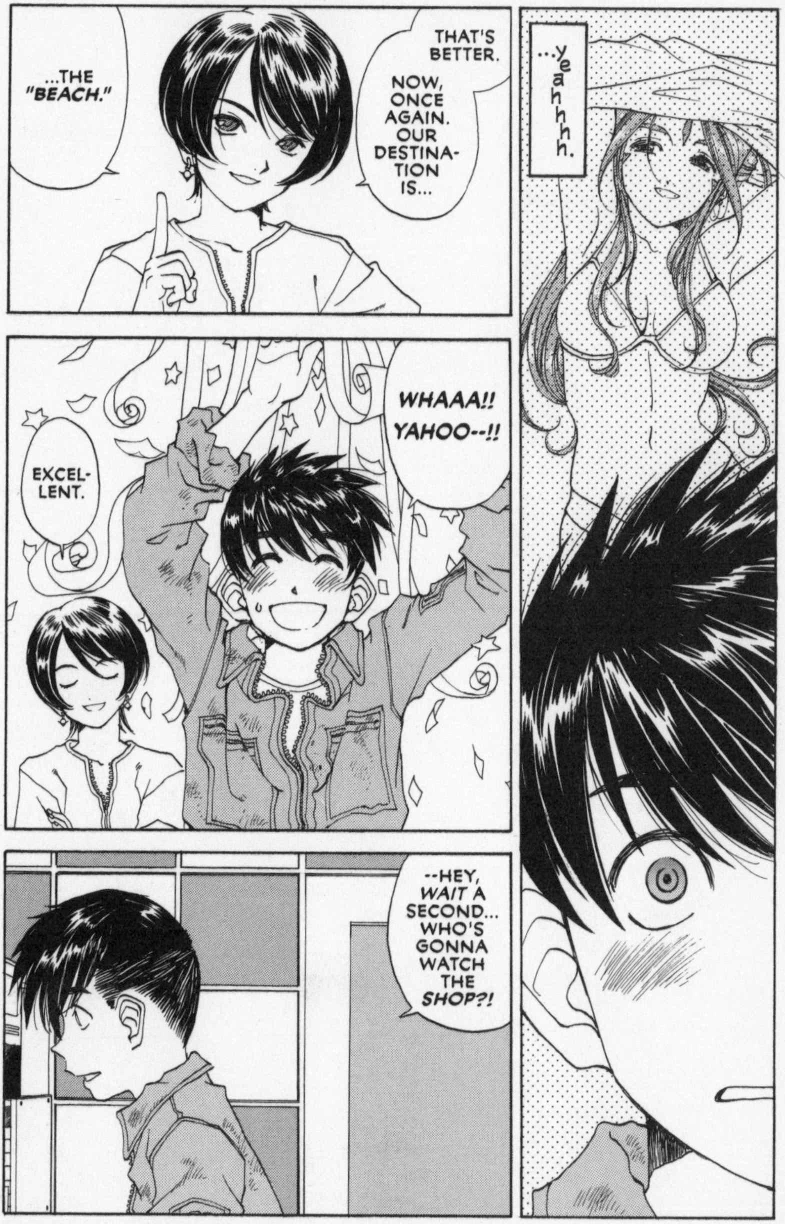
...yeahhh.
THAT'S BETTER.
NOW, ONCE AGAIN. OUR DESTINA-TION IS...
...THE "BEACH."
WHAAA!! YAHOO--!!
EXCEL-LENT.
--HEY, WAIT A SECOND... WHO'S GONNA WATCH THE SHOP?!

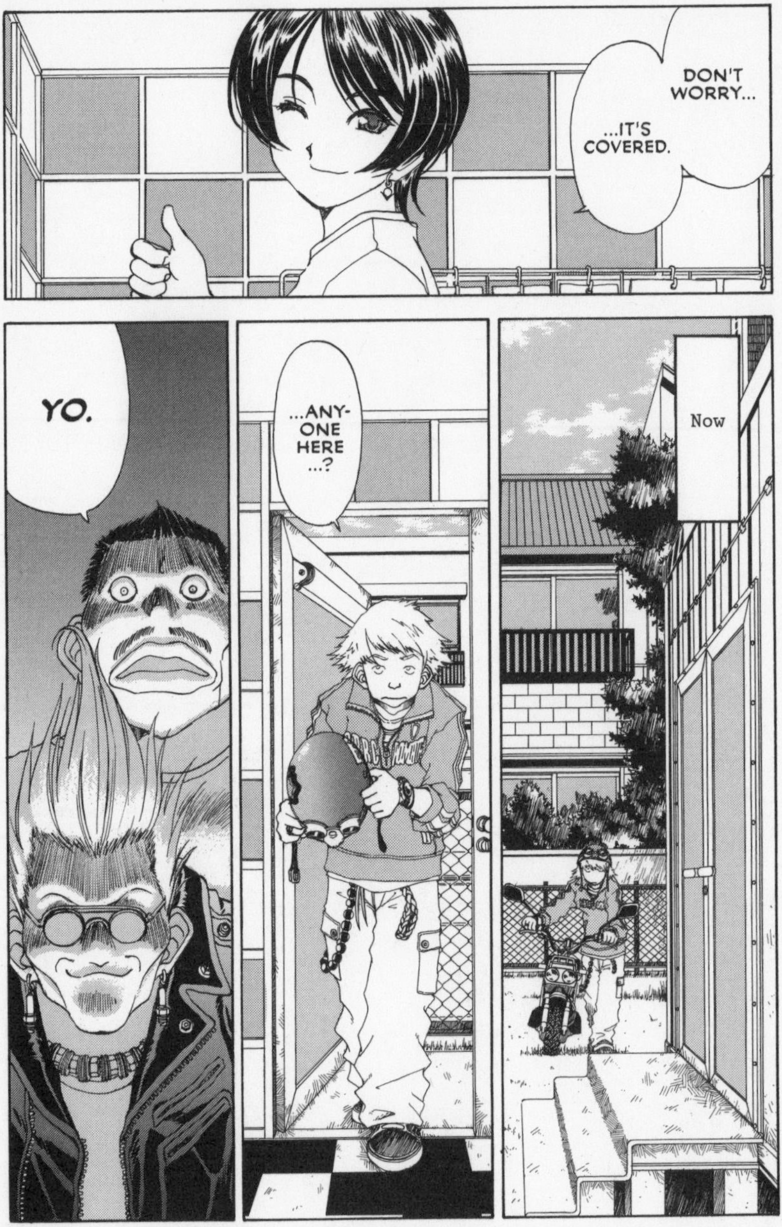
DON'T WORRY...
...IT'S COVERED.
Now
...ANY-ONE HERE ...?
YO.

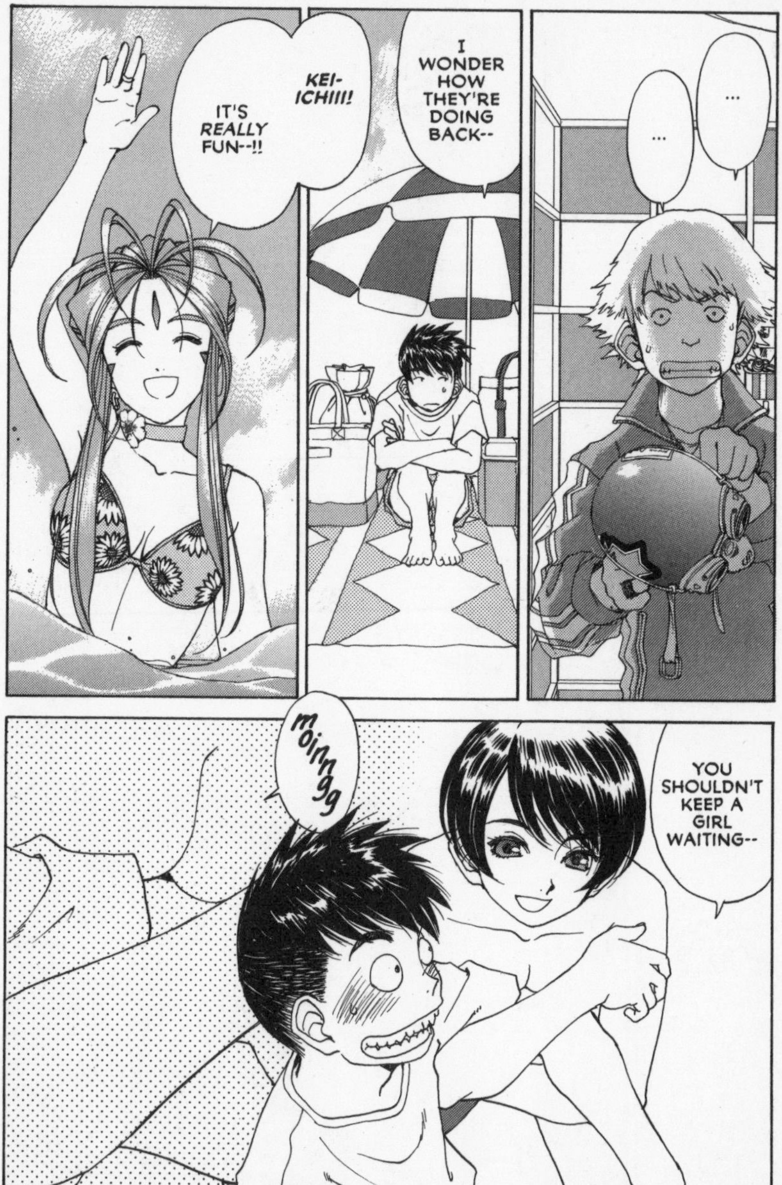
...
...
I WONDER HOW THEY'RE DOING BACK--
KEI-ICHIII!
IT'S *REALLY* FUN--!!
YOU SHOULDN'T KEEP A GIRL WAITING--
moinngg

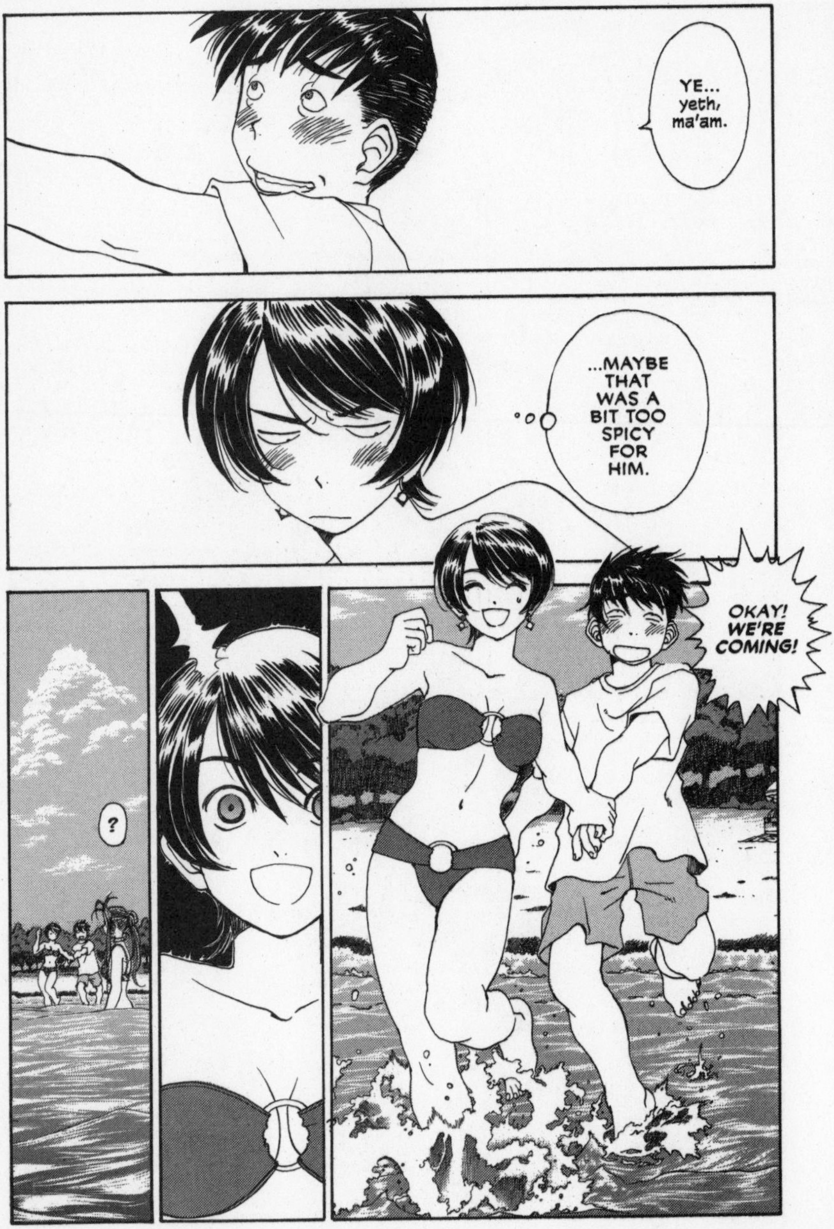
YE... yeth, ma'am.
...MAYBE THAT WAS A BIT TOO SPICY FOR HIM.
OKAY! WE'RE COMING!
?

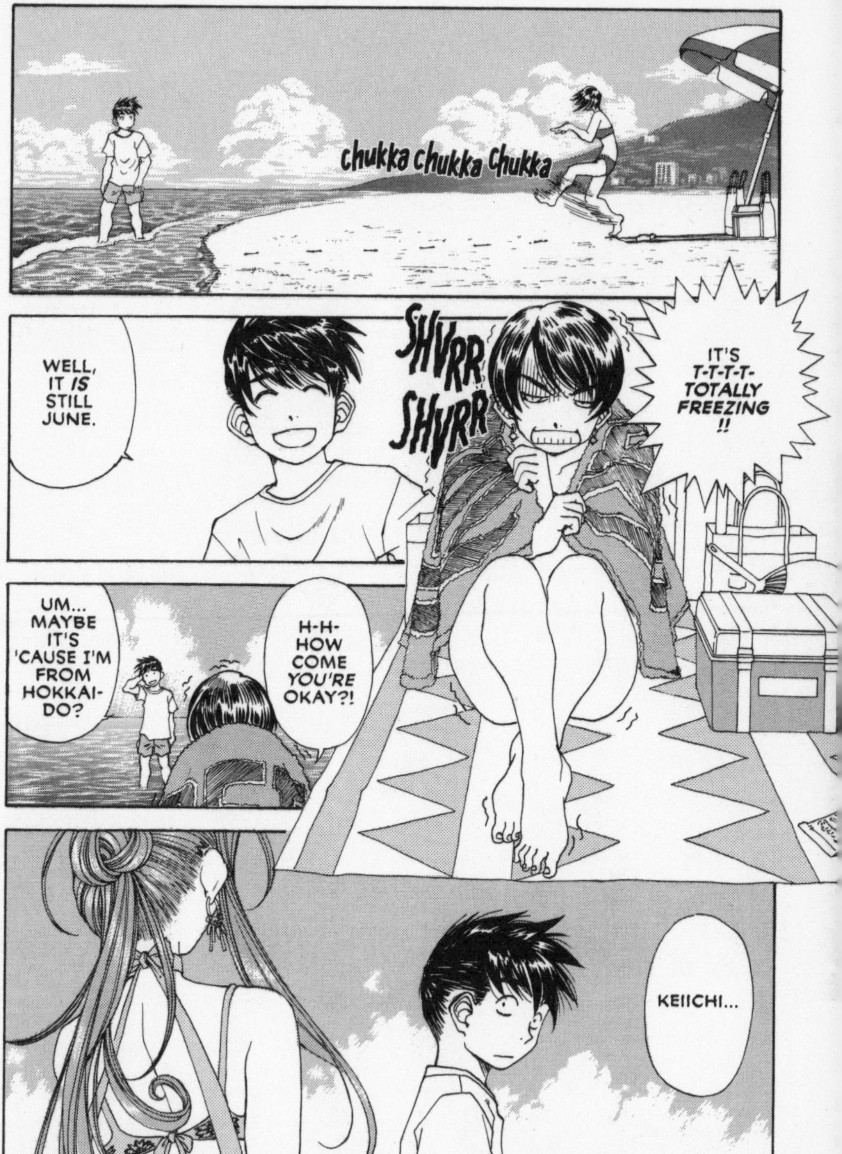
chukka chukka chukka
SHVRR SHVRR
IT'S T-T-T-T-TOTALLY FREEZING!!
WELL, IT *IS* STILL JUNE.
H-H-HOW COME *YOU'RE* OKAY?!
UM... MAYBE IT'S 'CAUSE I'M FROM HOKKAI-DO?
KEIICHI...

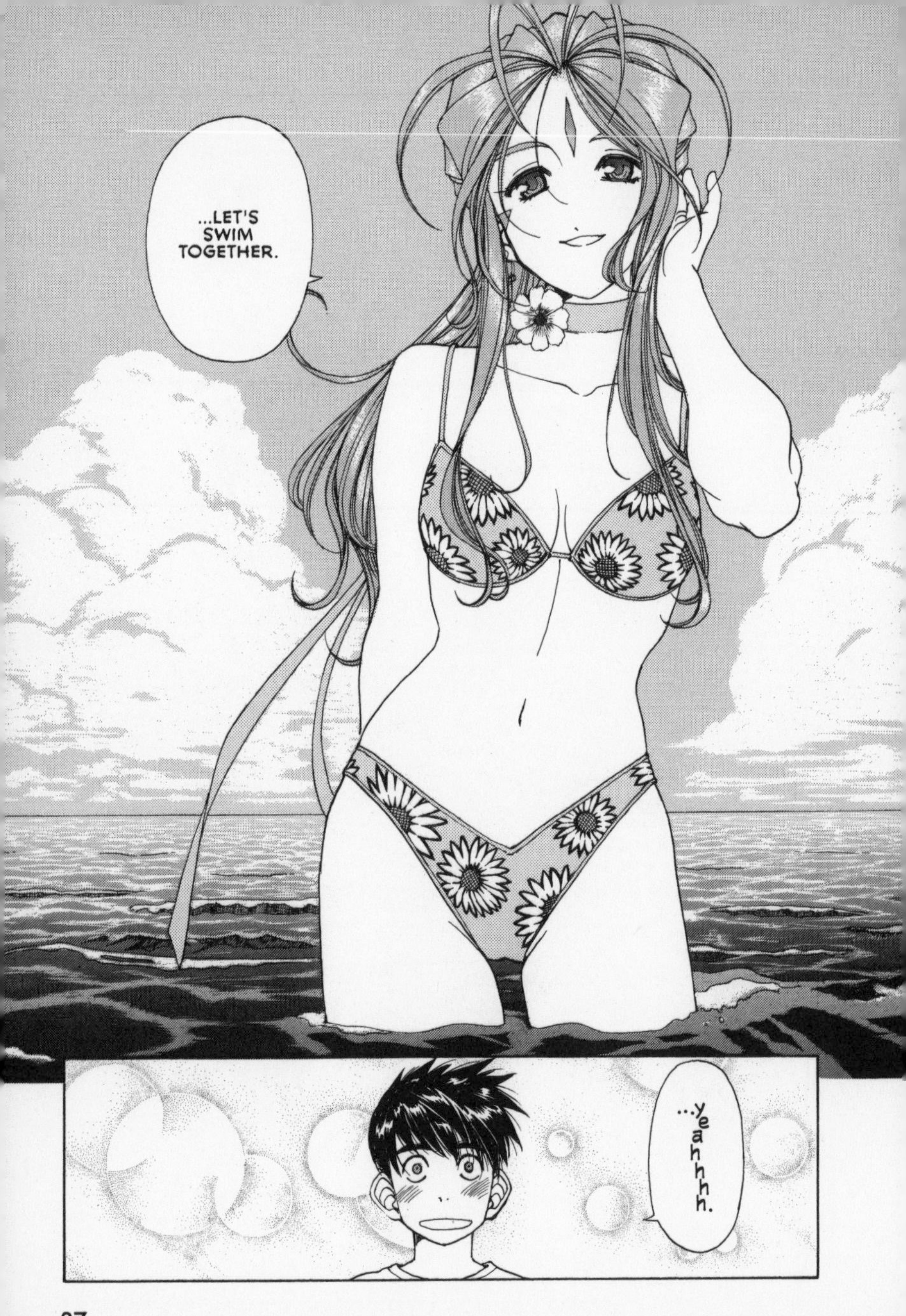
...LET'S SWIM TOGETHER.
...yeahhhh.

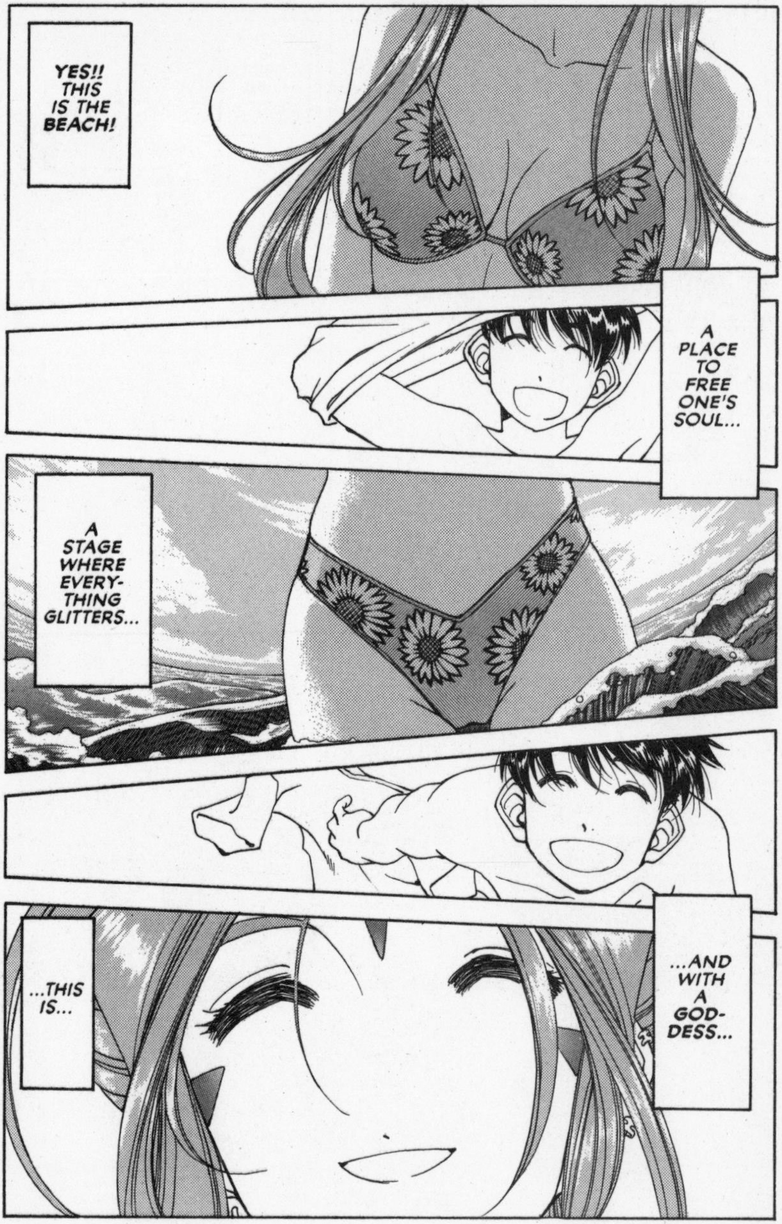
YES!! THIS IS THE BEACH!
A PLACE TO FREE ONE'S SOUL...
A STAGE WHERE EVERY-THING GLITTERS...
...AND WITH A GOD-DESS...
...THIS IS...

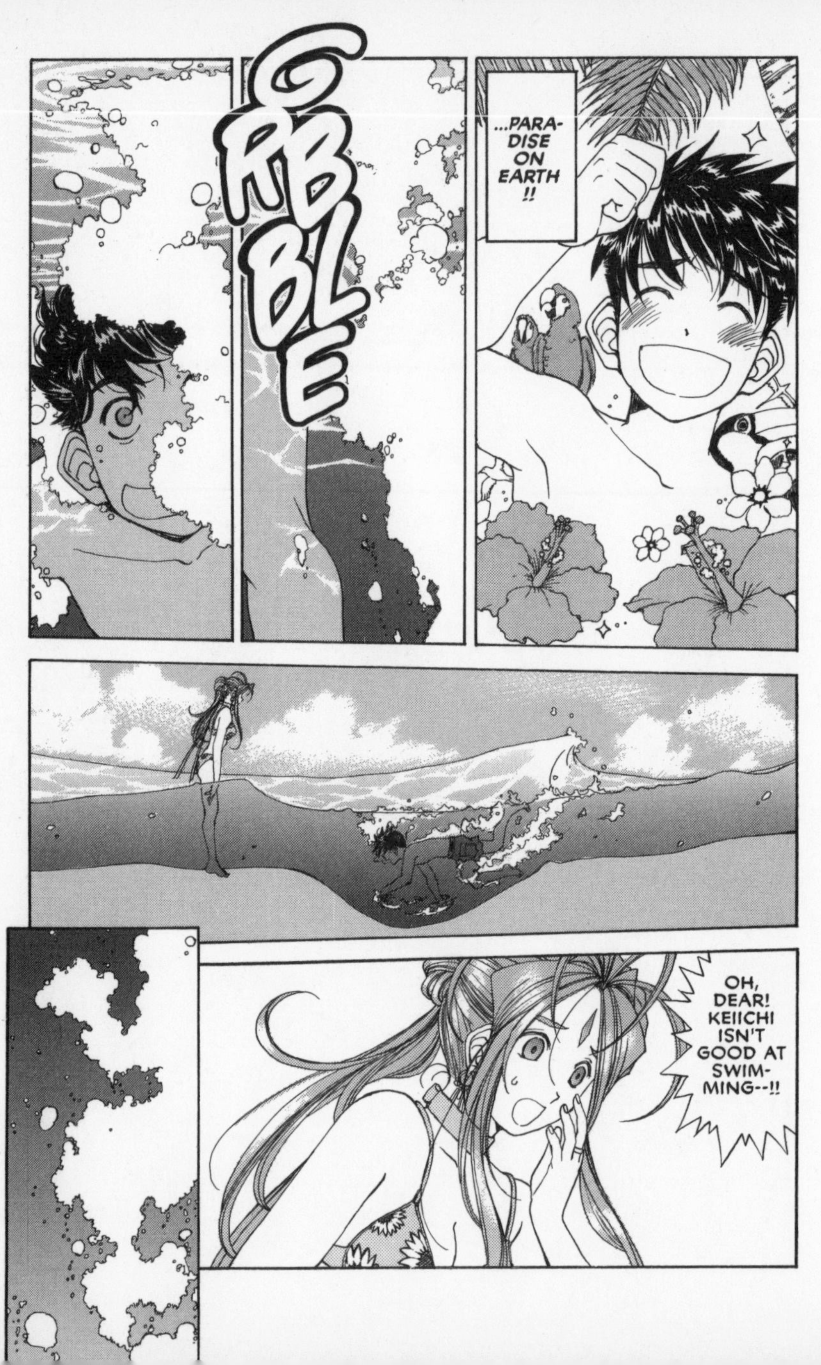
...PARADISE ON EARTH!!
GRBBLE
OH, DEAR! KEIICHI ISN'T GOOD AT SWIMMING--!!

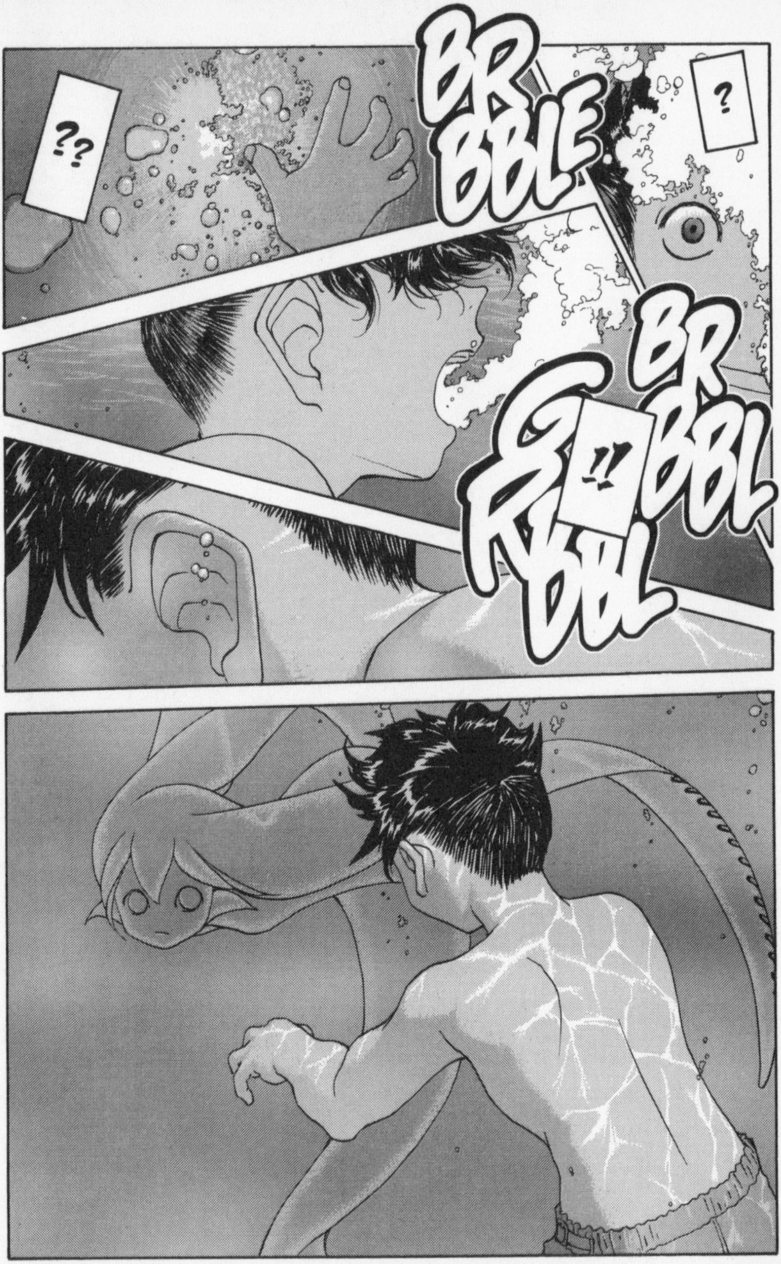
?
BR BBLE
??
BR BBL
!!
GR BBL

CHAPTER 203

First Encounter

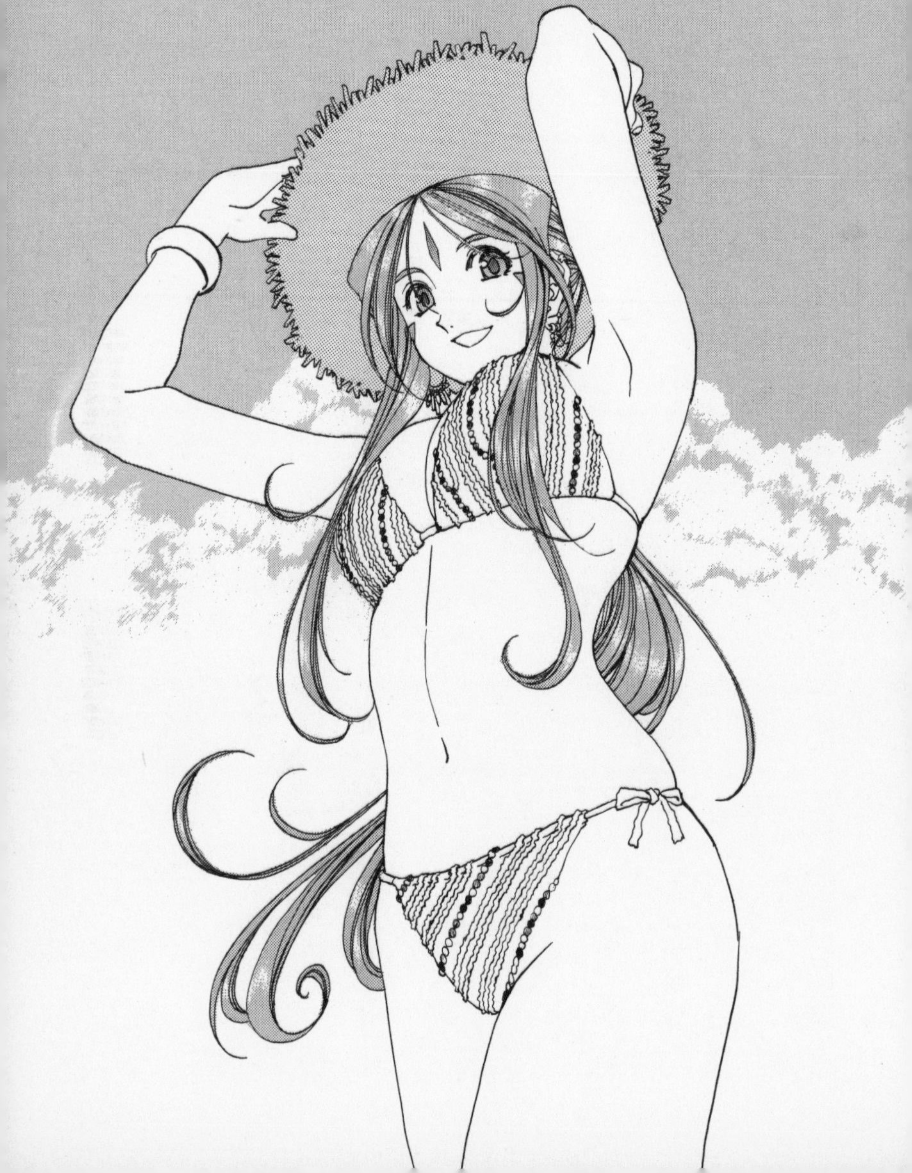

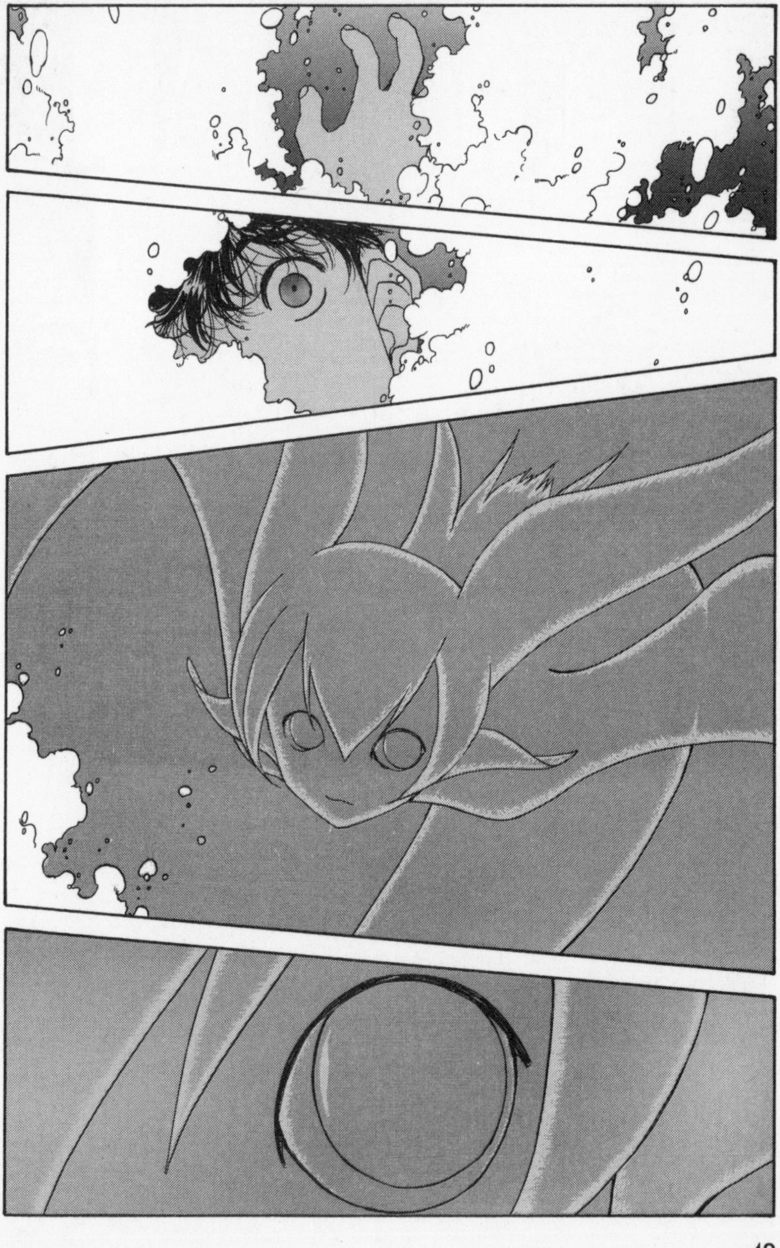

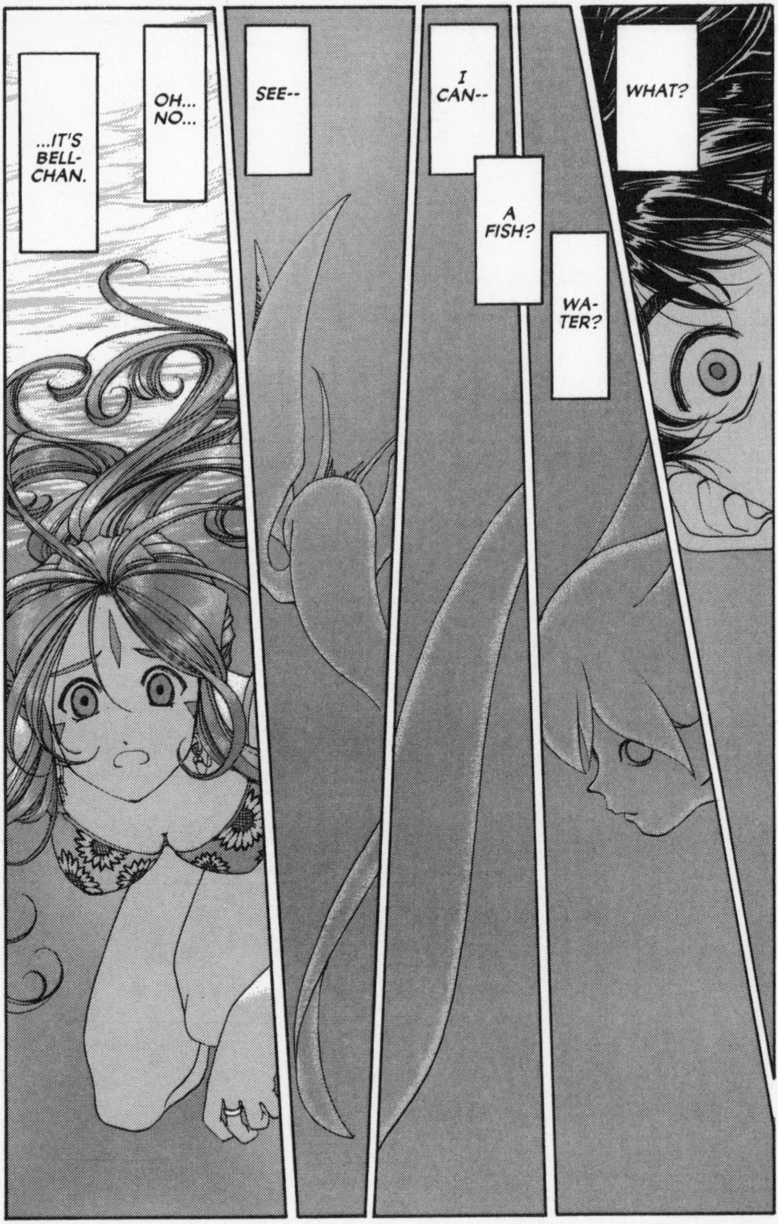
WHAT?
WA-TER?
A FISH?
I CAN--
SEE--
OH... NO...
...IT'S BELL-CHAN.

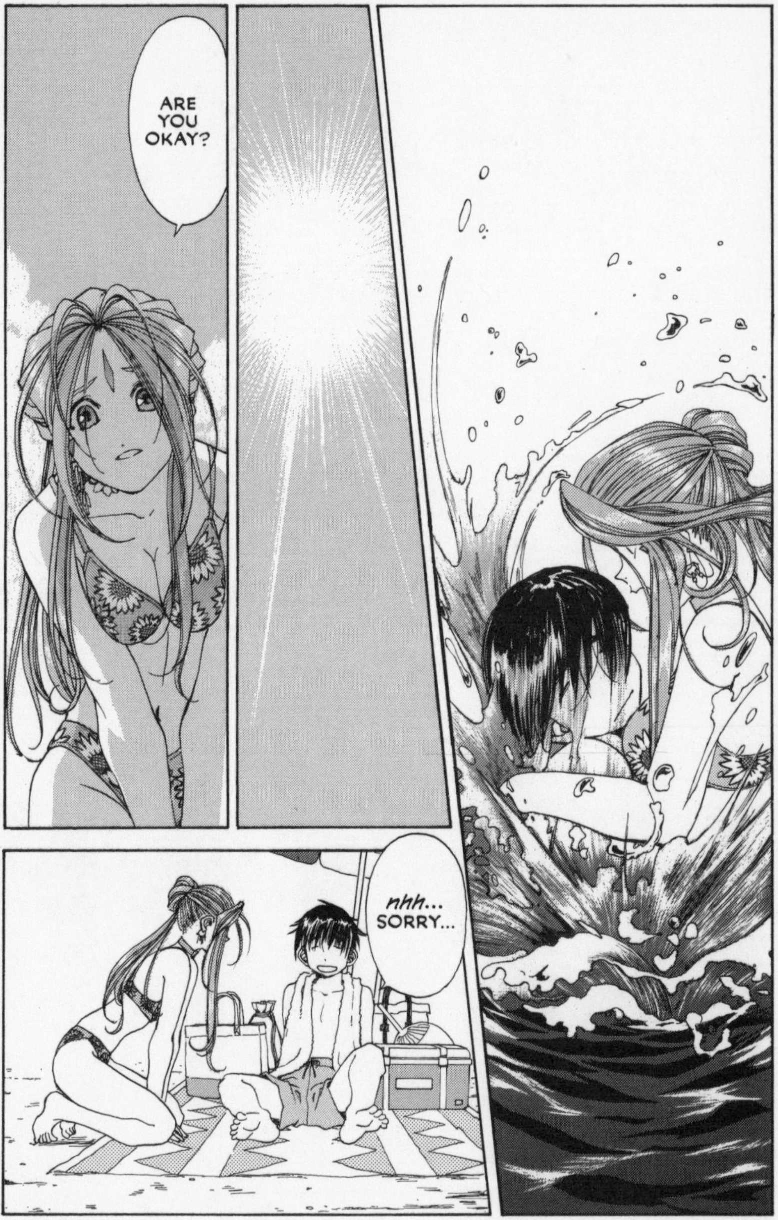
ARE YOU OKAY?
nhh... SORRY...

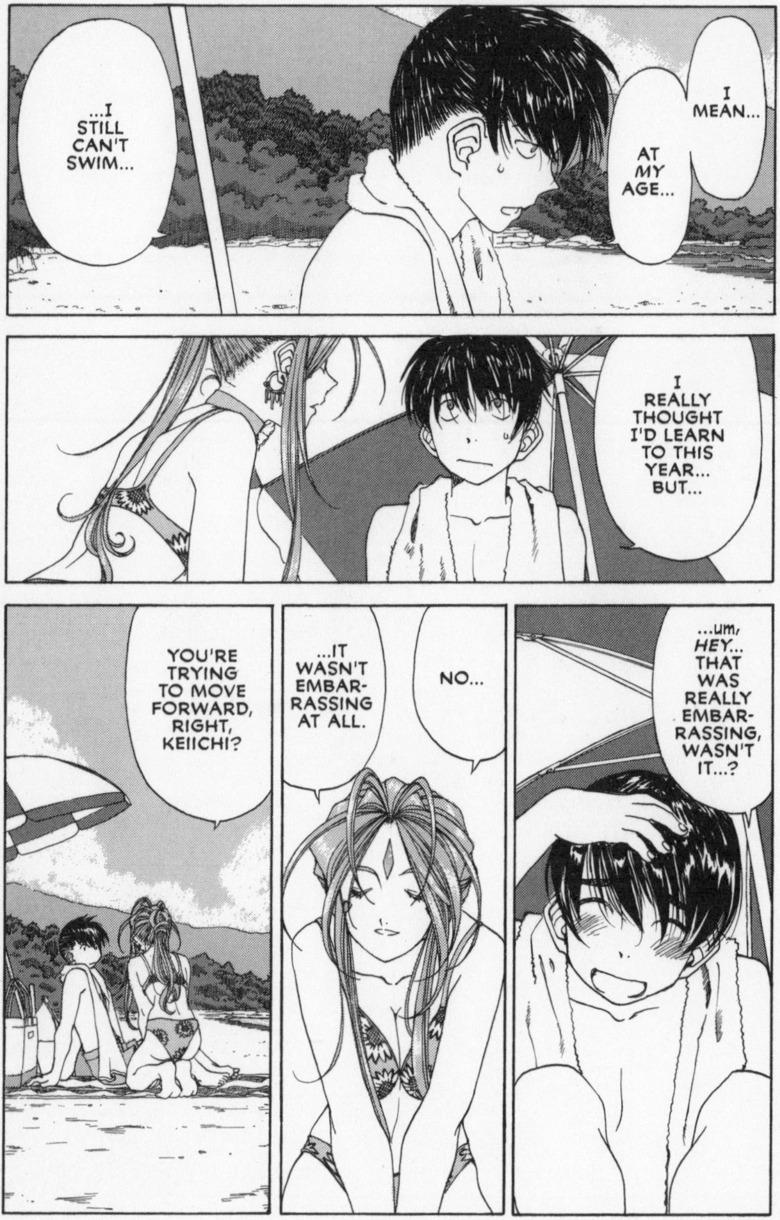
I MEAN...
AT MY AGE...
...I STILL CAN'T SWIM...
I REALLY THOUGHT I'D LEARN TO THIS YEAR... BUT...
...um, *HEY*... THAT WAS REALLY EMBARRASSING, WASN'T IT...?
NO...
...IT WASN'T EMBARRASSING AT ALL.
YOU'RE TRYING TO MOVE FORWARD, RIGHT, KEIICHI?

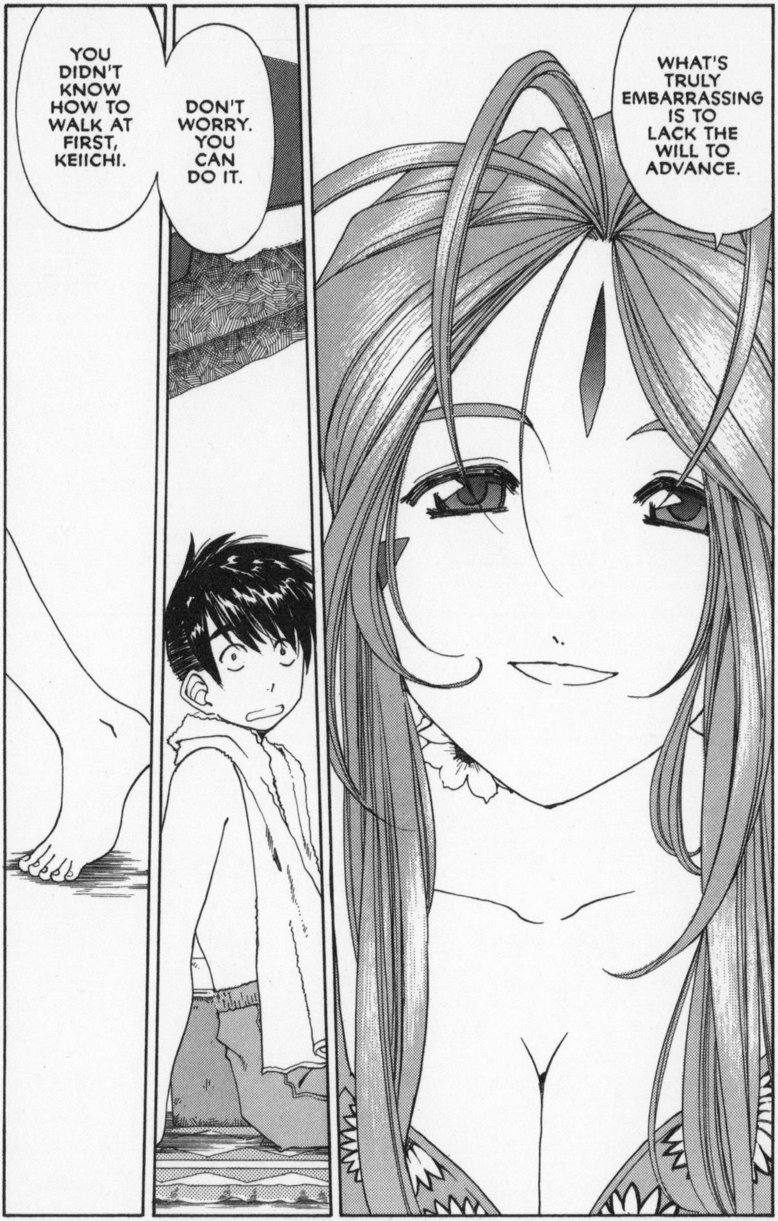
WHAT'S TRULY EMBARRASSING IS TO LACK THE WILL TO ADVANCE.
DON'T WORRY. YOU CAN DO IT.
YOU DIDN'T KNOW HOW TO WALK AT FIRST, KEIICHI.

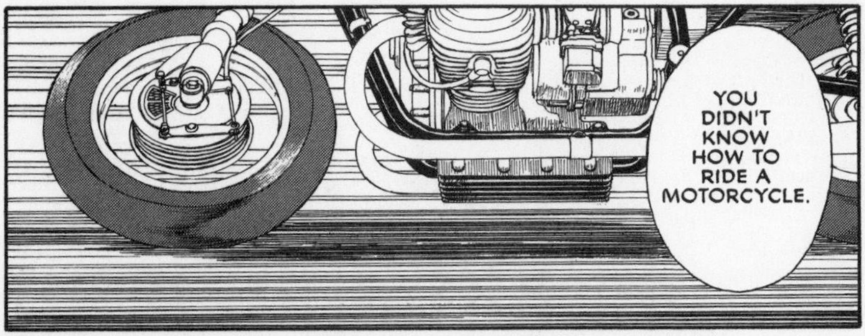
YOU DIDN'T KNOW HOW TO RIDE A MOTORCYCLE.

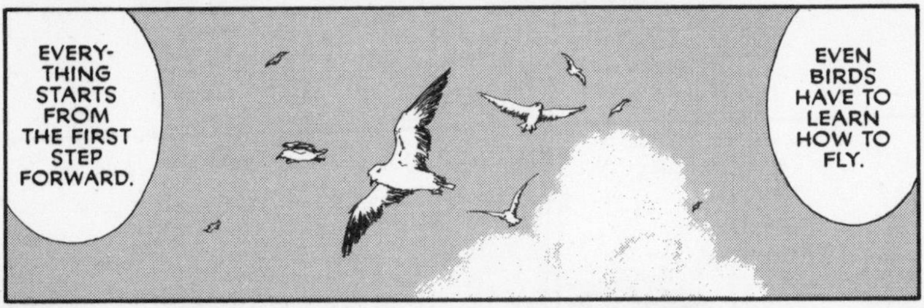
EVEN BIRDS HAVE TO LEARN HOW TO FLY.
EVERY-THING STARTS FROM THE FIRST STEP FORWARD.

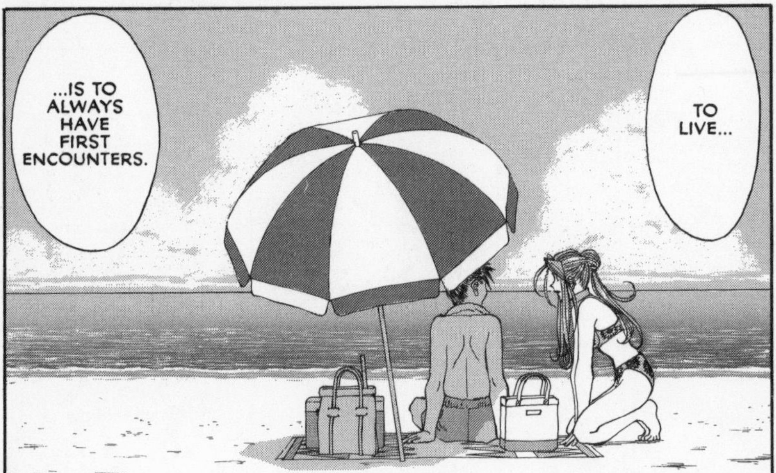
TO LIVE...
...IS TO ALWAYS HAVE FIRST ENCOUNTERS.

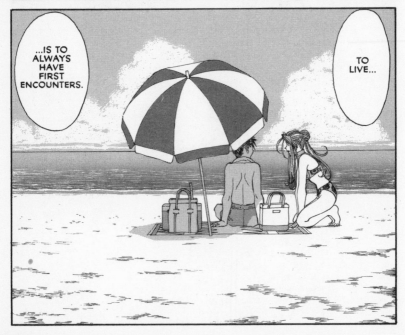

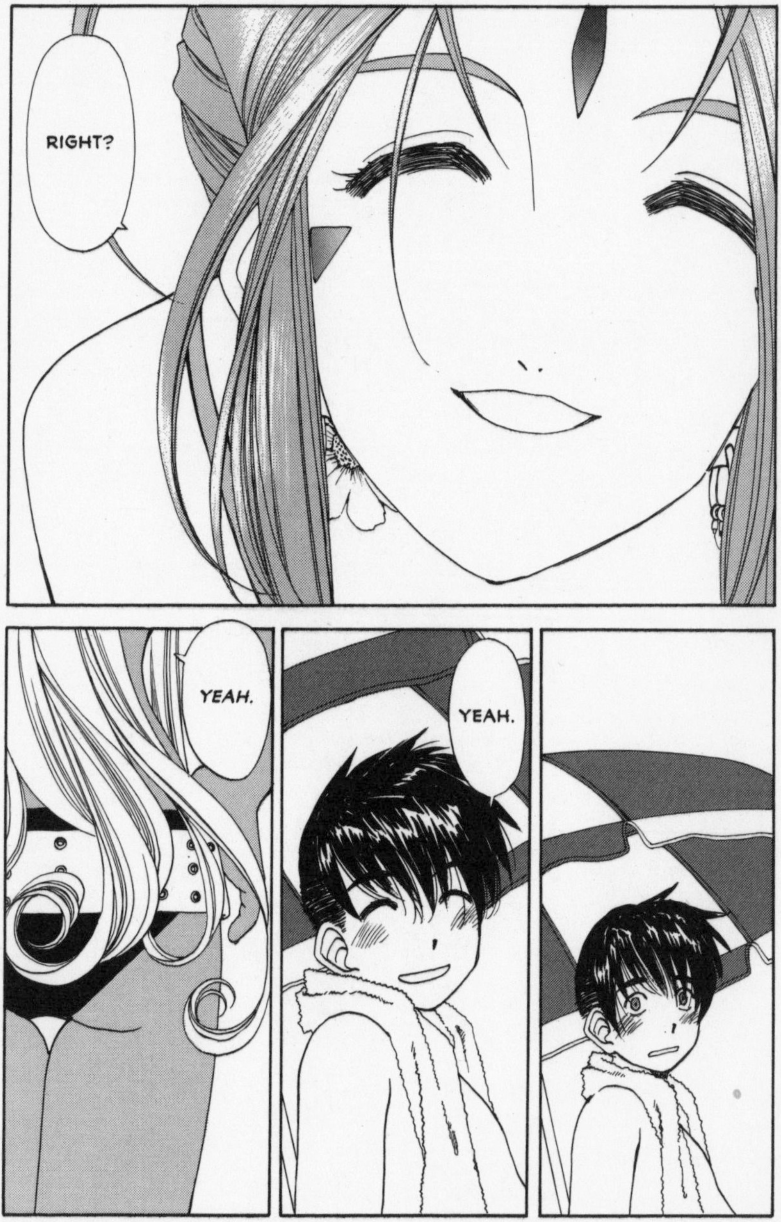
RIGHT?
YEAH.
YEAH.

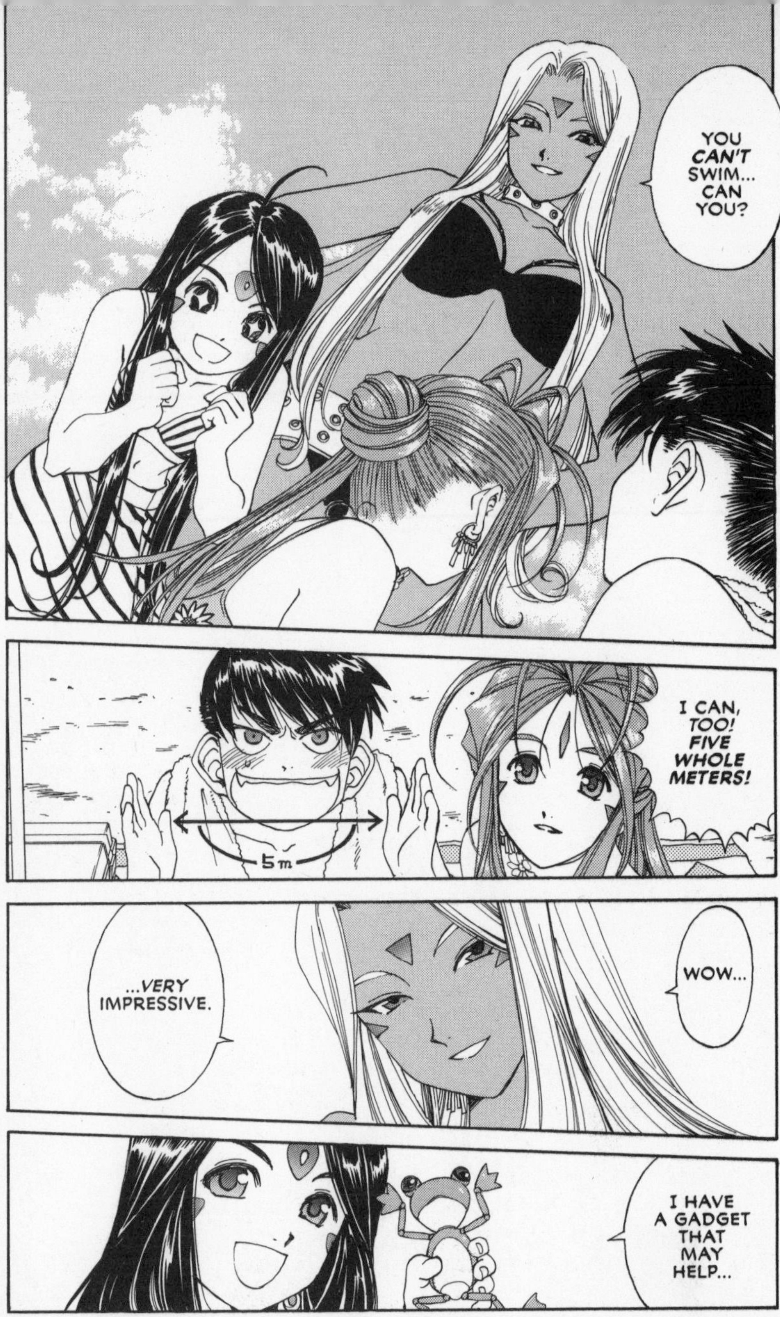
YOU CAN'T SWIM... CAN YOU?
I CAN, TOO! FIVE WHOLE METERS!
5m
WOW...
...VERY IMPRESSIVE.
I HAVE A GADGET THAT MAY HELP...

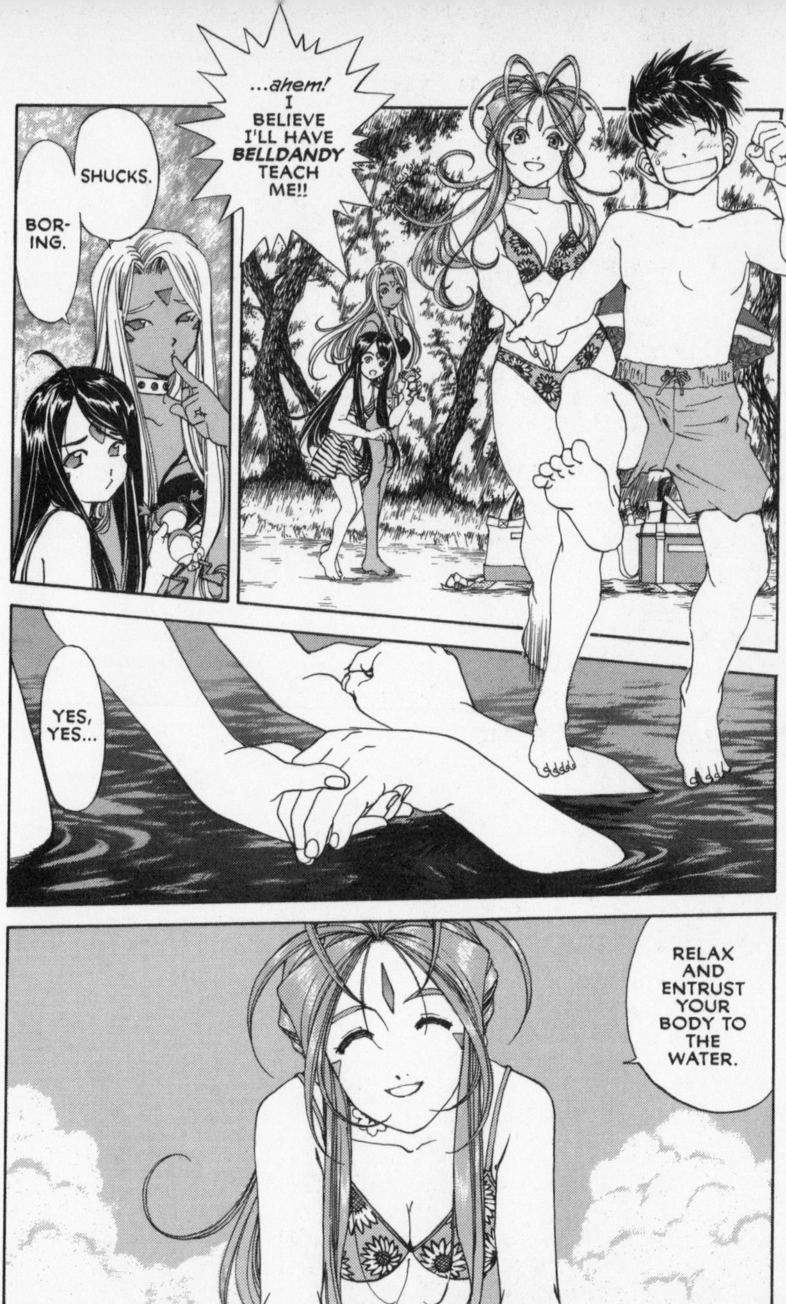
...ahem! I BELIEVE I'LL HAVE BELLDANDY TEACH ME!!
SHUCKS.
BOR-ING.
YES, YES...
RELAX AND ENTRUST YOUR BODY TO THE WATER.

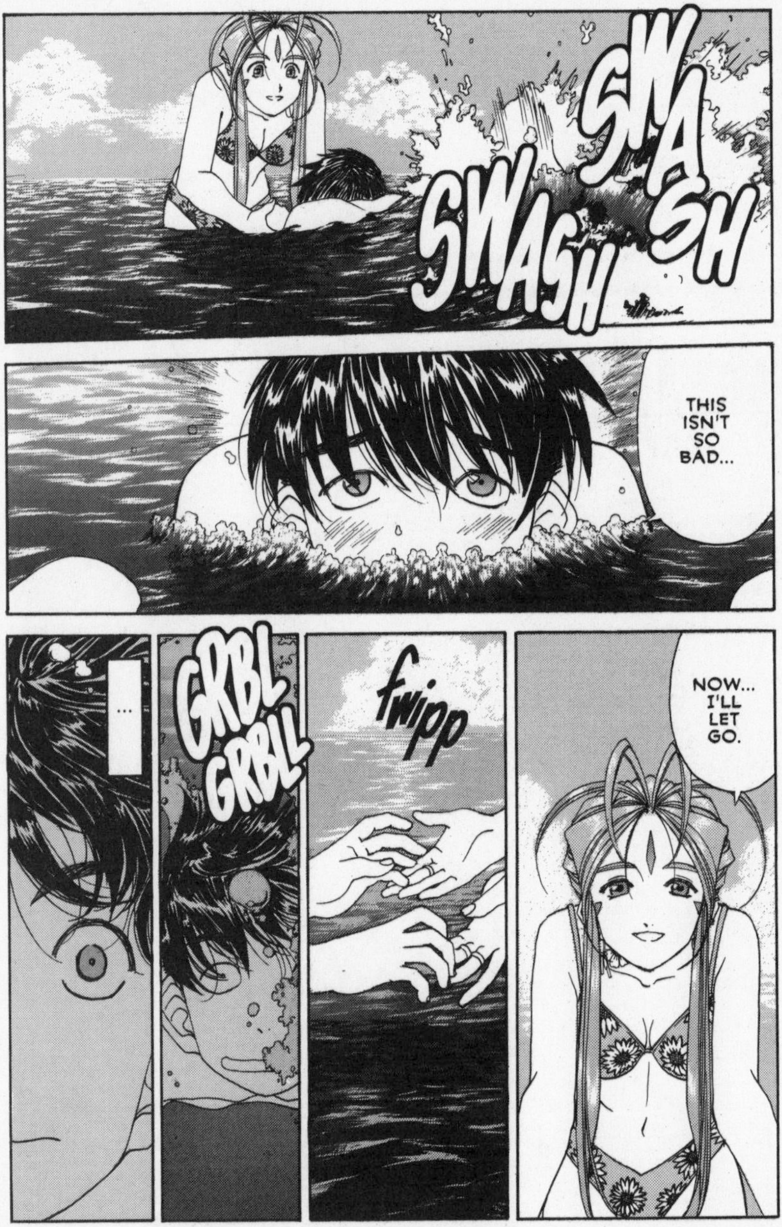
SWASH
SWASH
THIS ISN'T SO BAD...
NOW... I'LL LET GO.
fwipp
GRBL GRBL
...

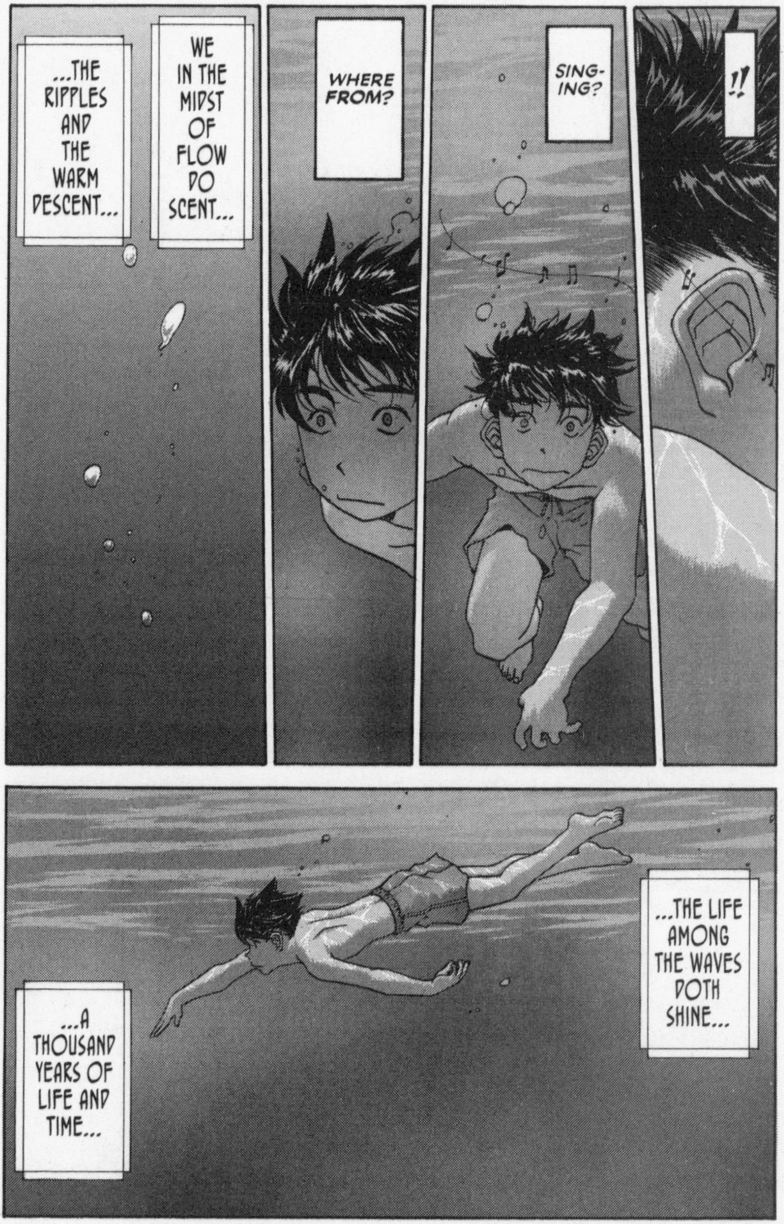
!!
SING-ING?
WHERE FROM?
WE IN THE MIDST OF FLOW DO SCENT...
...THE RIPPLES AND THE WARM DESCENT...
...THE LIFE AMONG THE WAVES DOTH SHINE...
...A THOUSAND YEARS OF LIFE AND TIME...

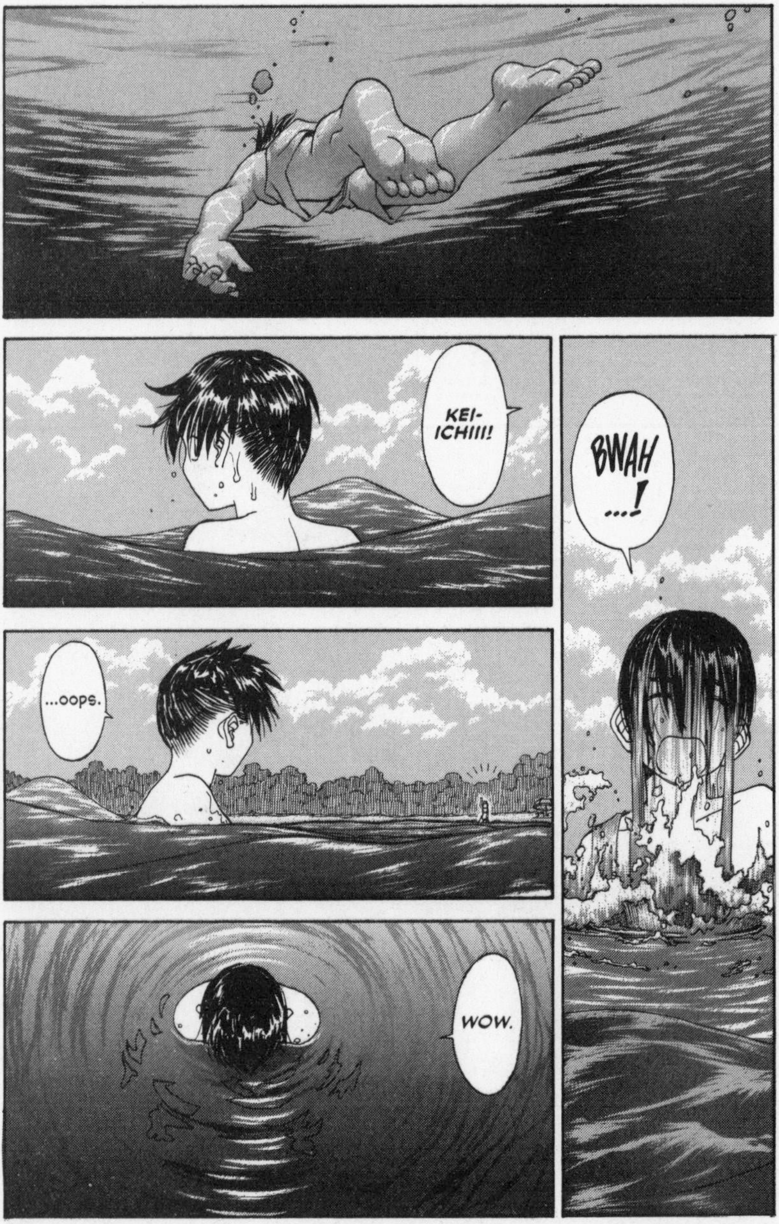
BWAH ...!
KEI-ICHIII!
...oops.
WOW.

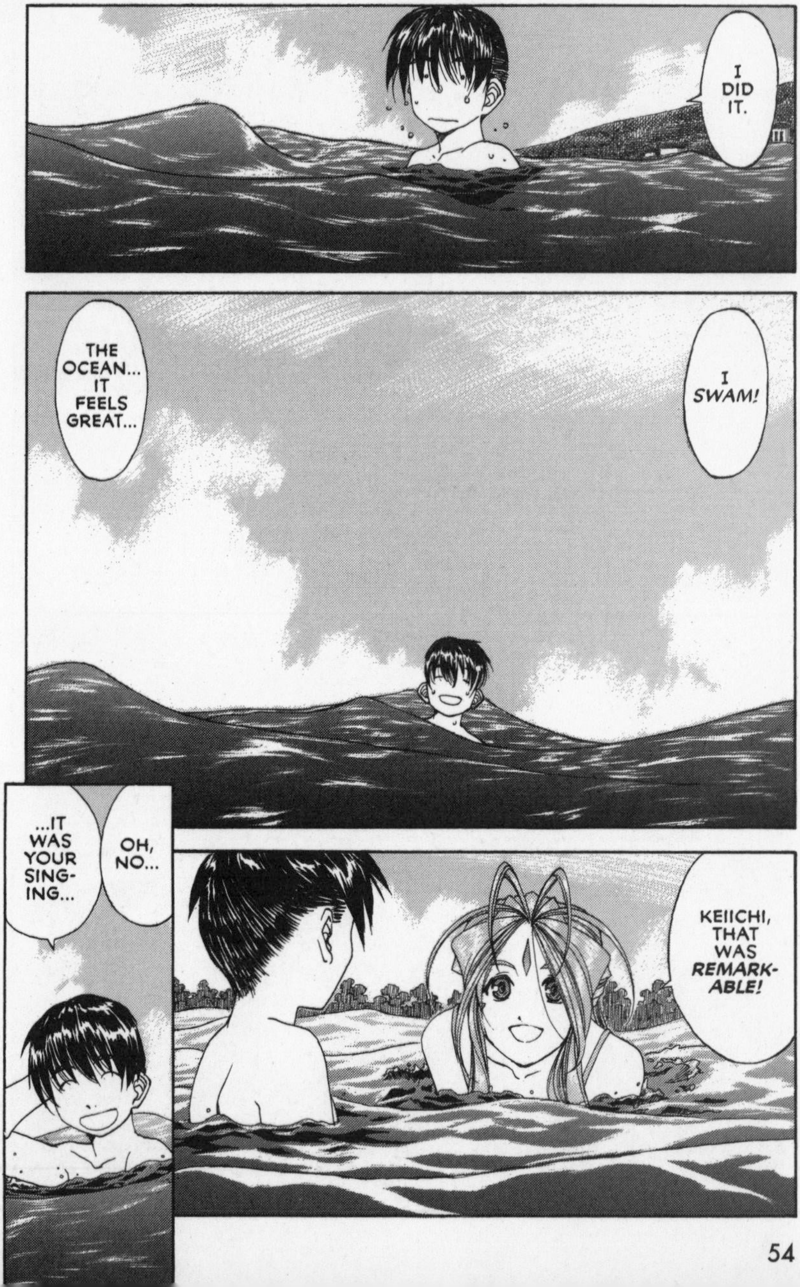
I DID IT.
I *SWAM!*
THE OCEAN... IT FEELS GREAT...
KEIICHI, THAT WAS *REMARKABLE!*
OH, NO...
...IT WAS YOUR SINGING...

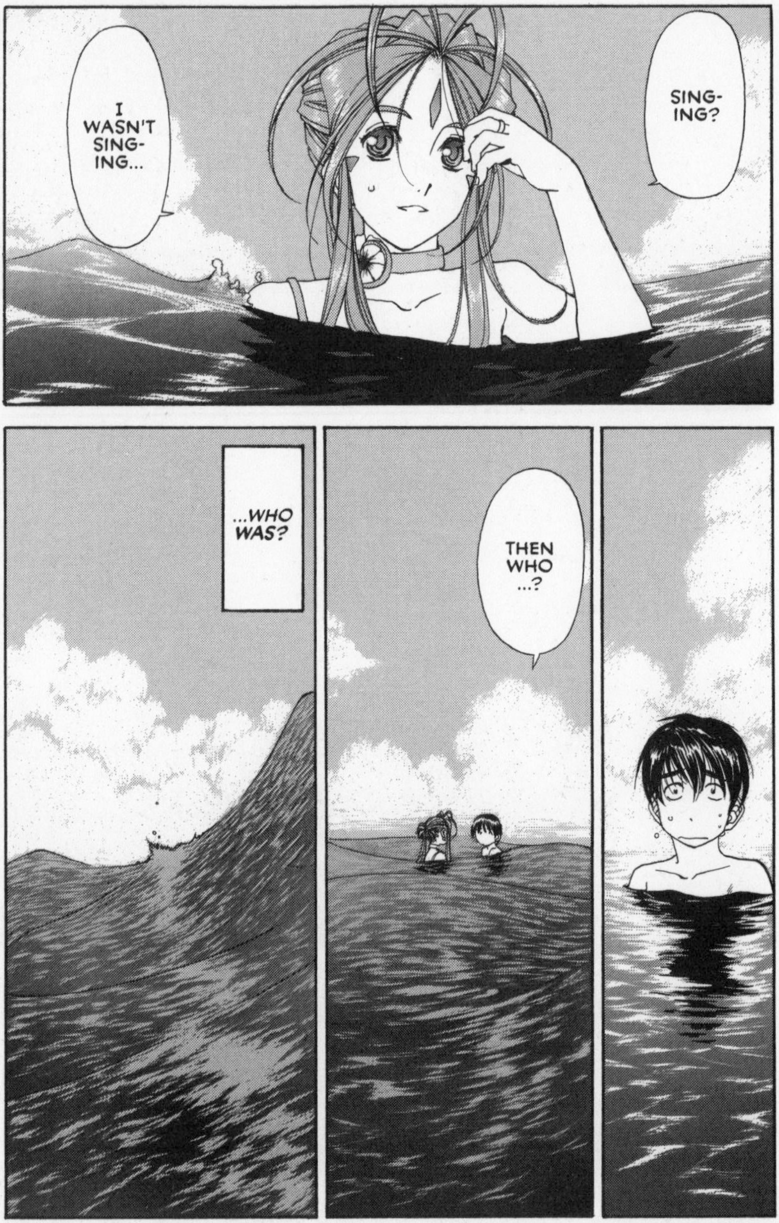
SING-ING?
I WASN'T SING-ING...
THEN WHO ...?
...WHO WAS?

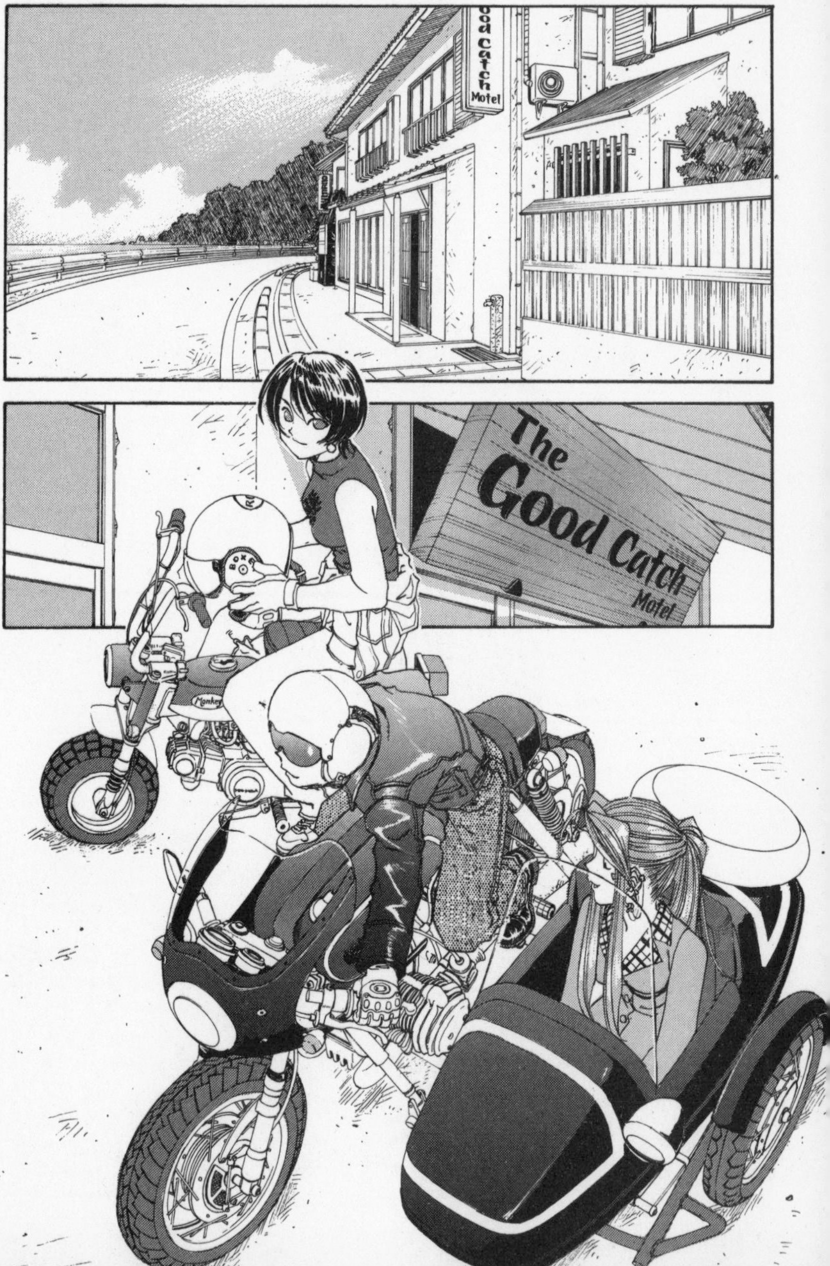
ood Catch
Motel
The
Good Catch
Motel
Monkey

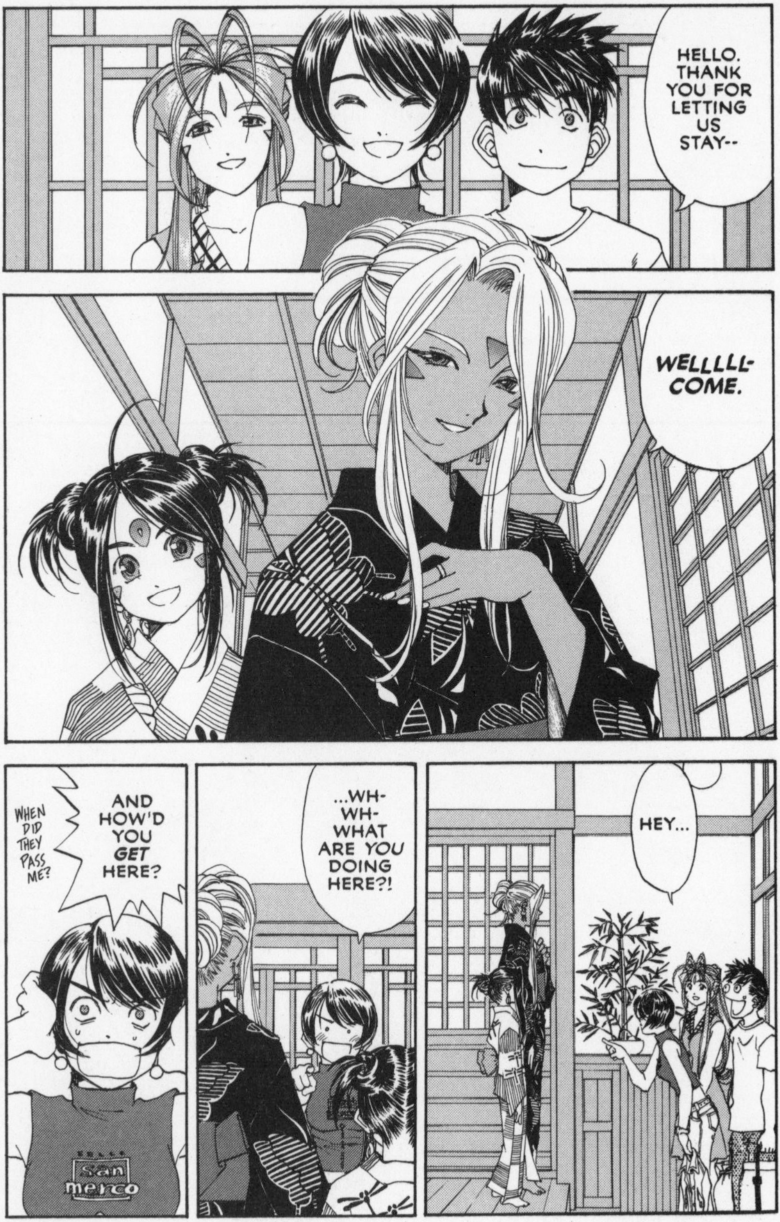
HELLO. THANK YOU FOR LETTING US STAY--
WELLLLL-COME.
HEY...
...WH- WH- WHAT ARE YOU DOING HERE?!
AND HOW'D YOU GET HERE?
WHEN DID THEY PASS ME?
San marco

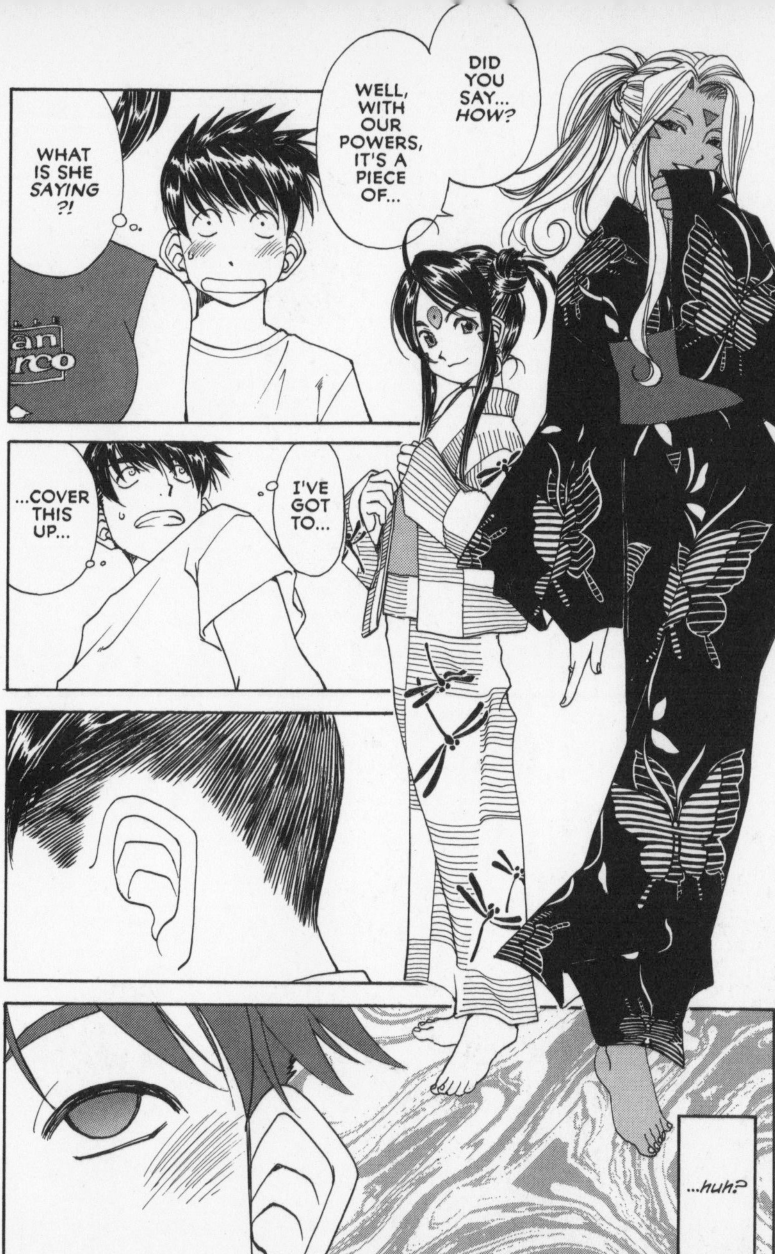
DID YOU SAY... *HOW?*
WELL, WITH OUR POWERS, IT'S A PIECE OF...
WHAT IS SHE *SAYING* ?!
I'VE GOT TO...
...COVER THIS UP...
...huh?

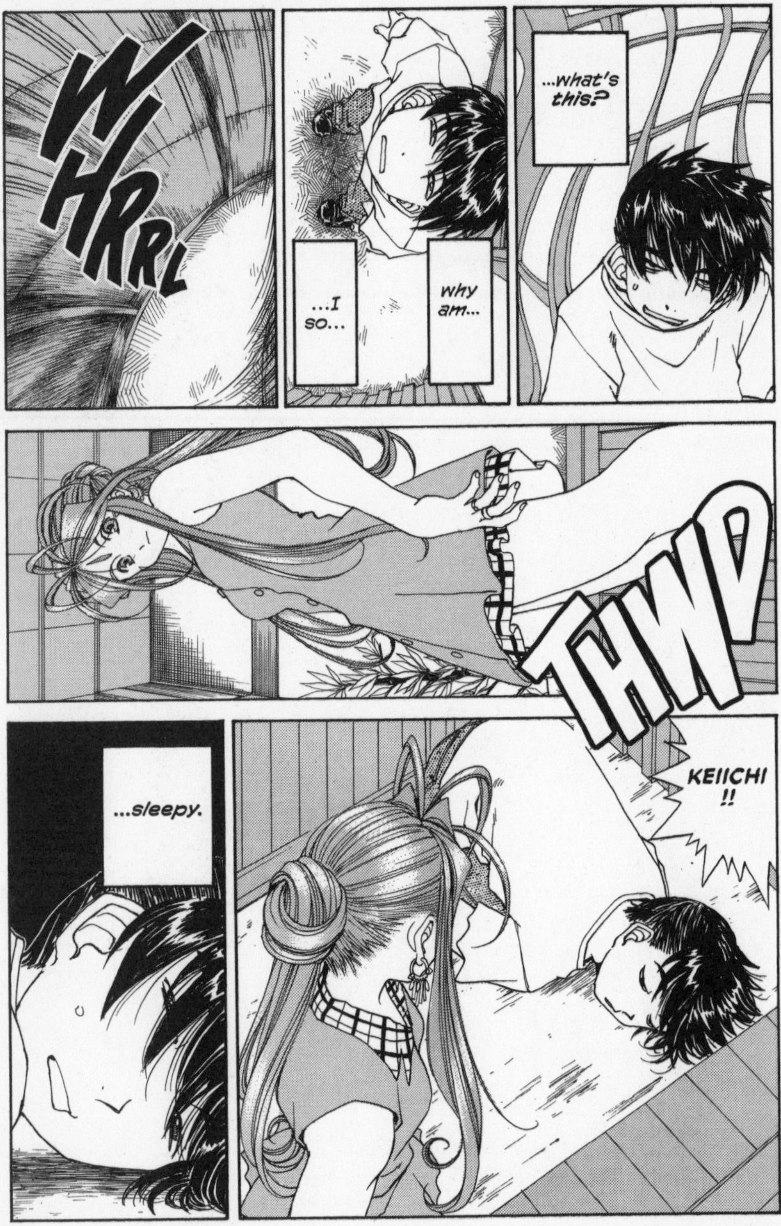
...what's this?
why am...
...I so...
WHRRL
THWD
KEIICHI !!
...sleepy.

...the song...

THE BUBBLES RISE...

it's...

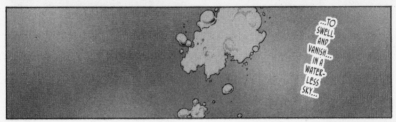

...TO SWELL AND VANISH... IN A WATER- LESS SKY...

...HUH?

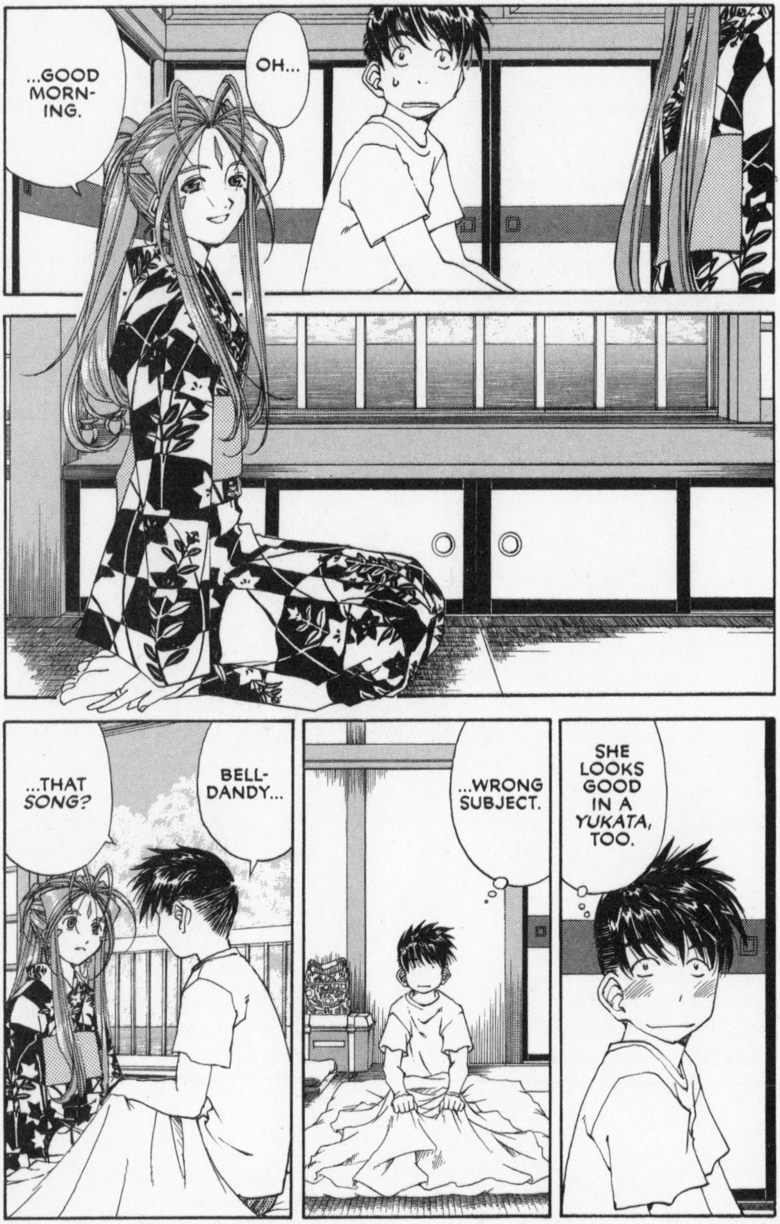
OH...
...GOOD MORNING.
SHE LOOKS GOOD IN A *YUKATA*, TOO.
...WRONG SUBJECT.
BELL-DANDY...
...THAT *SONG*?

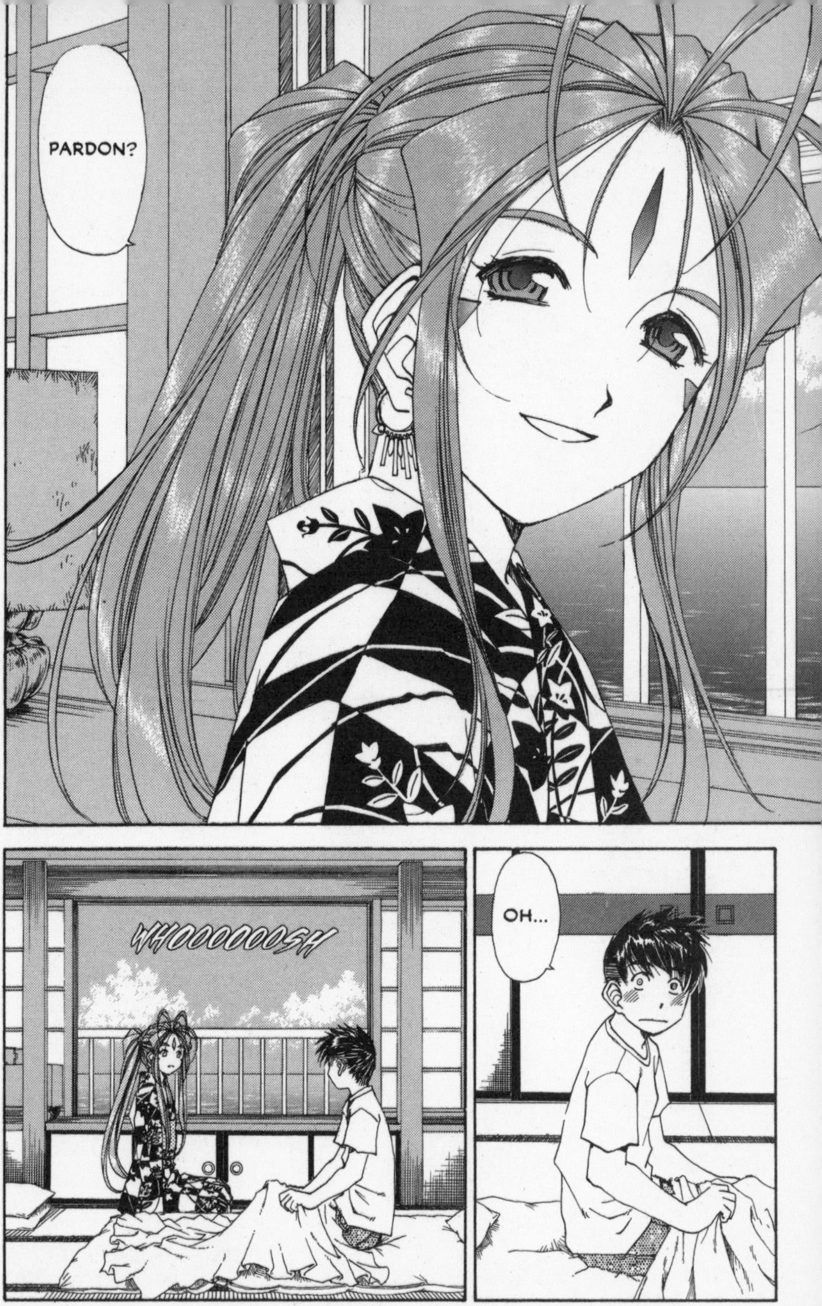
PARDON?
OH...
WHOOOOOOOSH

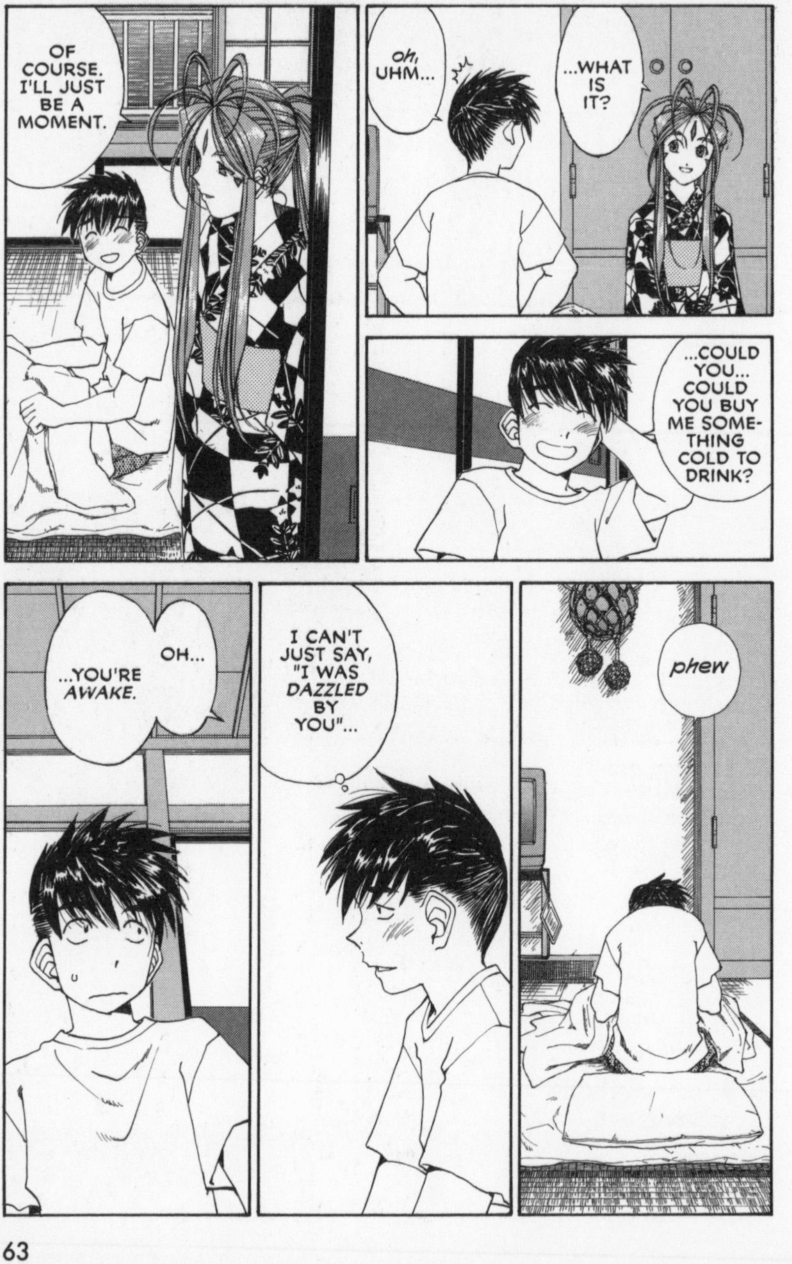
...WHAT IS IT?
oh, UHM...
...COULD YOU... COULD YOU BUY ME SOME-THING COLD TO DRINK?
OF COURSE. I'LL JUST BE A MOMENT.
phew
I CAN'T JUST SAY, "I WAS *DAZZLED* BY YOU"...
OH...
...YOU'RE *AWAKE.*

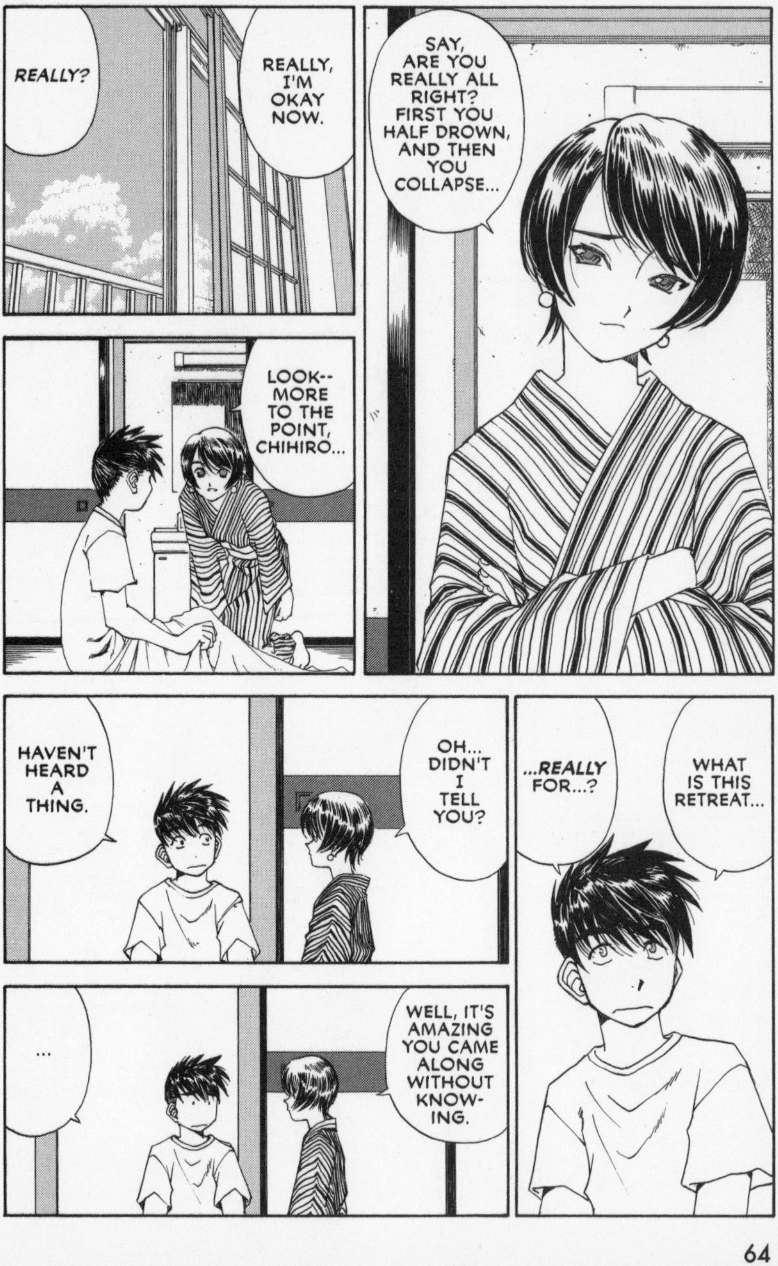
SAY, ARE YOU REALLY ALL RIGHT? FIRST YOU HALF DROWN, AND THEN YOU COLLAPSE...
REALLY, I'M OKAY NOW.
REALLY?
LOOK-- MORE TO THE POINT, CHIHIRO...
WHAT IS THIS RETREAT...
...*REALLY* FOR...?
OH... DIDN'T I TELL YOU?
HAVEN'T HEARD A THING.
WELL, IT'S AMAZING YOU CAME ALONG WITHOUT KNOW-ING.
...

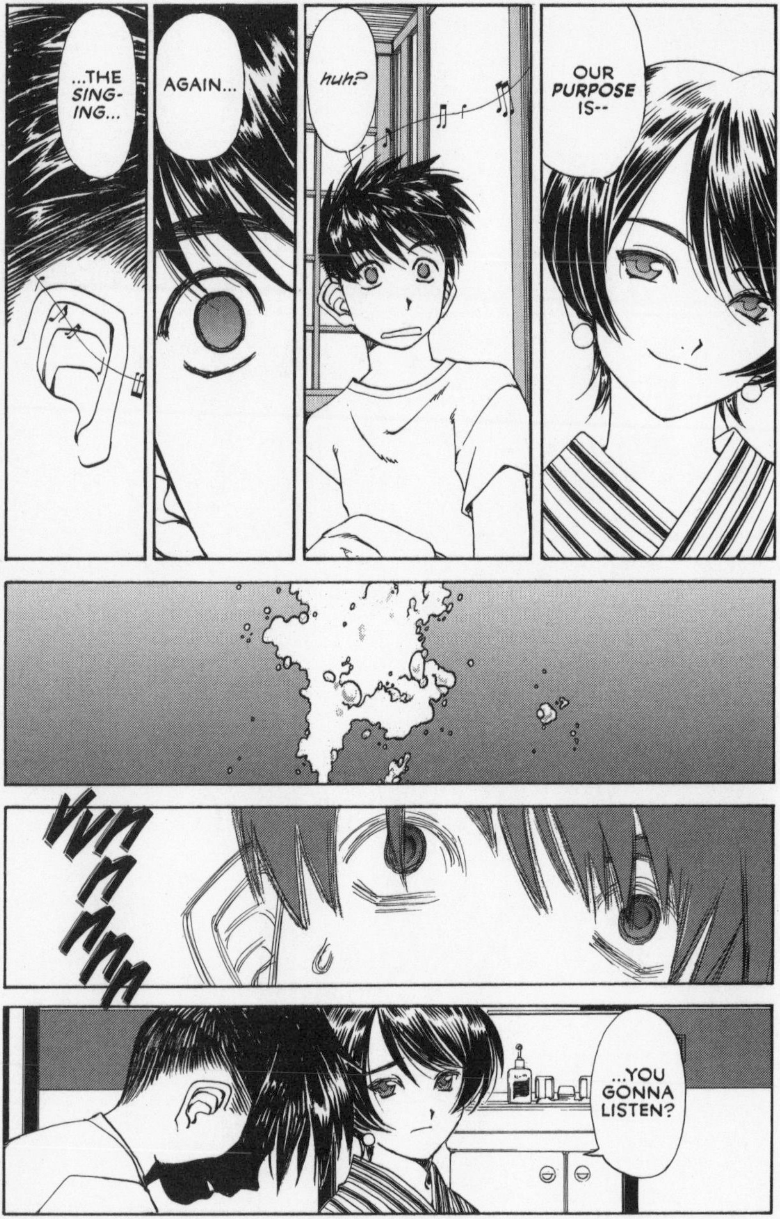
OUR PURPOSE IS--
huh?
AGAIN...
...THE SING-ING...
...YOU GONNA LISTEN?

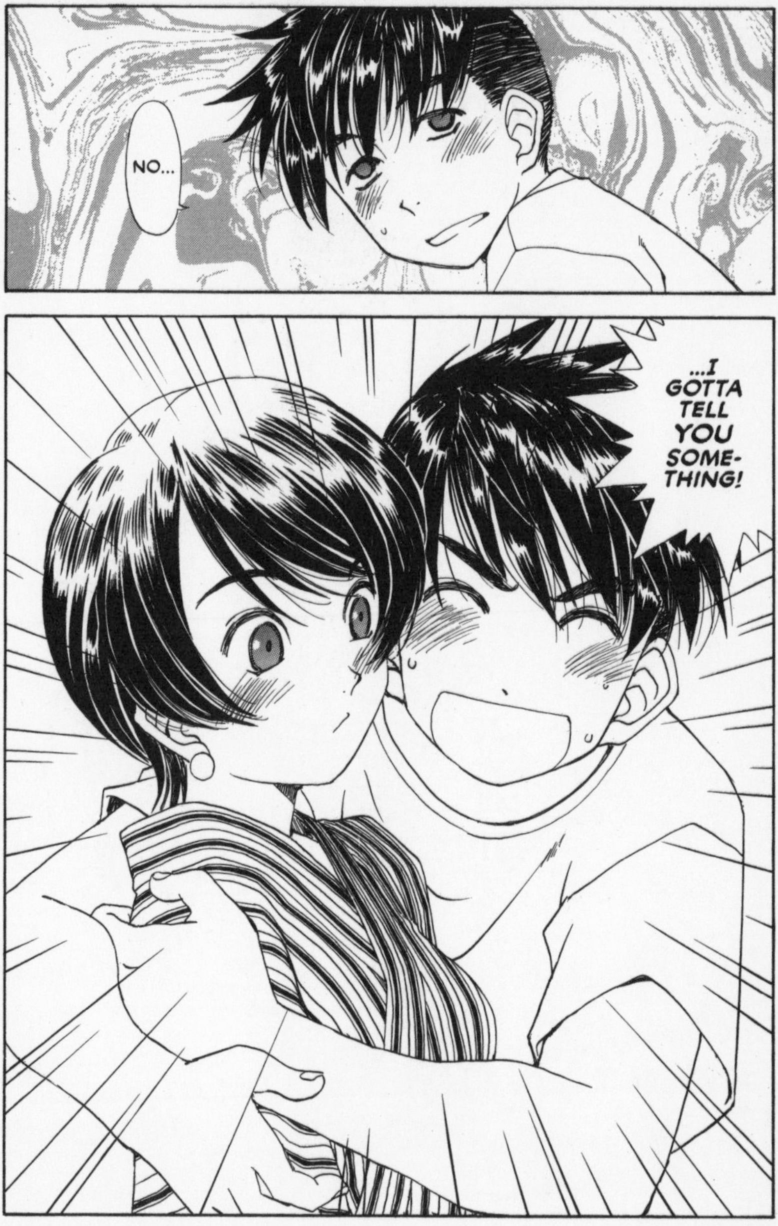
NO...
...I GOTTA TELL YOU SOME-THING!

CHAPTER 204

Sounds That Reach, Voices That Don't

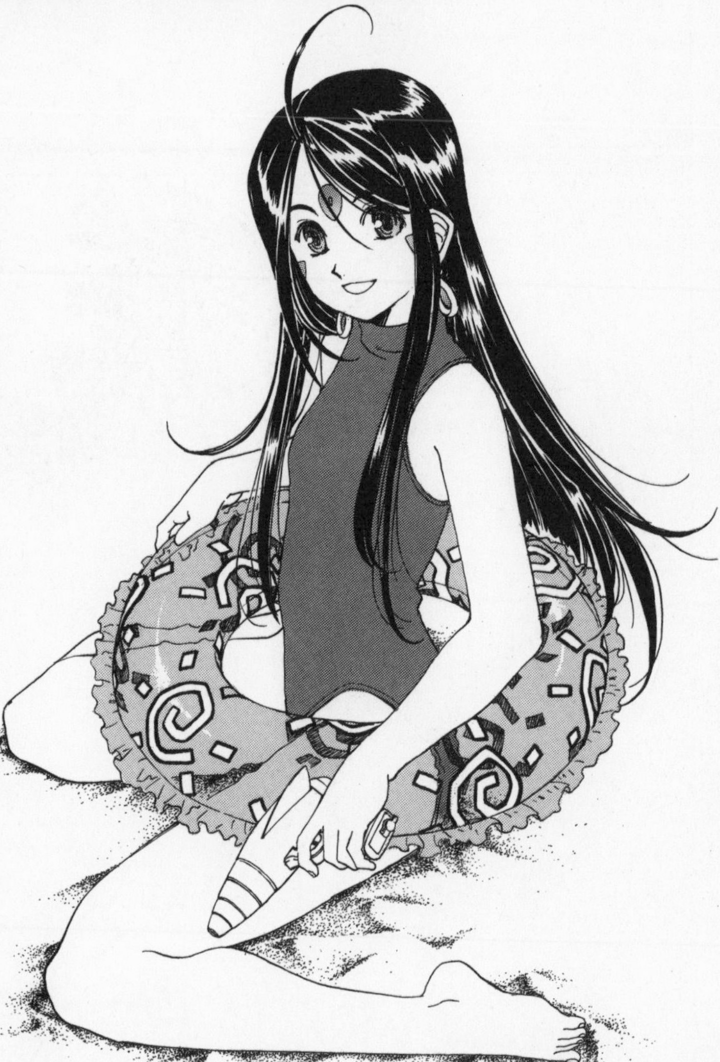

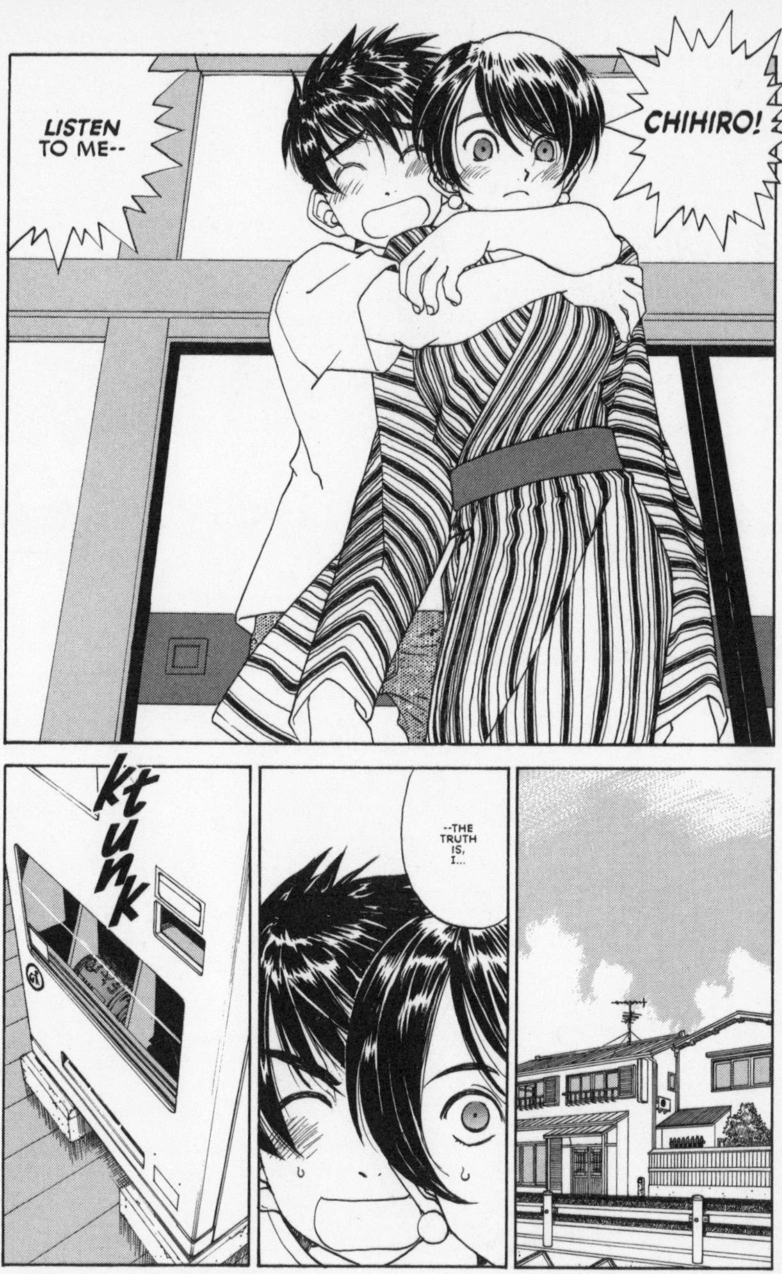
CHIHIRO!
LISTEN TO ME--
--THE TRUTH IS, I...
ktunk

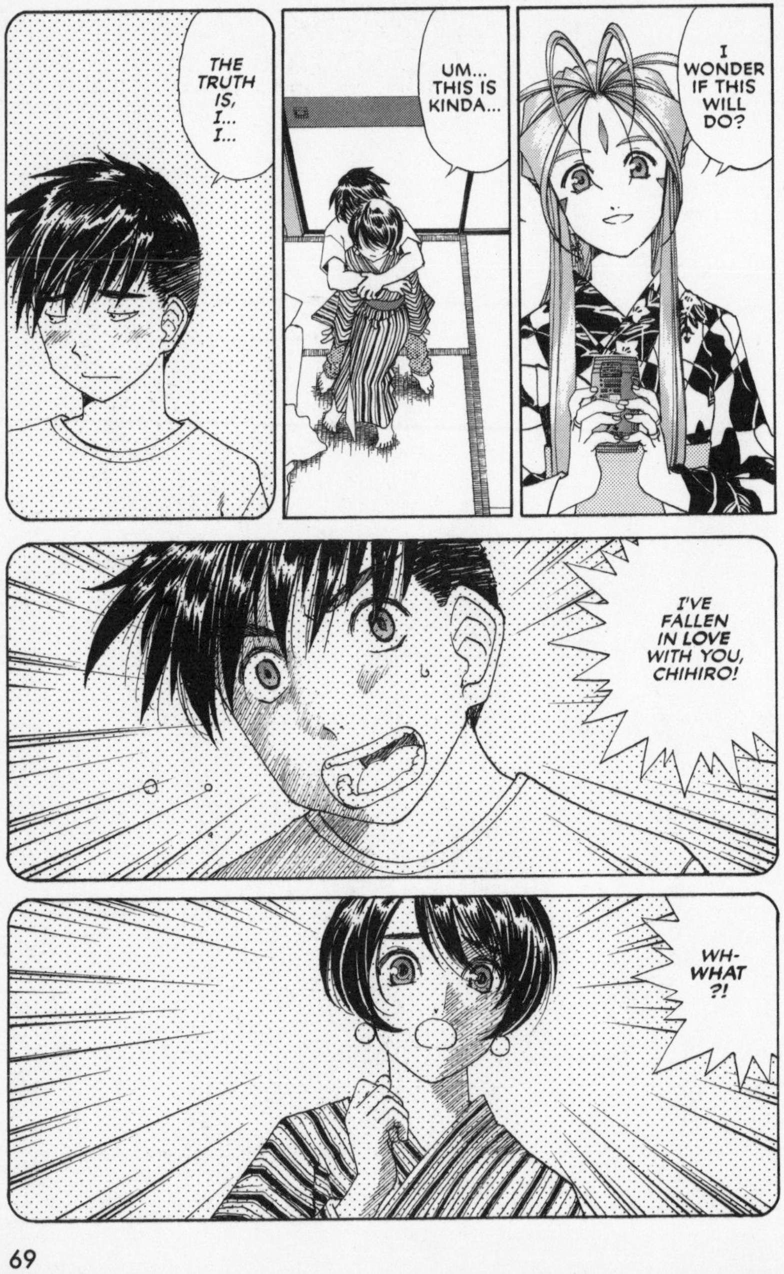
I WONDER IF THIS WILL DO?
UM... THIS IS KINDA...
THE TRUTH IS, I... I...
I'VE FALLEN IN LOVE WITH YOU, CHIHIRO!
WH-WHAT?!

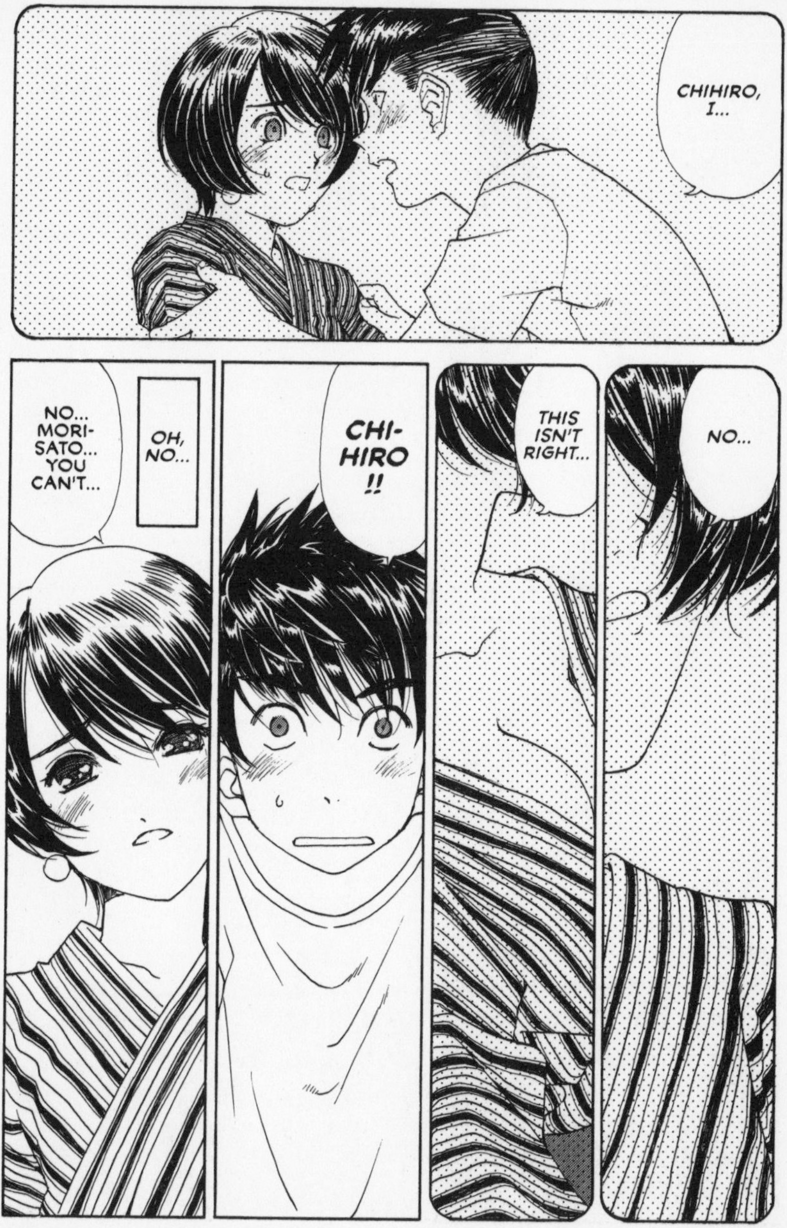
CHIHIRO, I...
NO...
THIS ISN'T RIGHT...
CHI-HIRO !!
OH, NO...
NO... MORI-SATO... YOU CAN'T...

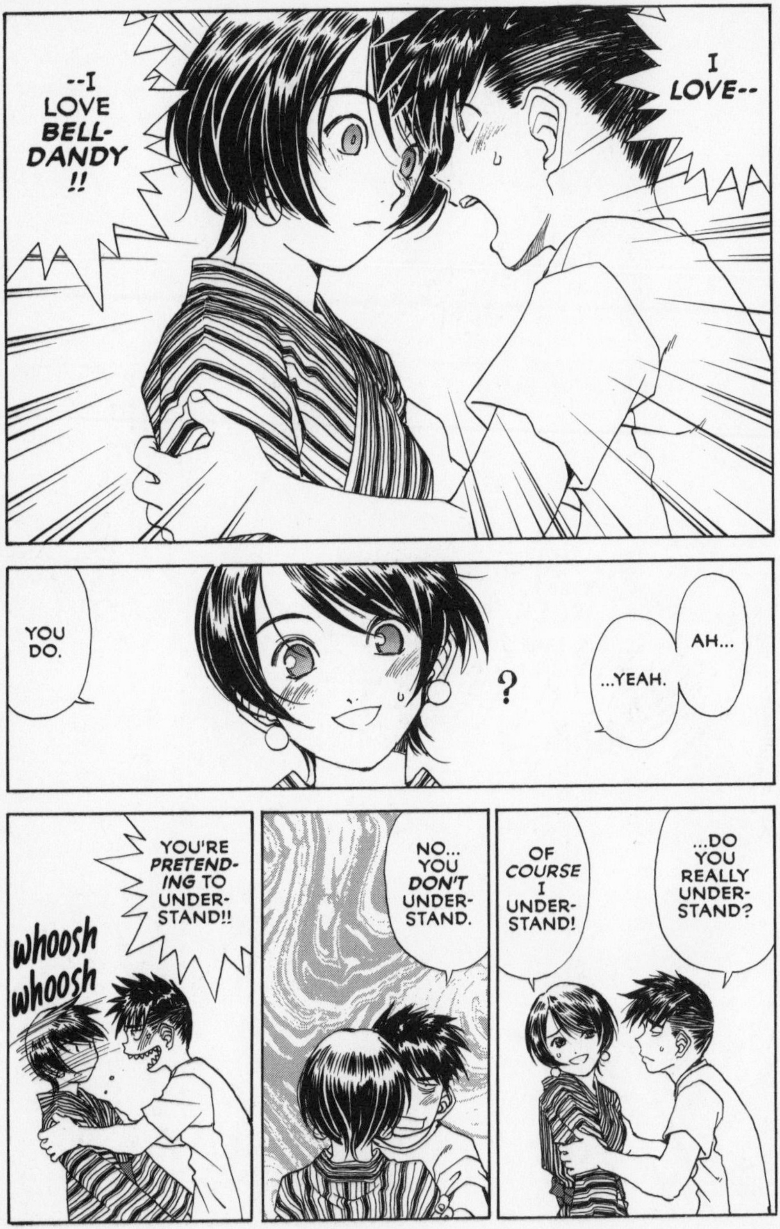
I LOVE--
--I LOVE BELL-DANDY!!
AH...
...YEAH.
?
YOU DO.
...DO YOU REALLY UNDER-STAND?
OF COURSE I UNDER-STAND!
NO... YOU DON'T UNDER-STAND.
YOU'RE PRETEND-ING TO UNDER-STAND!!
whoosh whoosh

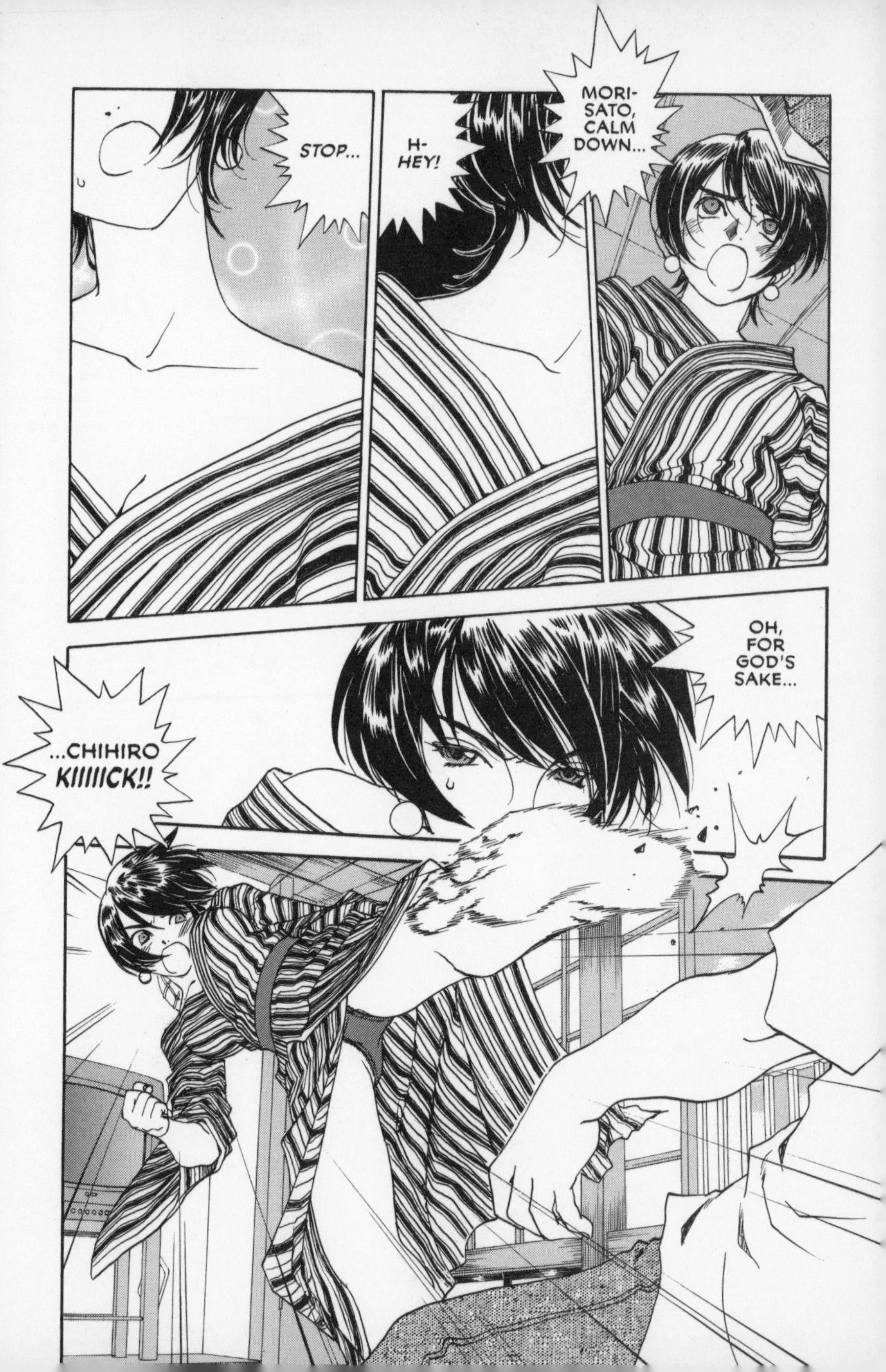
MORI-SATO, CALM DOWN...
H-HEY!
STOP...
OH, FOR GOD'S SAKE...
...CHIHIRO KIIIIICK!!

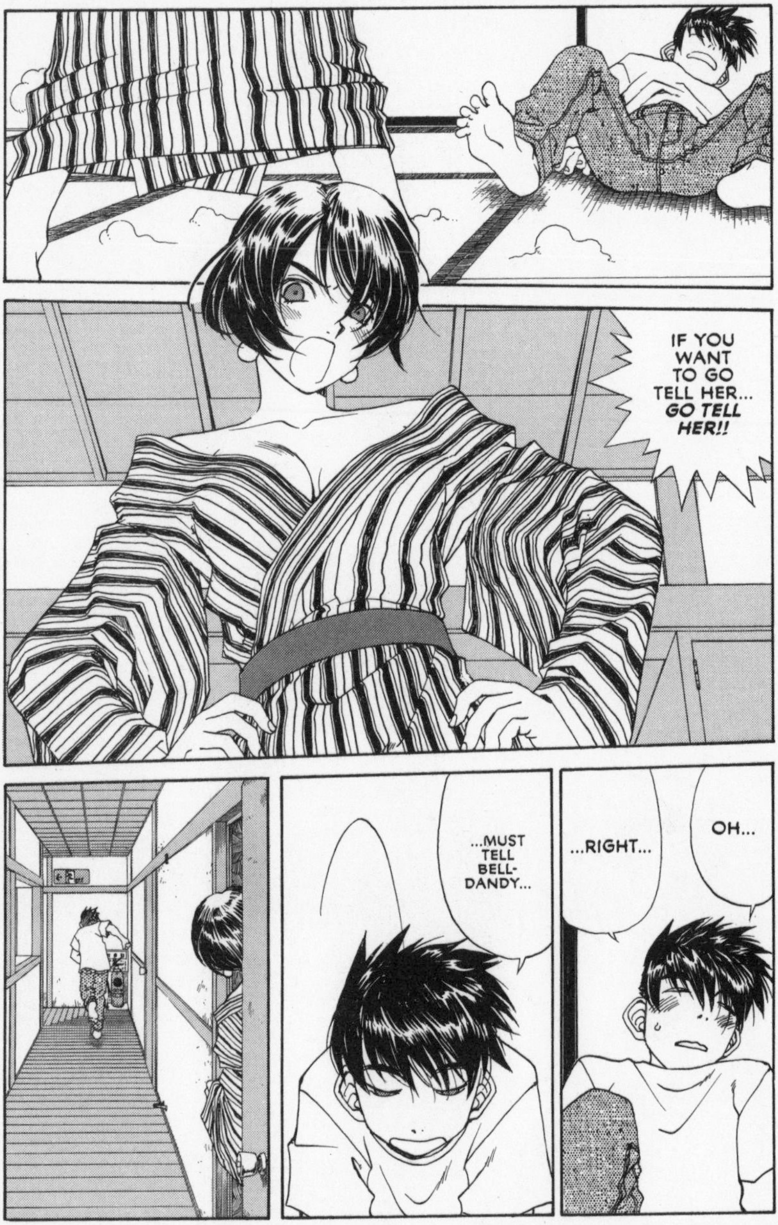
IF YOU WANT TO GO TELL HER... GO TELL HER!!
OH...
...RIGHT...
...MUST TELL BELL-DANDY...

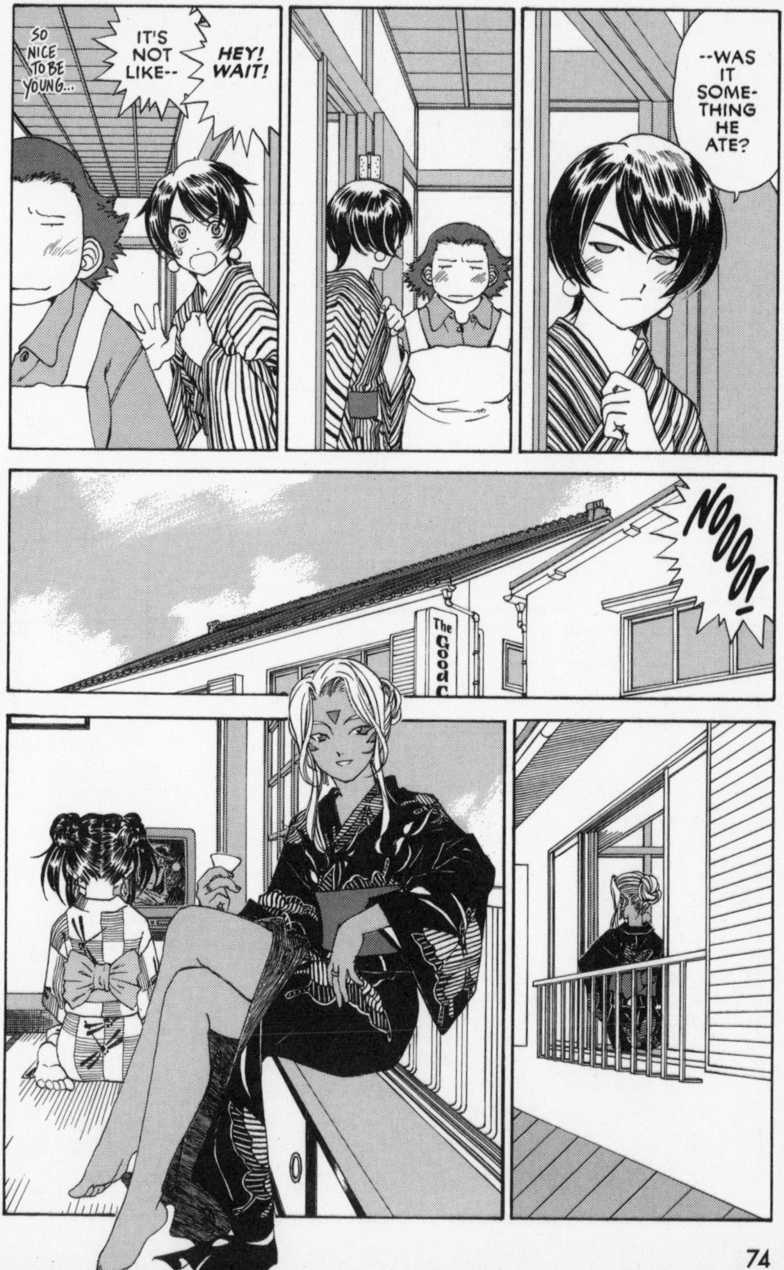
--WAS IT SOMETHING HE ATE?
HEY! WAIT!
IT'S NOT LIKE--
SO NICE TO BE YOUNG...
NOOOO!

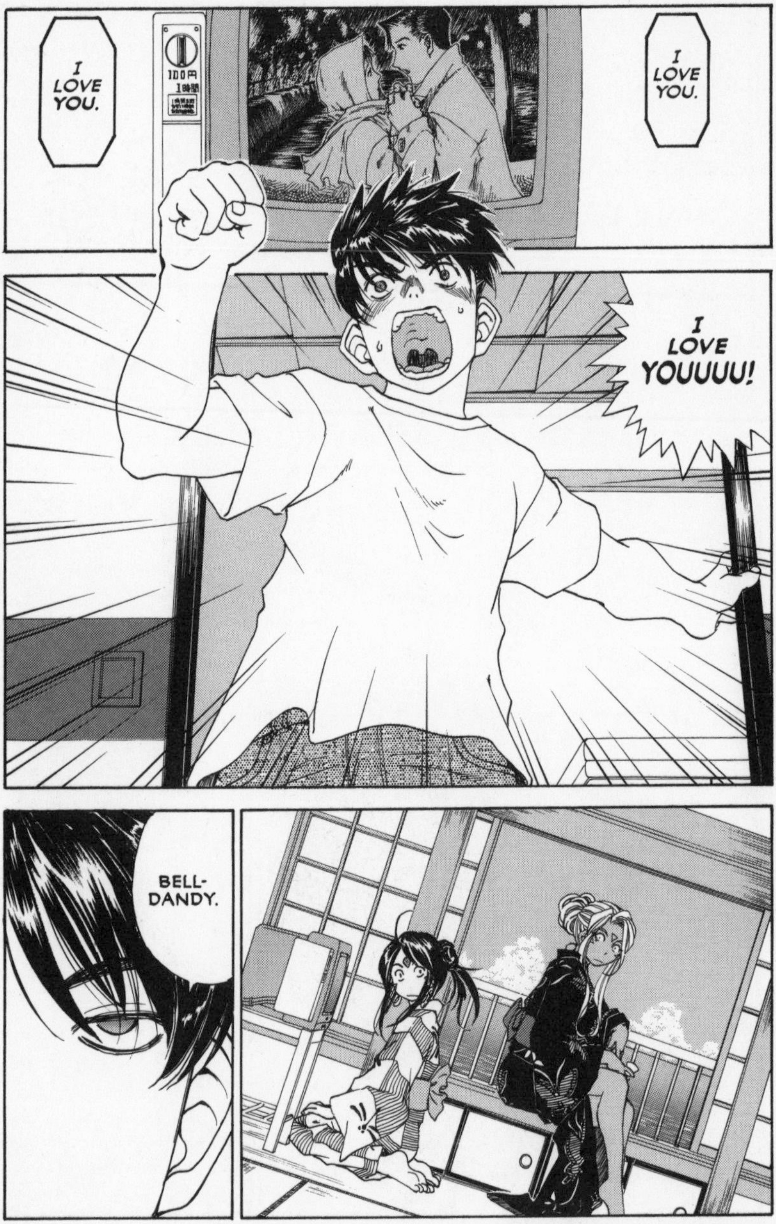
I LOVE YOU.
I LOVE YOU.
I LOVE YOUUUU!
BELL-DANDY.

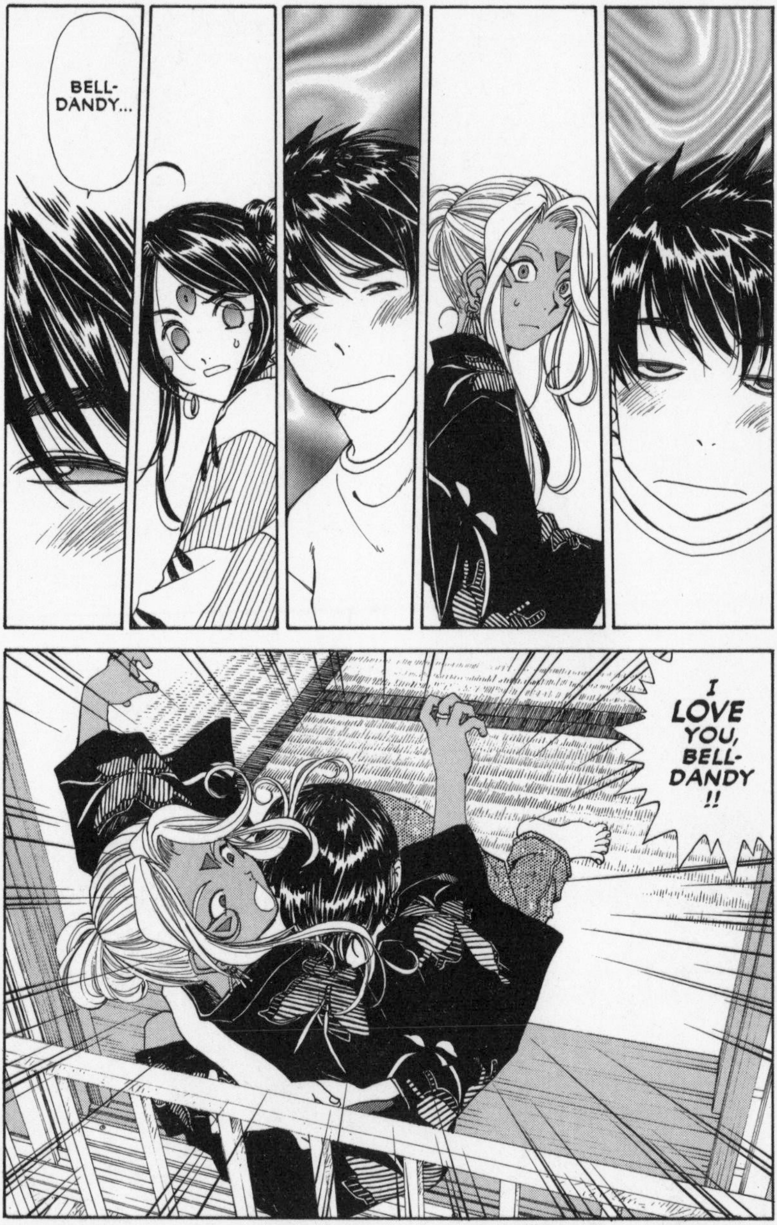
BELL-
DANDY...
I LOVE YOU, BELL-DANDY !!

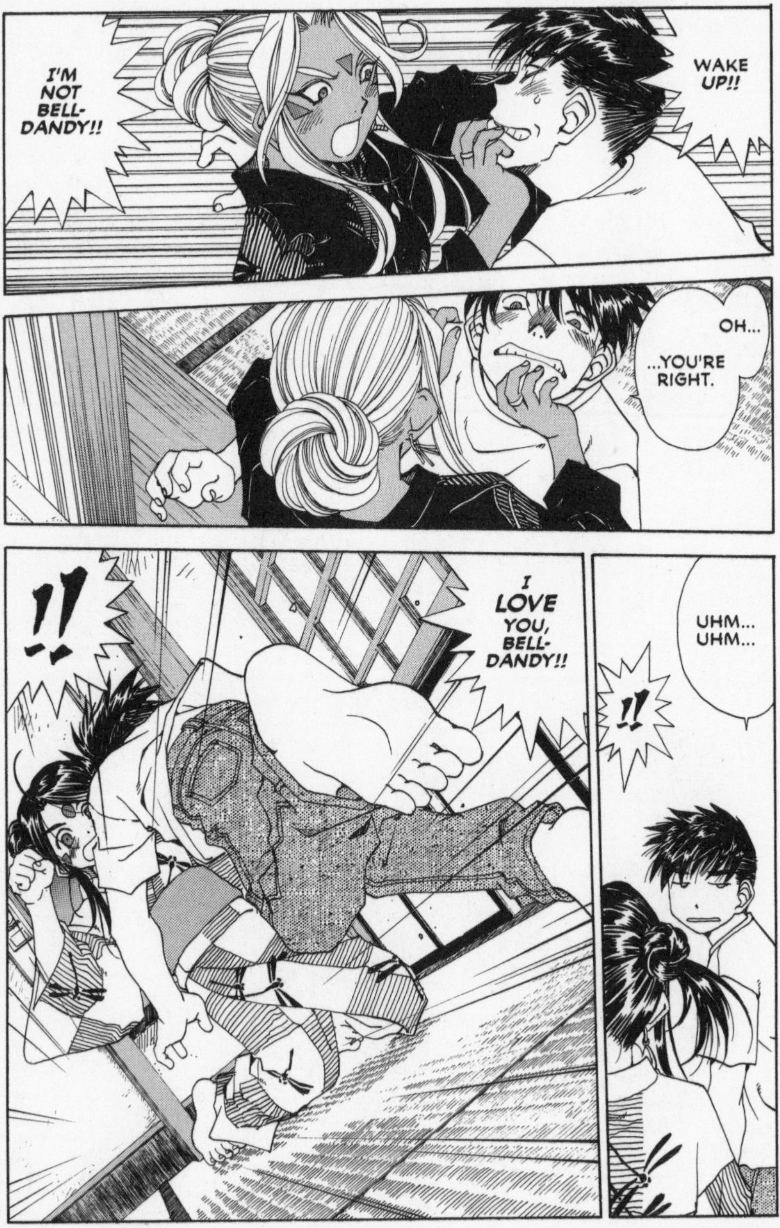
WAKE UP!!
I'M NOT BELL-DANDY!!
OH...
...YOU'RE RIGHT.
UHM... UHM...
!!
I LOVE YOU, BELL-DANDY!!
!!

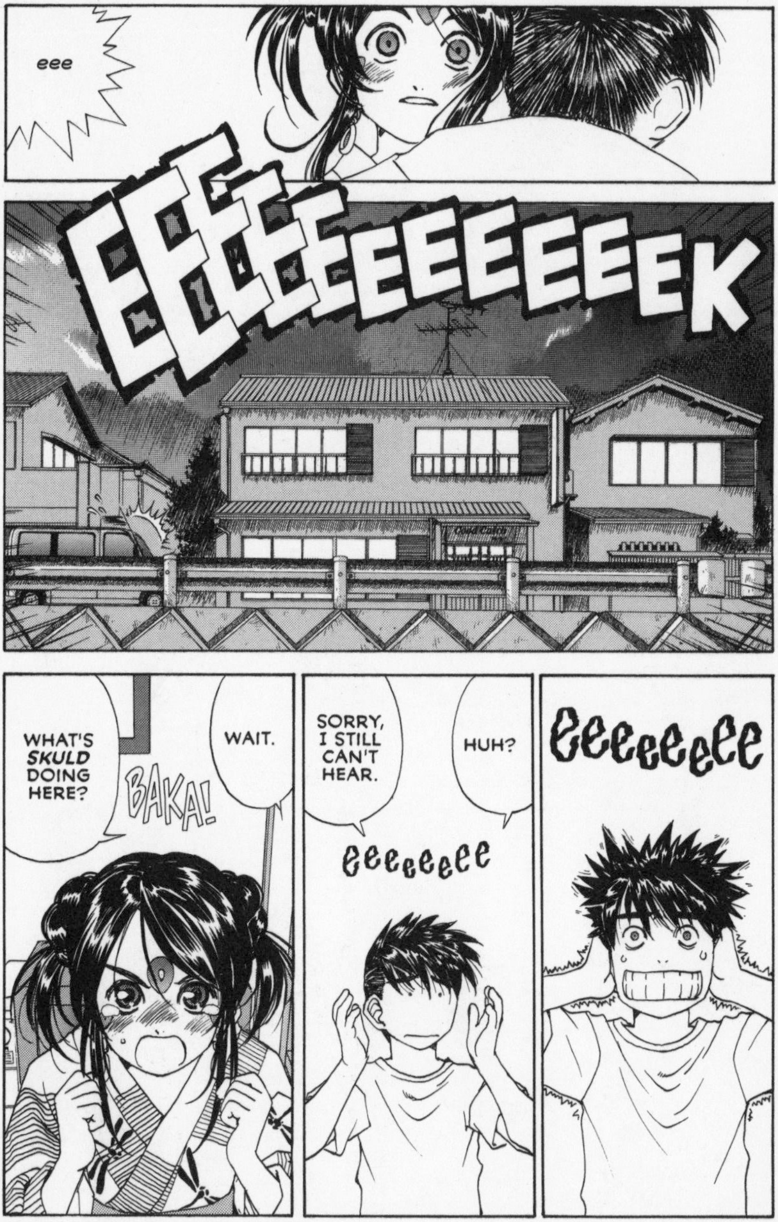
eee
EEEEEEEEEEEK
eeeeeeee
HUH?
SORRY, I STILL CAN'T HEAR.
eeeeeeeee
WAIT.
WHAT'S *SKULD* DOING HERE?
BAKA!

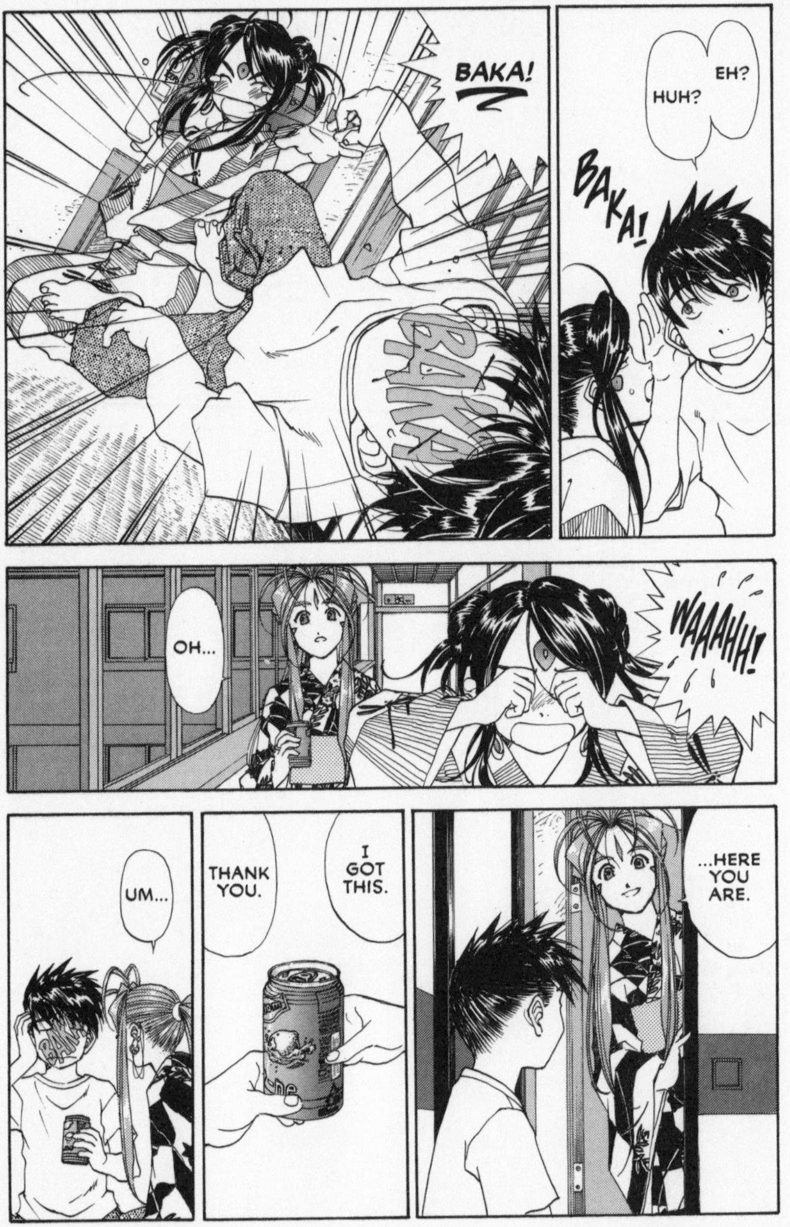
EH?
HUH?
BAKA!
BAKA!
BAKA
WAAAHH!
OH...
...HERE YOU ARE.
I GOT THIS.
THANK YOU.
UM...

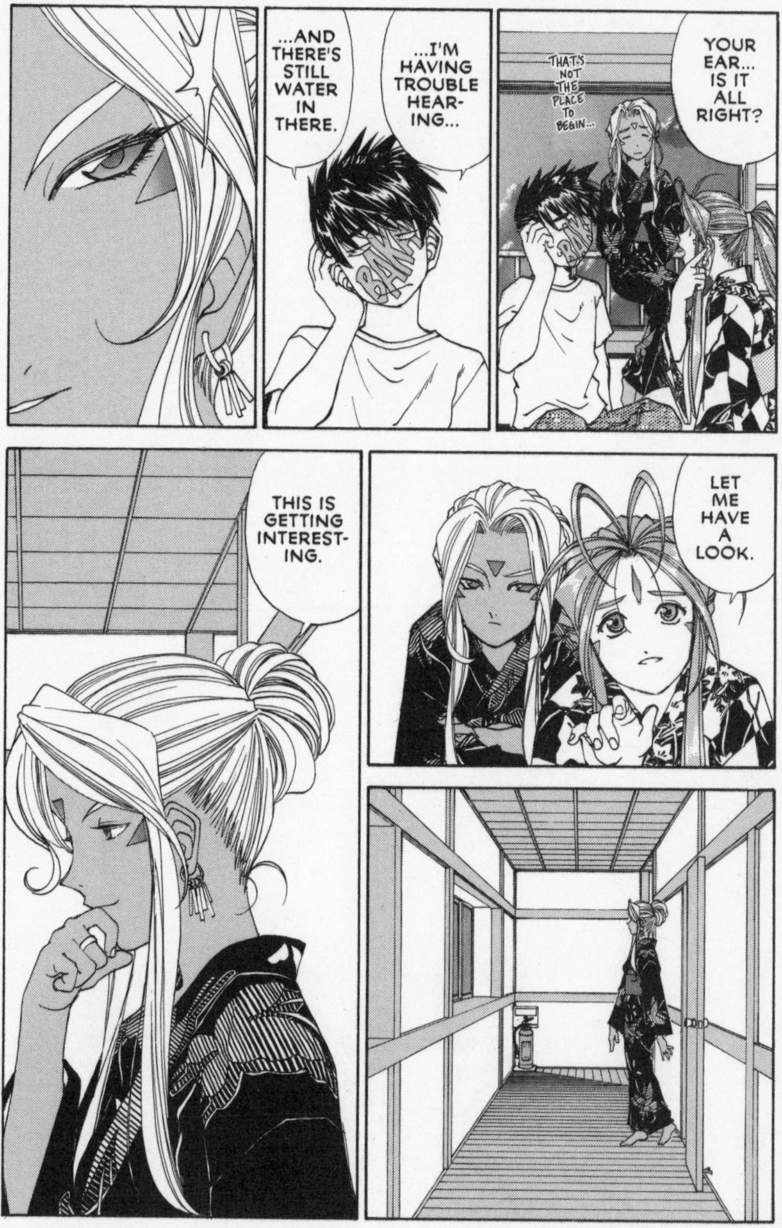
YOUR EAR... IS IT ALL RIGHT?
THAT'S NOT THE PLACE TO BEGIN...
...I'M HAVING TROUBLE HEAR-ING...
...AND THERE'S STILL WATER IN THERE.
LET ME HAVE A LOOK.
THIS IS GETTING INTEREST-ING.

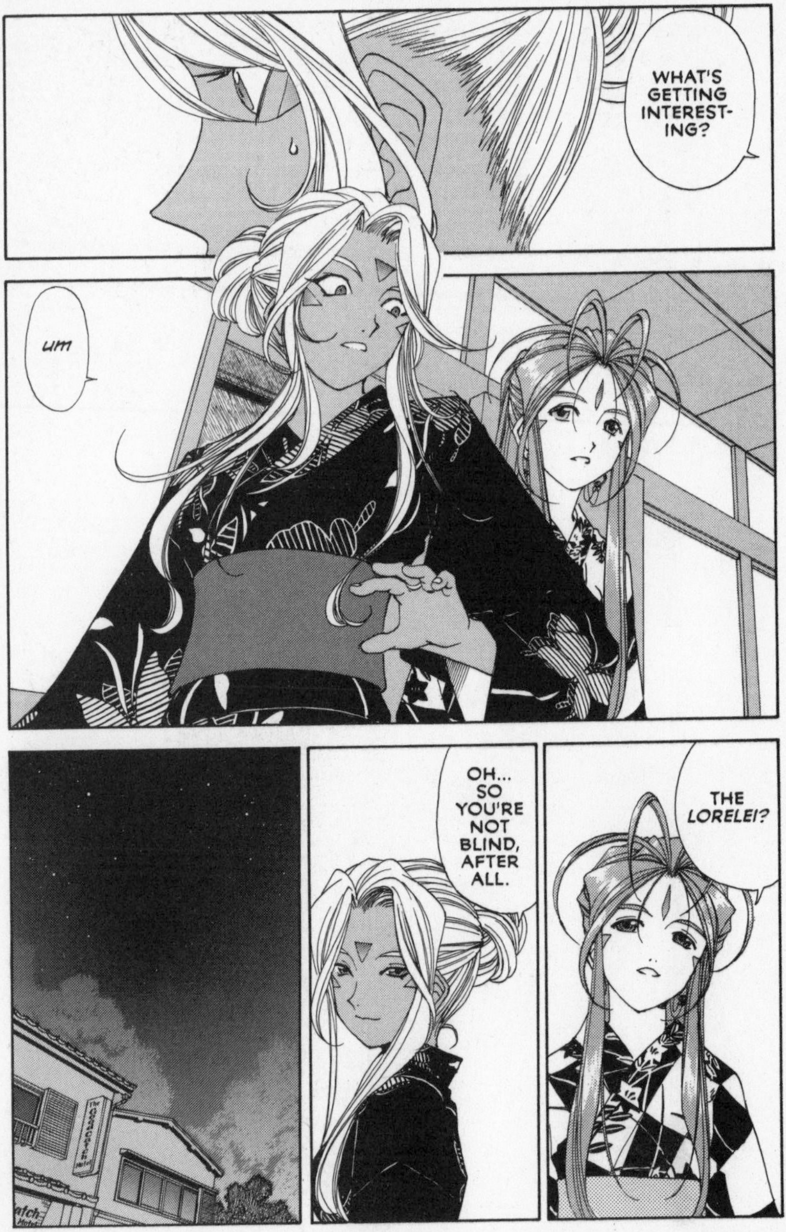
WHAT'S GETTING INTEREST-ING?
um
THE *LORELEI?*
OH... SO YOU'RE NOT BLIND, AFTER ALL.

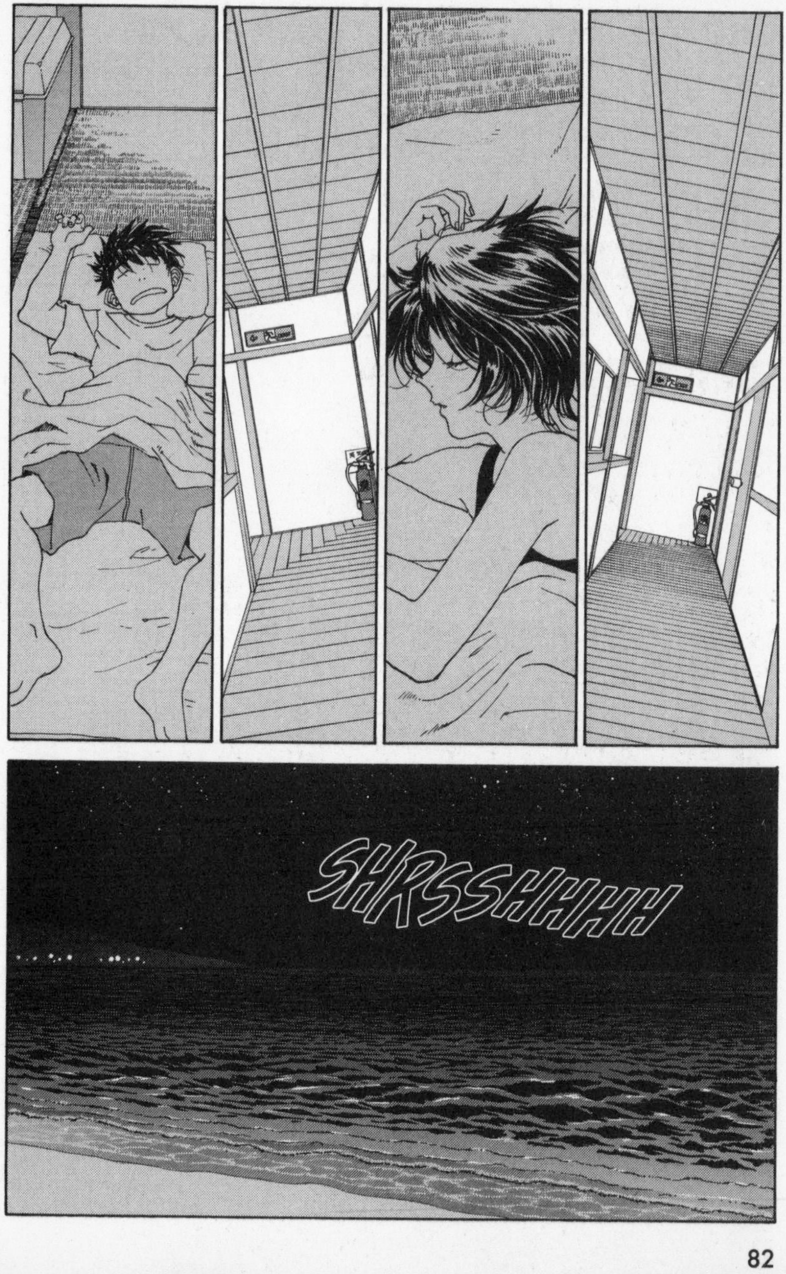
SHRSSHHHH

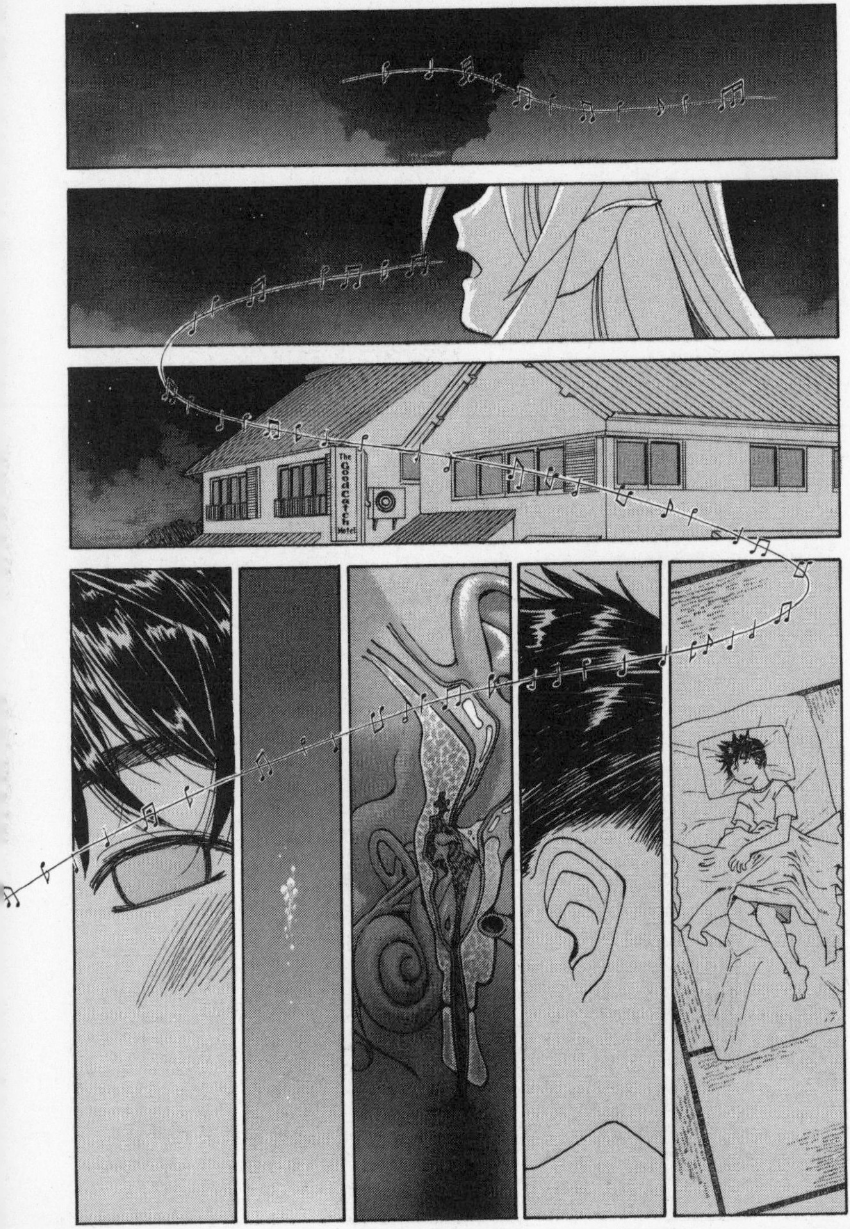
The
Hotel

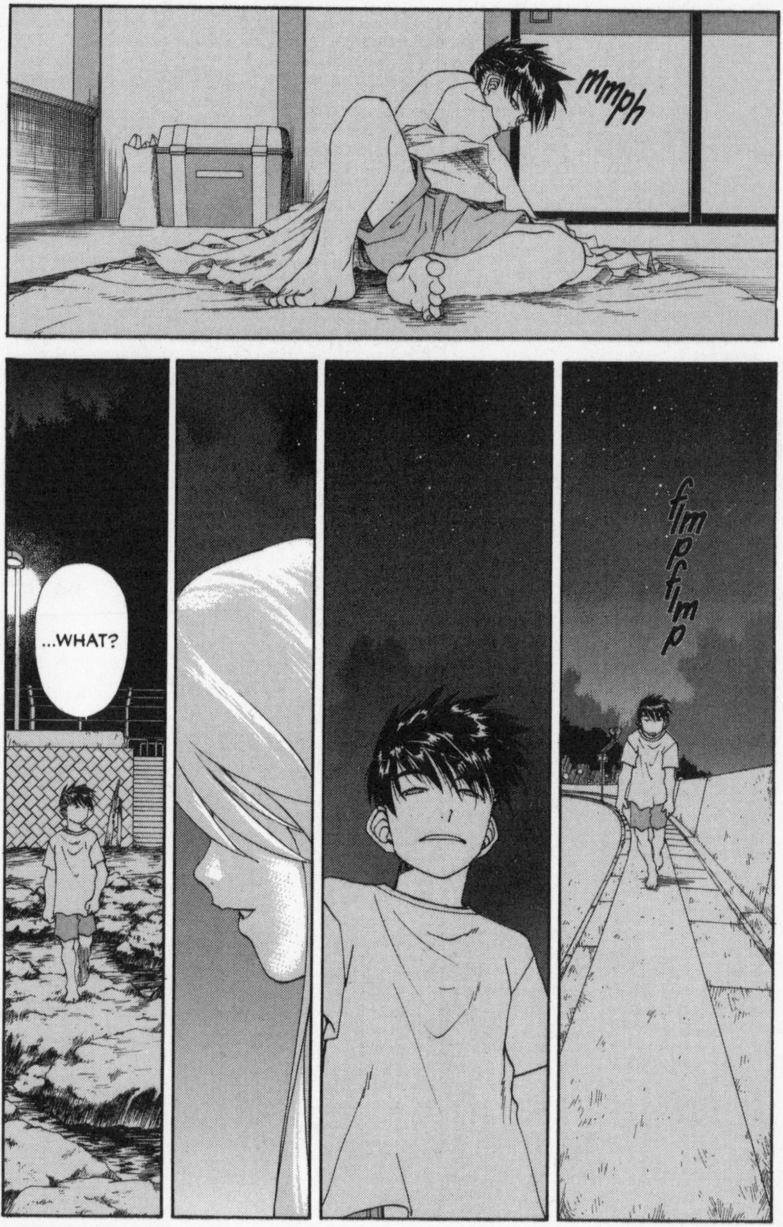
mmph
flmp flmp
...WHAT?

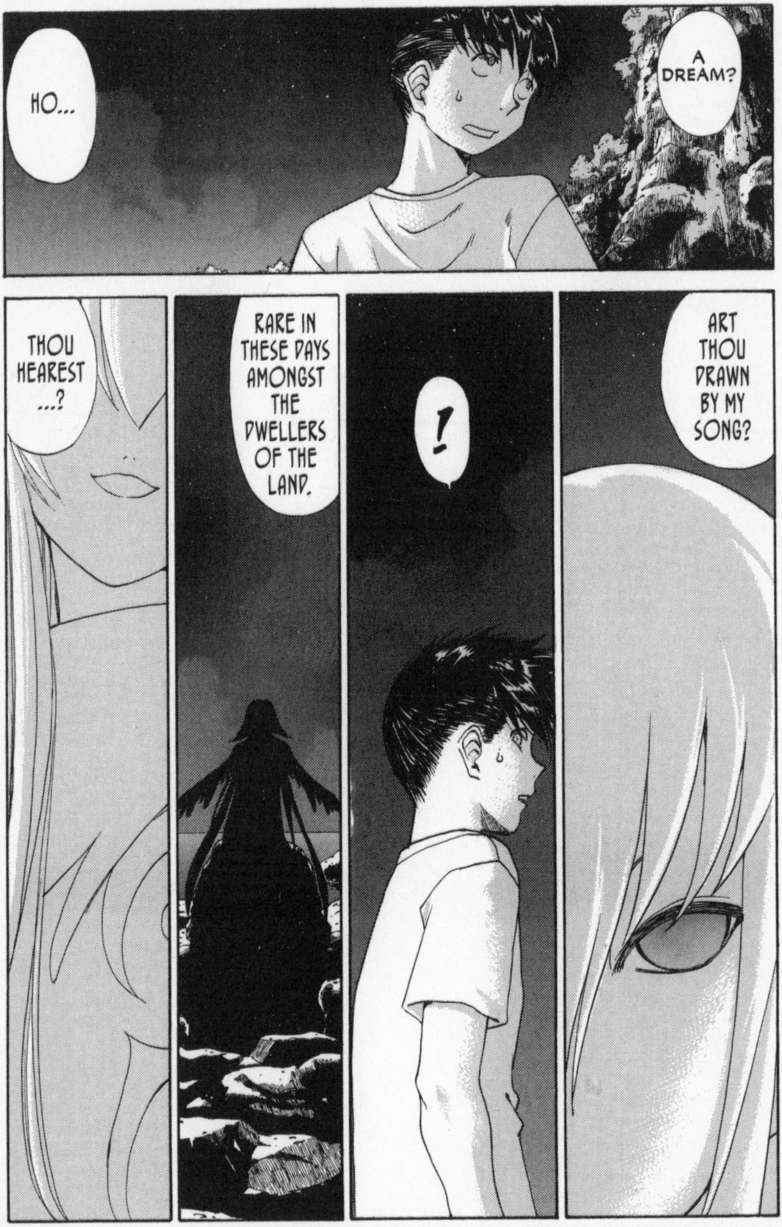
A DREAM?
HO...
ART THOU DRAWN BY MY SONG?
!
RARE IN THESE DAYS AMONGST THE DWELLERS OF THE LAND.
THOU HEAREST ...?

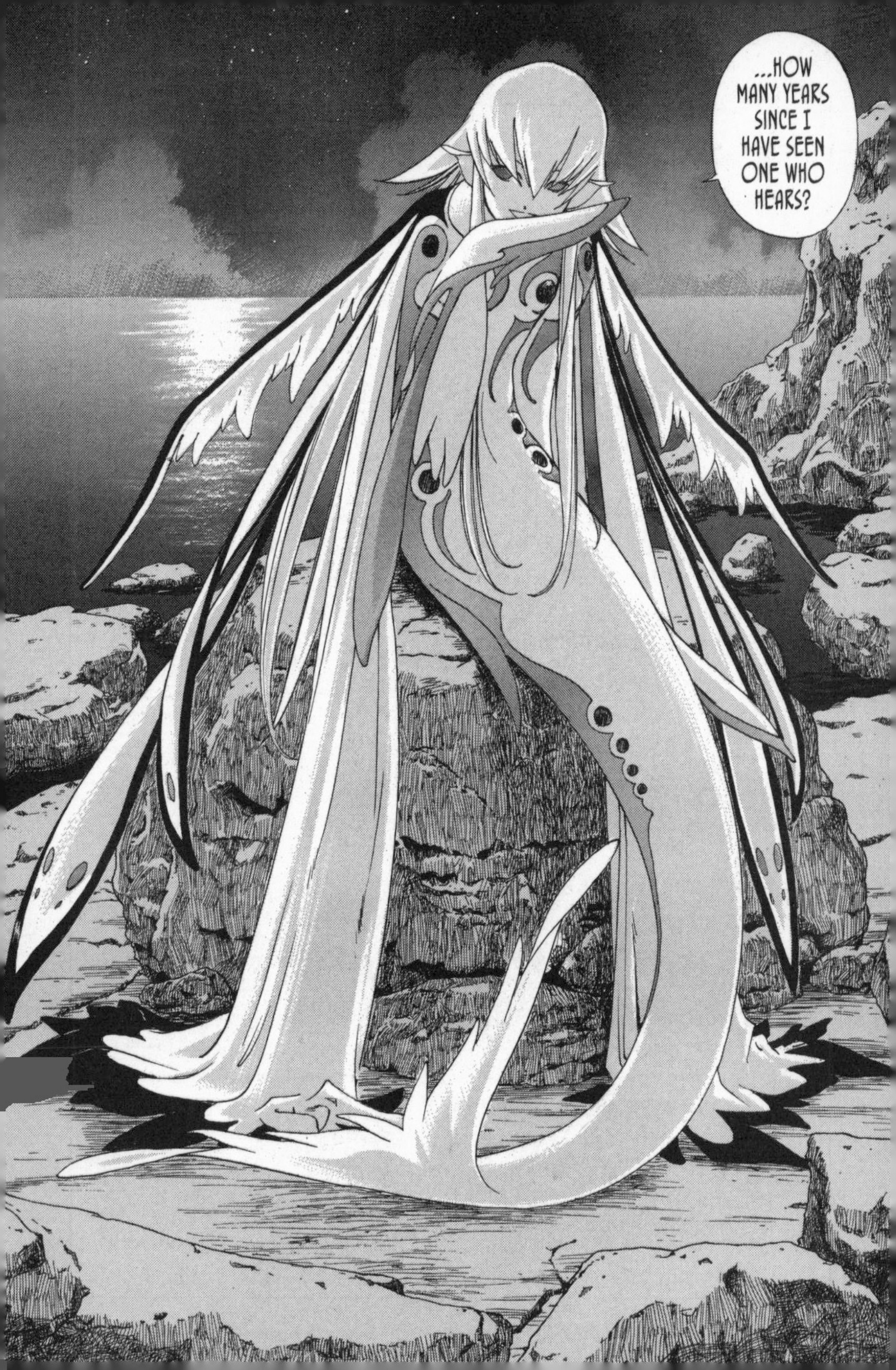
...HOW MANY YEARS SINCE I HAVE SEEN ONE WHO HEARS?

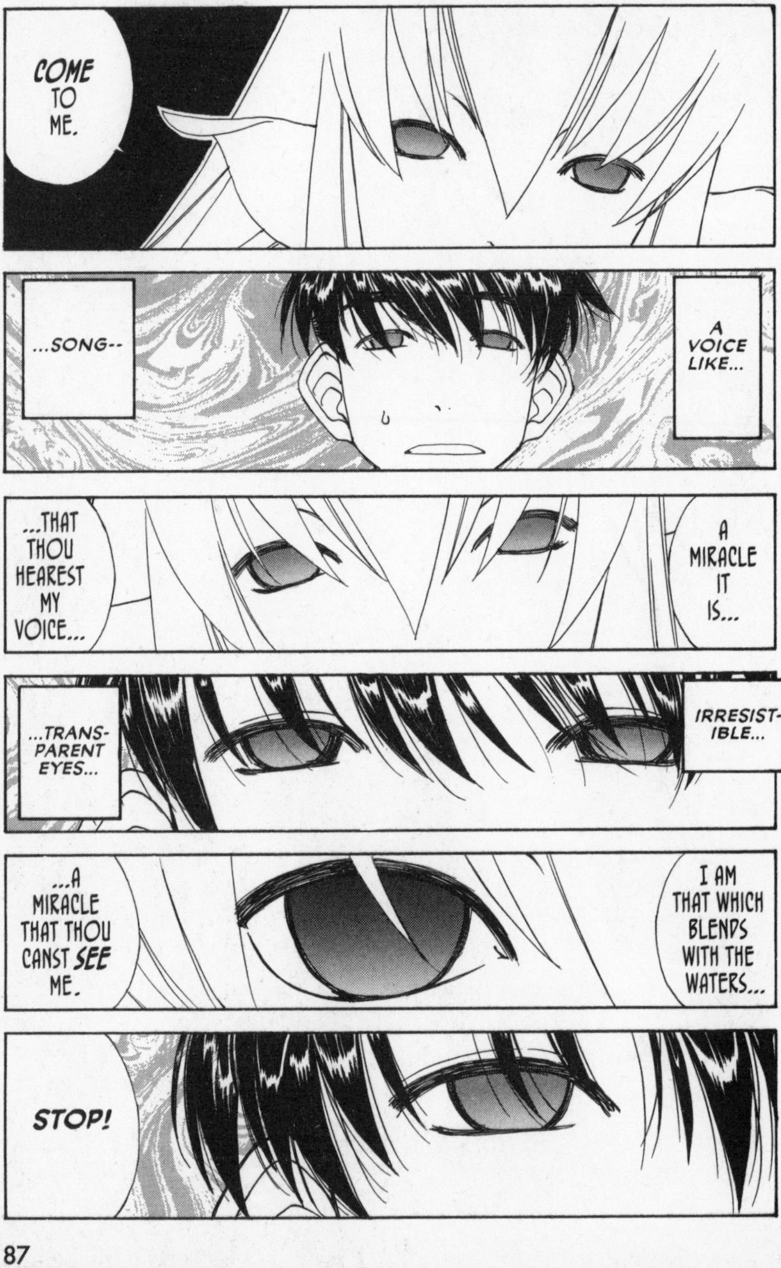
COME TO ME.
A VOICE LIKE...
...SONG--
A MIRACLE IT IS...
...THAT THOU HEAREST MY VOICE...
IRRESISTIBLE...
...TRANSPARENT EYES...
I AM THAT WHICH BLENDS WITH THE WATERS...
...A MIRACLE THAT THOU CANST SEE ME.
STOP!

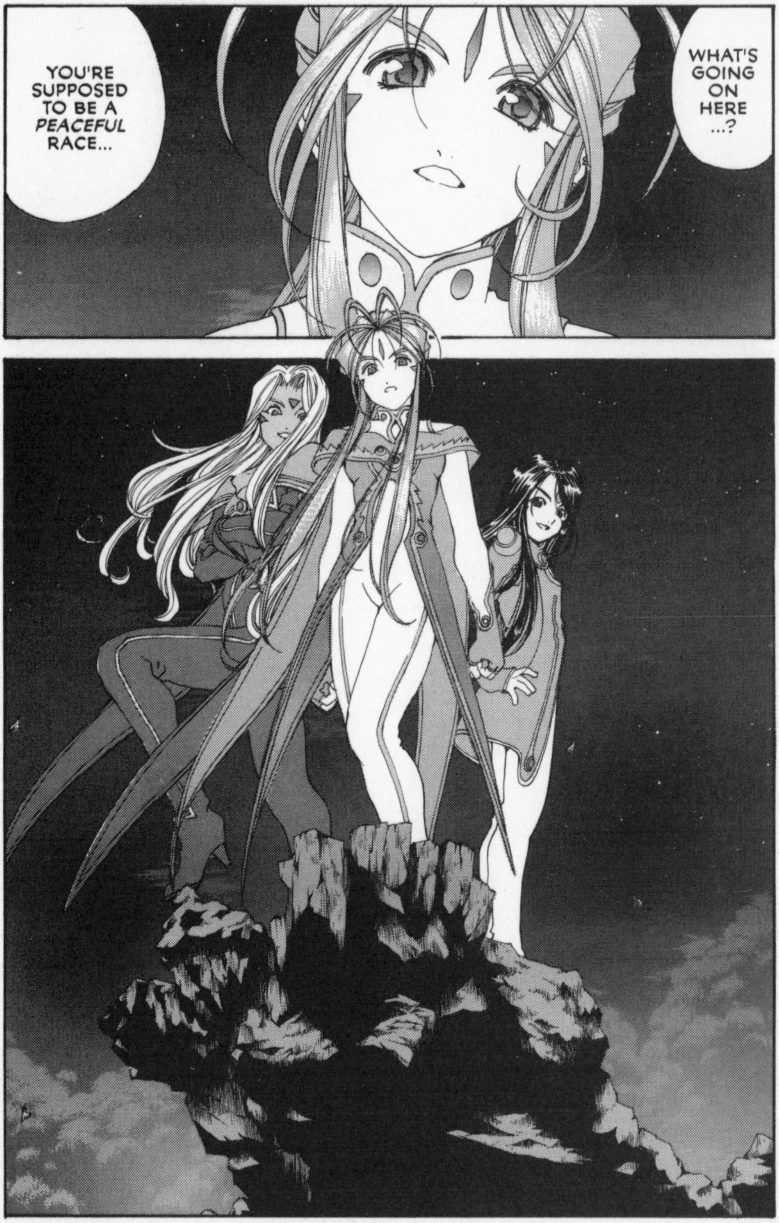
WHAT'S GOING ON HERE ...?
YOU'RE SUPPOSED TO BE A *PEACEFUL* RACE...

CHAPTER 205

Full-Clout Confrontation

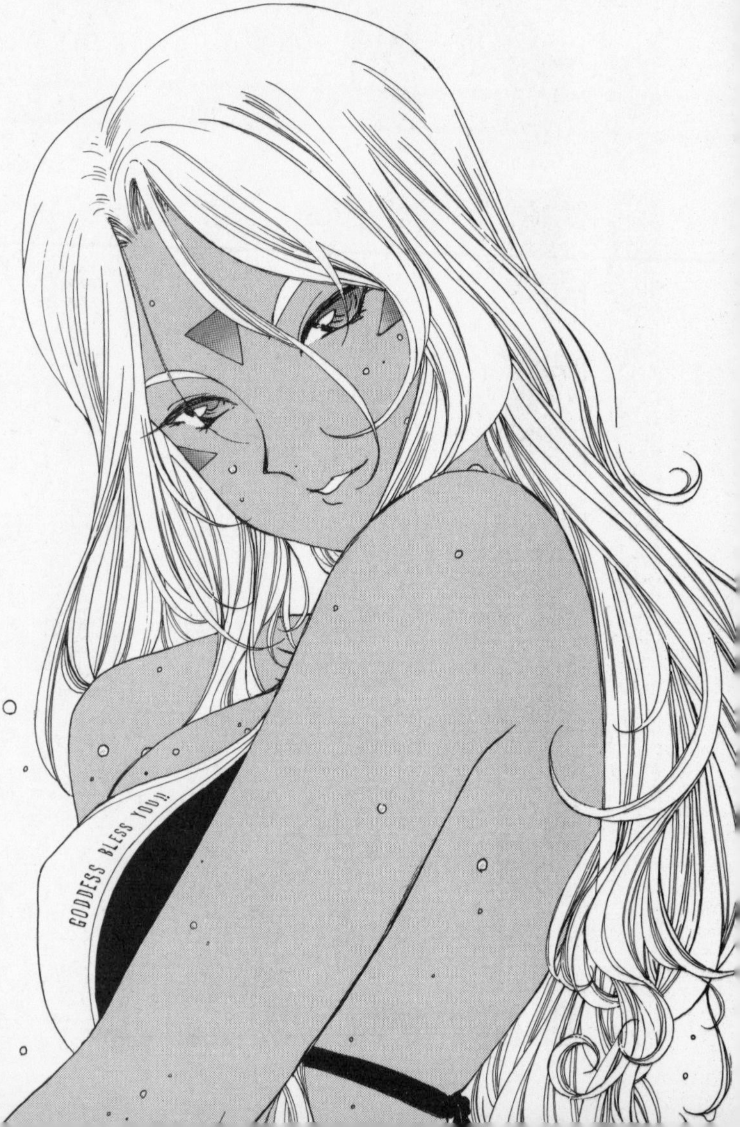
GODDESS BLESS YOU!!

QUEER THAT THOU ACCUSE US, YE FROM THE LAND OF THE GODS.
ART THOU NOT ACCUSTOMED TO BE CALM?
...AREN'T YOU...?

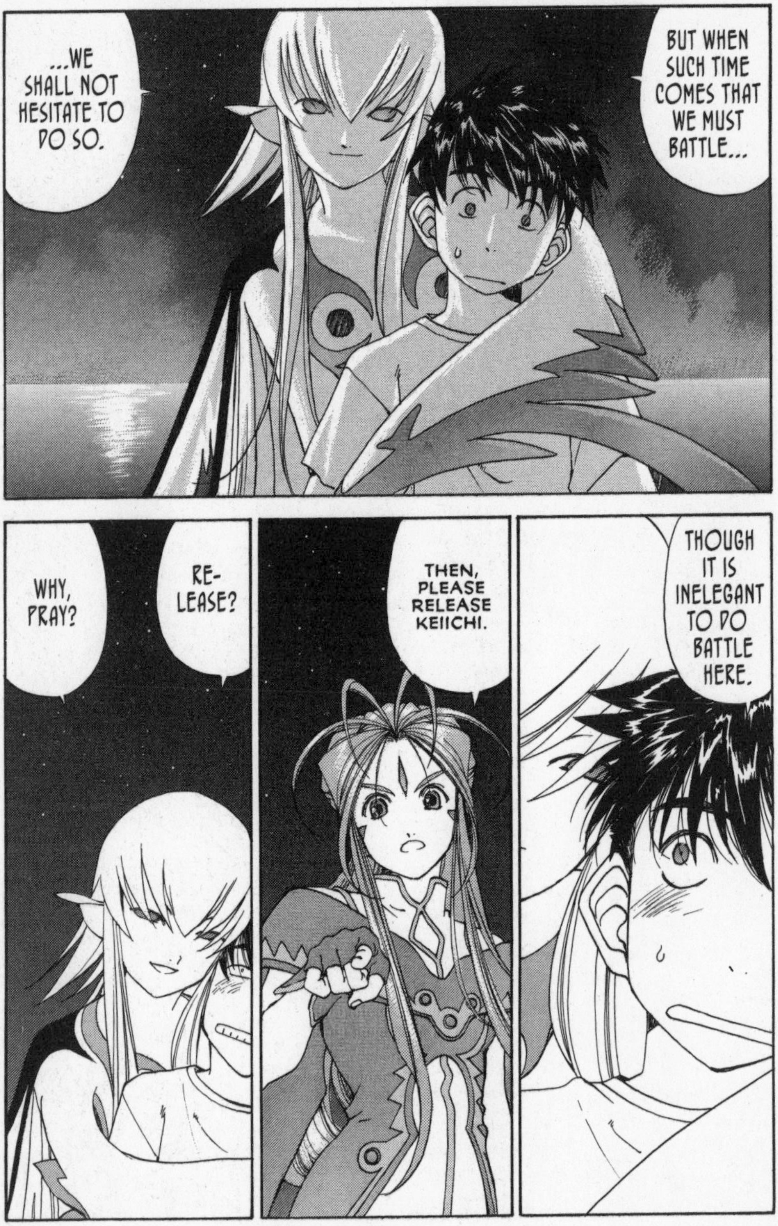
BUT WHEN SUCH TIME COMES THAT WE MUST BATTLE...
...WE SHALL NOT HESITATE TO DO SO.
THOUGH IT IS INELEGANT TO DO BATTLE HERE.
THEN, PLEASE RELEASE KEIICHI.
RE-LEASE?
WHY, PRAY?

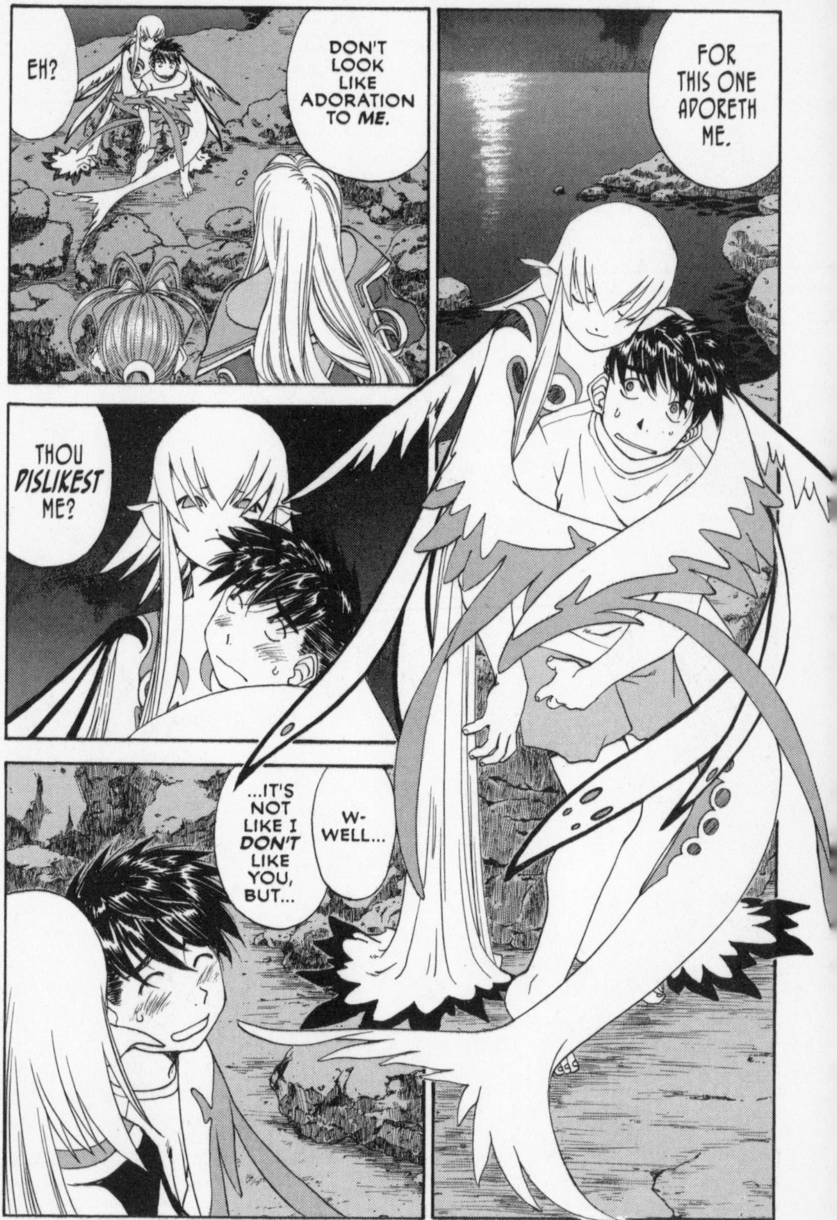
FOR THIS ONE ADORETH ME.
DON'T LOOK LIKE ADORATION TO *ME.*
EH?
THOU *DISLIKEST* ME?
W-WELL...
...IT'S NOT LIKE I *DON'T* LIKE YOU, BUT...

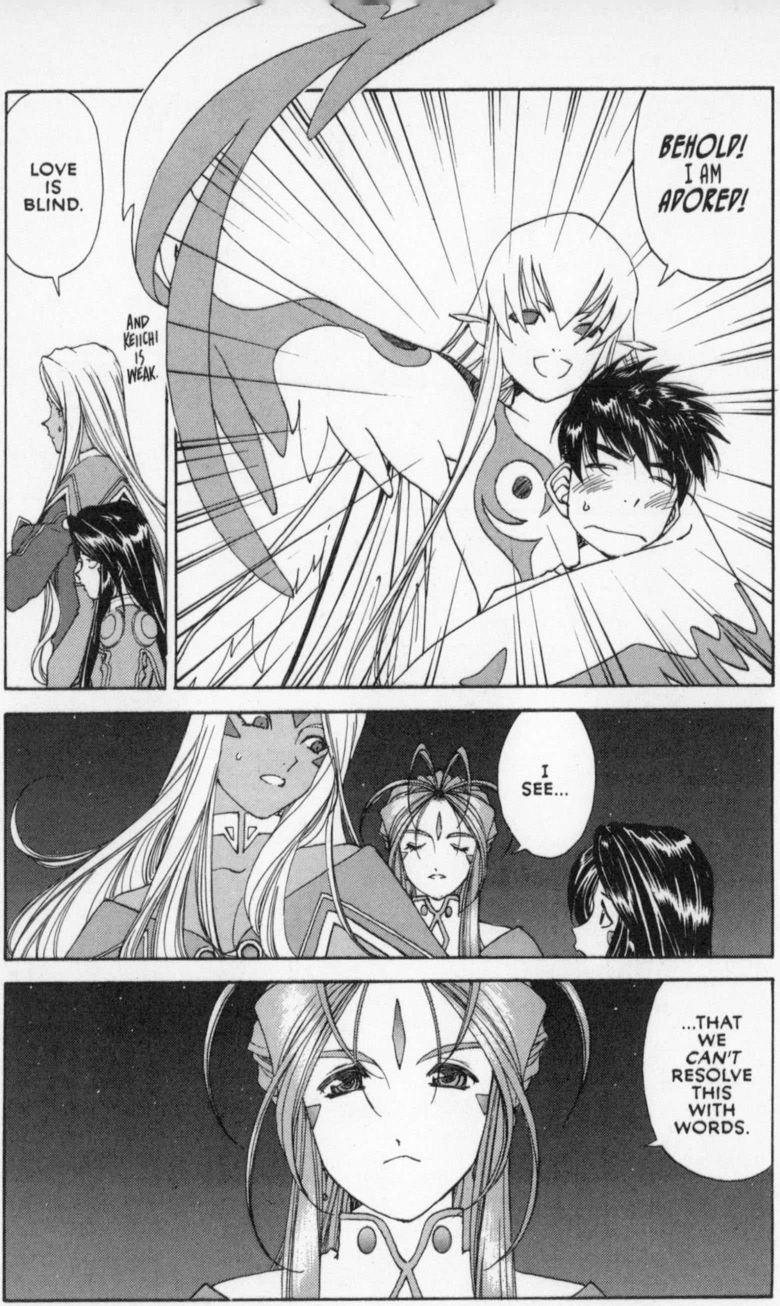
BEHOLD! I AM ADORED!
LOVE IS BLIND.
AND KEIICHI IS WEAK.
I SEE...
...THAT WE *CAN'T* RESOLVE THIS WITH WORDS.

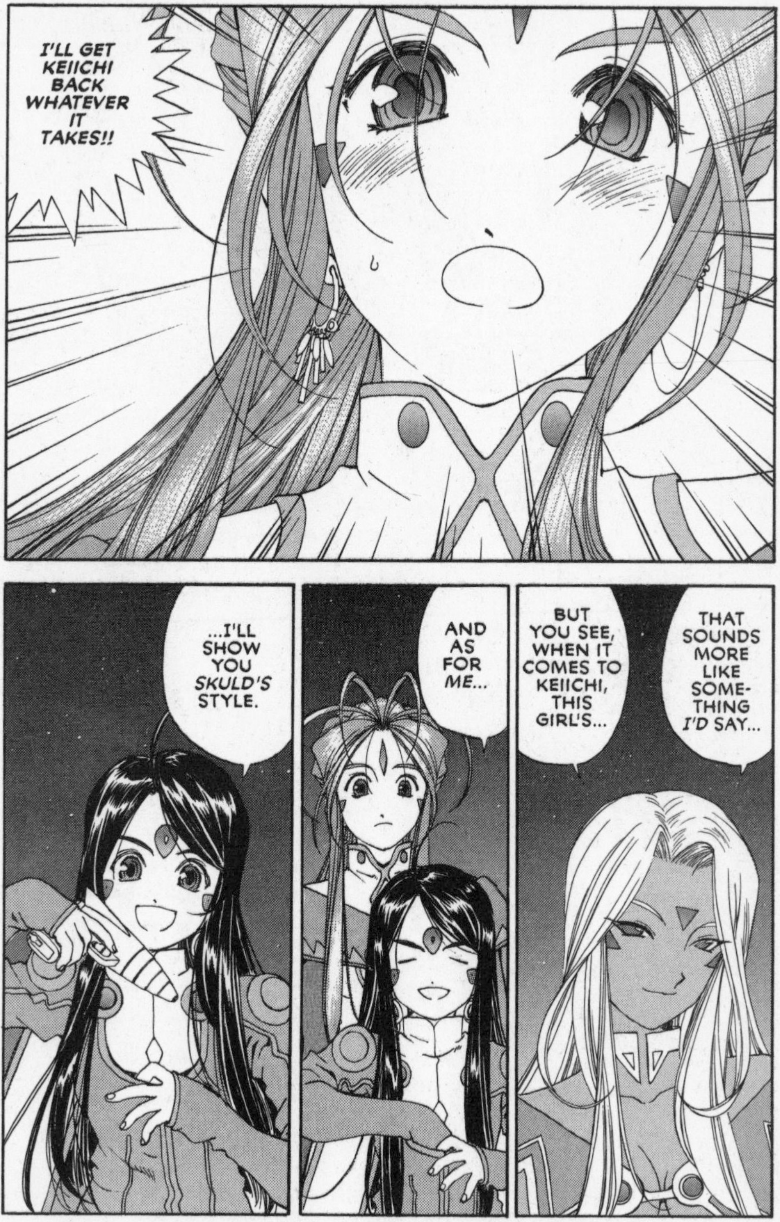

I'LL GET KEIICHI BACK WHATEVER IT TAKES!!
THAT SOUNDS MORE LIKE SOME-THING *I'D* SAY...
BUT YOU SEE, WHEN IT COMES TO KEIICHI, THIS GIRL'S...
AND AS FOR *ME*...
...I'LL SHOW YOU *SKULD'S* STYLE.

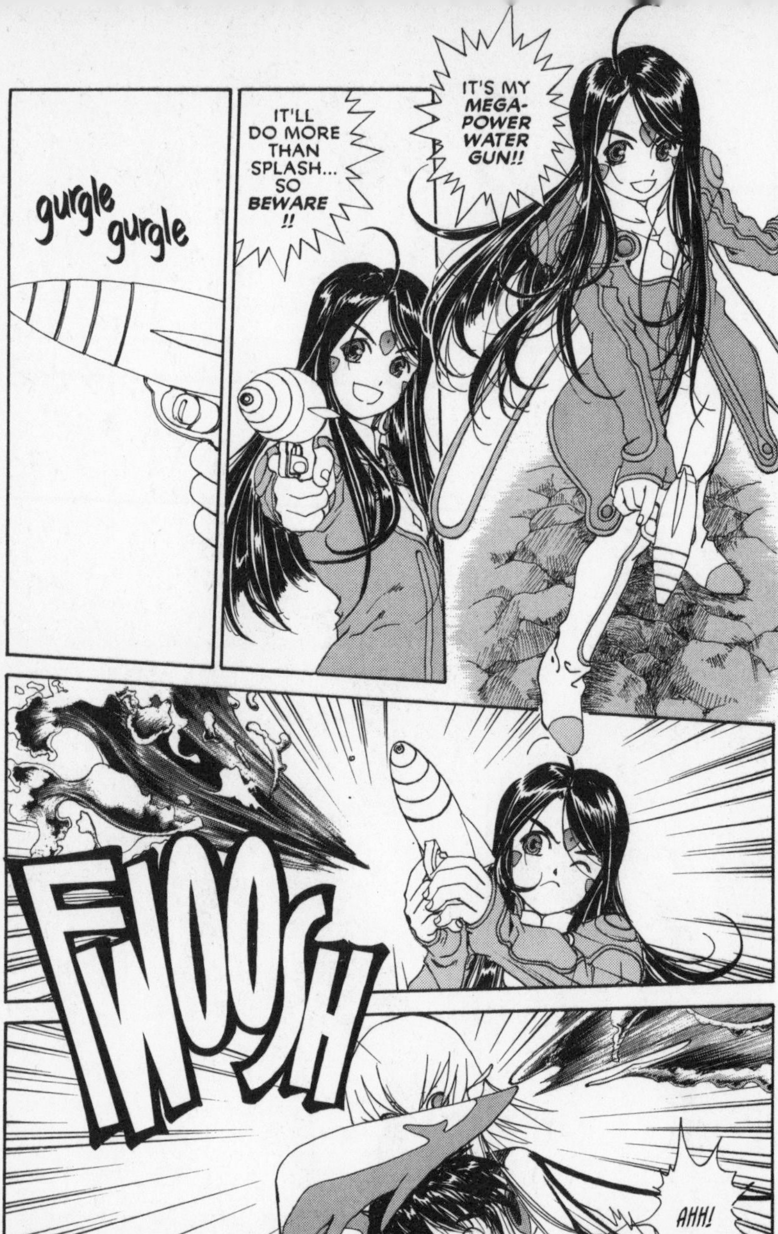

IT'S MY MEGA-POWER WATER GUN!!
IT'LL DO MORE THAN SPLASH... SO BEWARE!!
gurgle gurgle
FWOOSH
AHH!

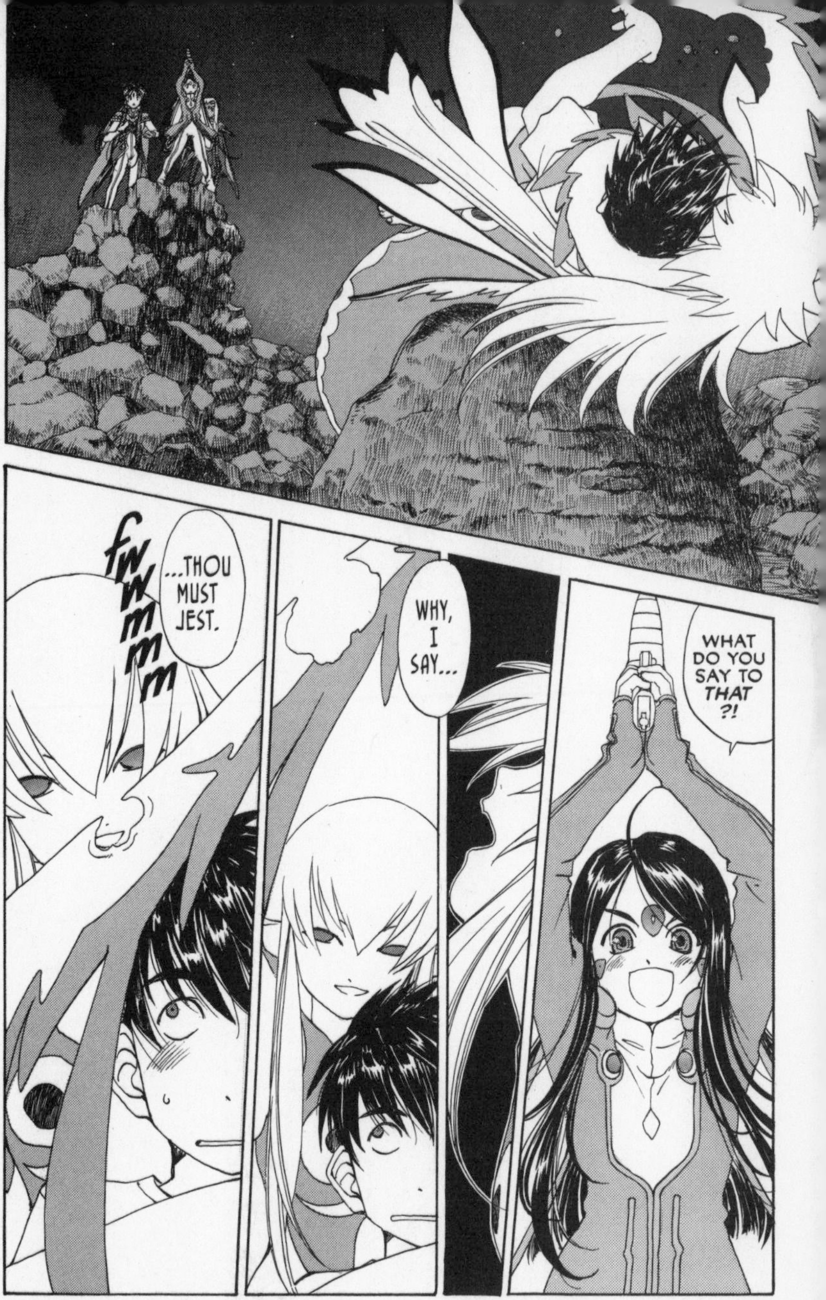
WHAT DO YOU SAY TO *THAT*?!
WHY, I SAY...
...THOU MUST JEST.
fwwmmm

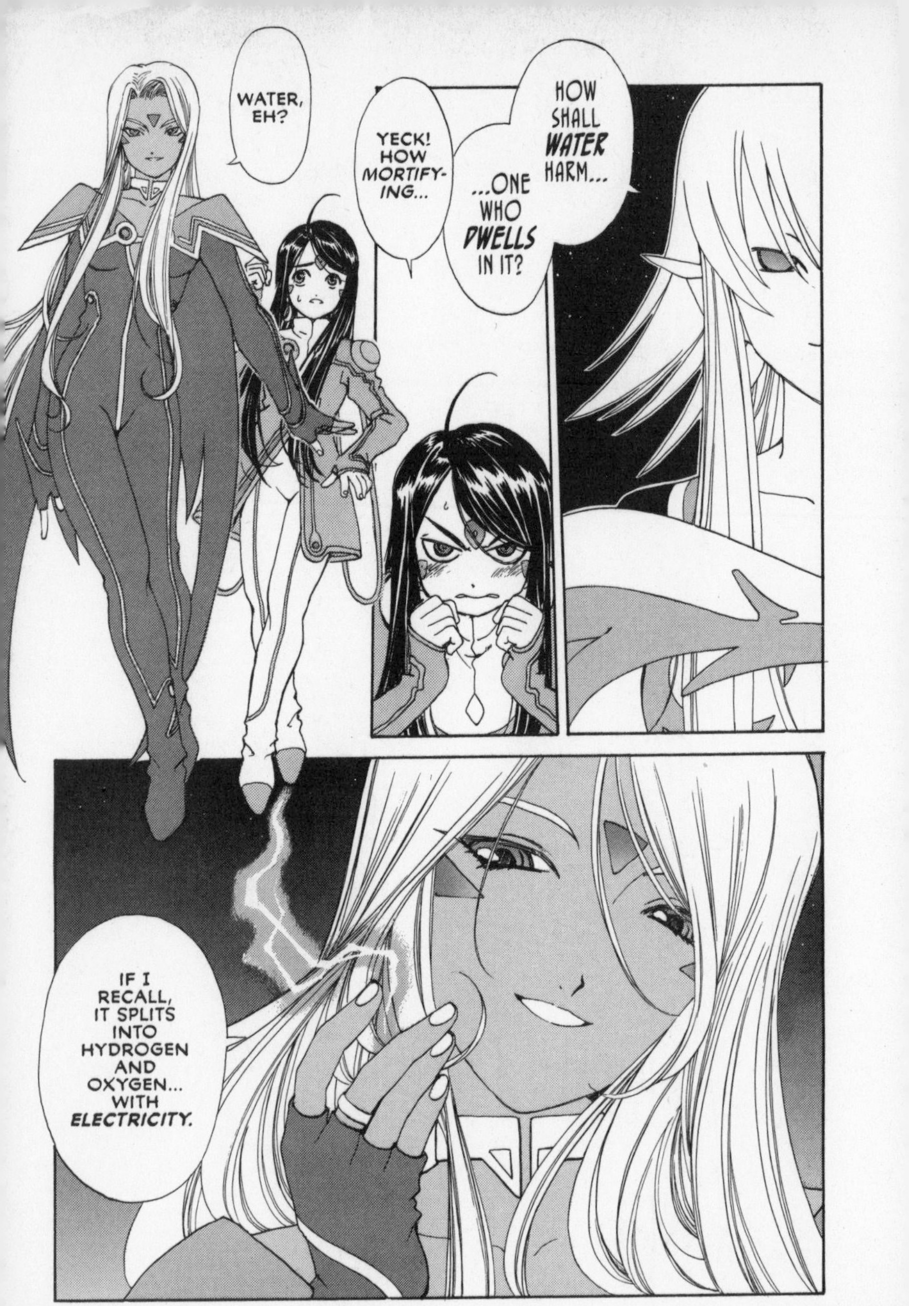
HOW SHALL WATER HARM...
...ONE WHO DWELLS IN IT?
YECK! HOW MORTIFYING...
WATER, EH?
IF I RECALL, IT SPLITS INTO HYDROGEN AND OXYGEN... WITH ELECTRICITY.

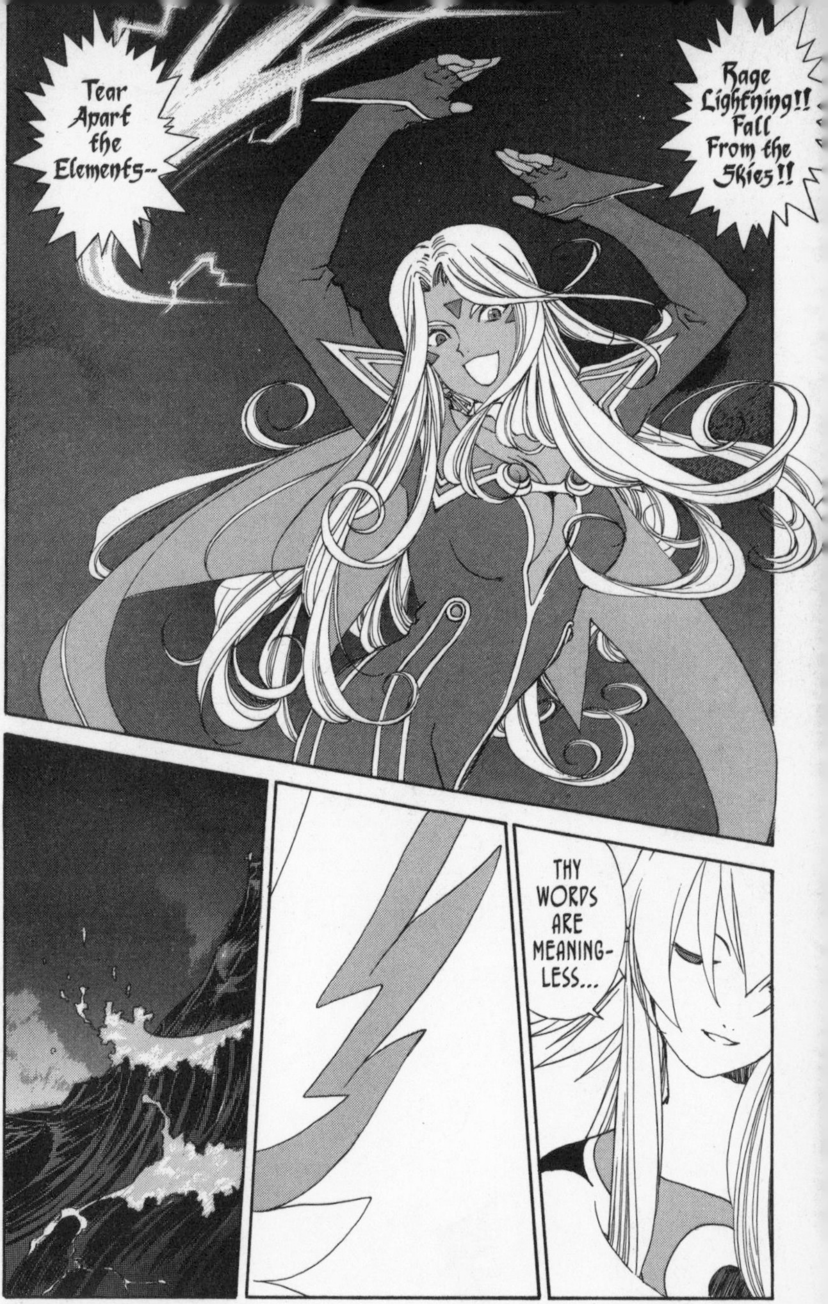
Rage Lightning!! Fall From the Skies!!
Tear Apart the Elements--
THY WORDS ARE MEANING-LESS...

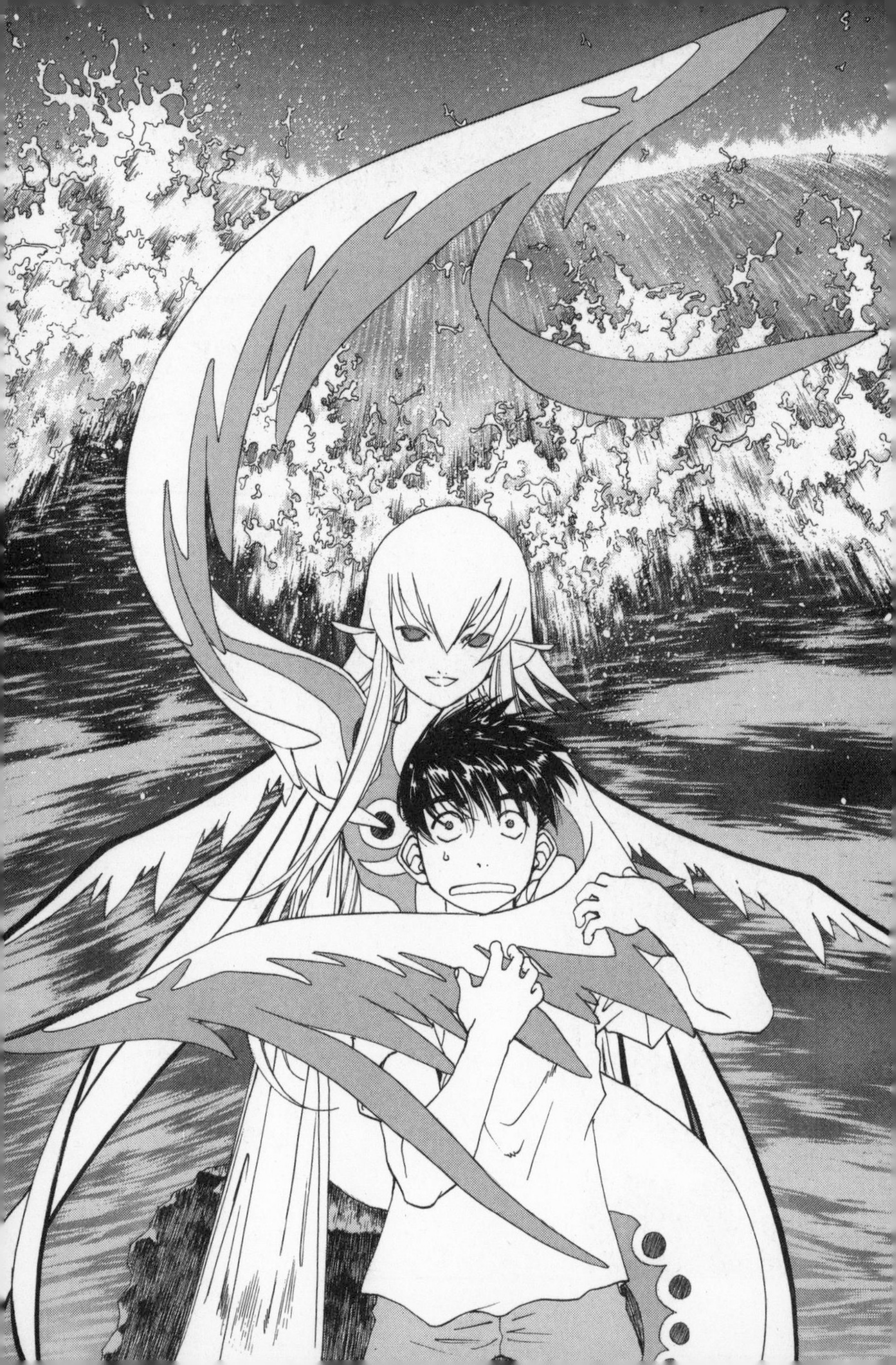

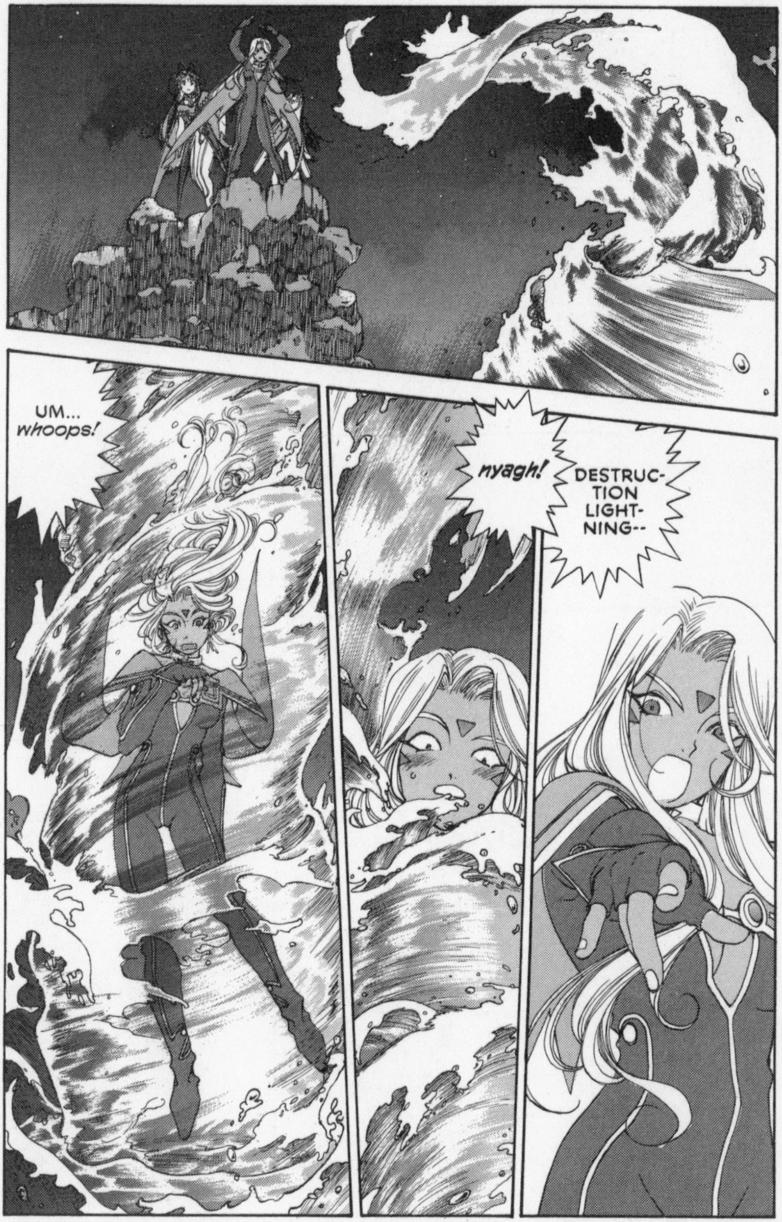
DESTRUC-TION LIGHT-NING--
nyagh!
UM... whoops!

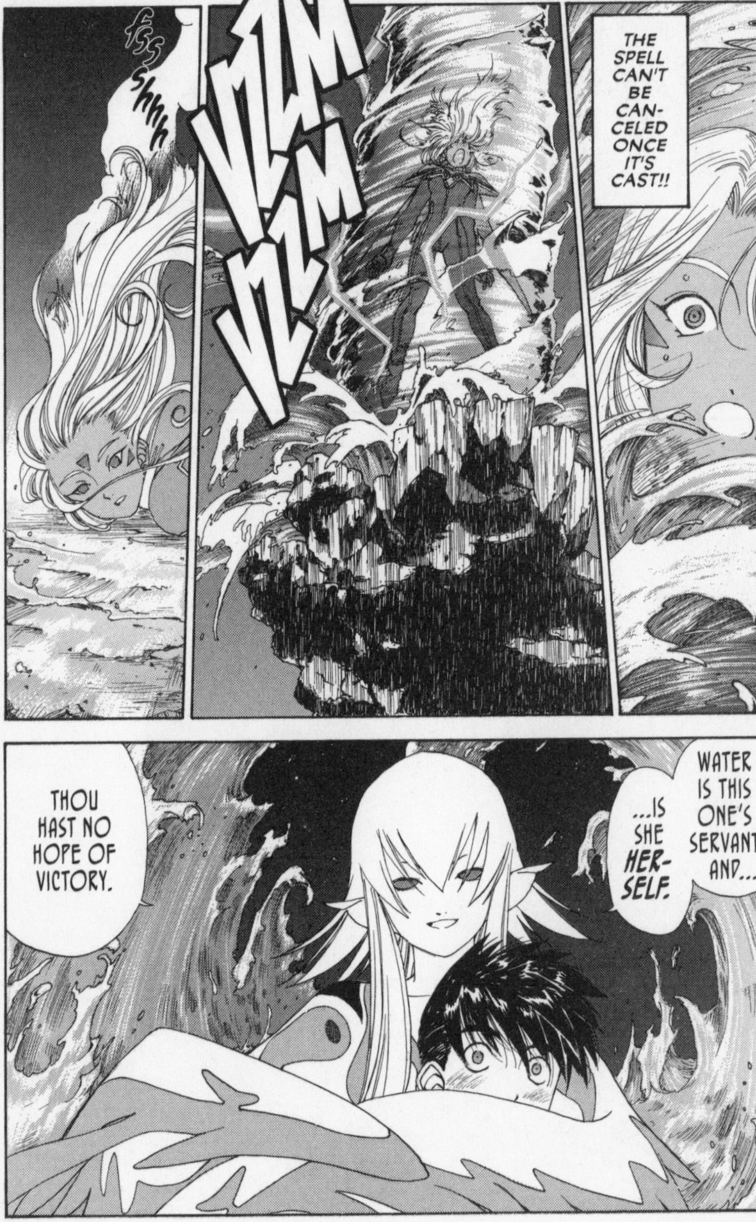
THE SPELL CAN'T BE CAN-CELED ONCE IT'S CAST!!
VZZM VZZM
fss shhh
WATER IS THIS ONE'S SERVANT AND...
...IS SHE HER-SELF.
THOU HAST NO HOPE OF VICTORY.

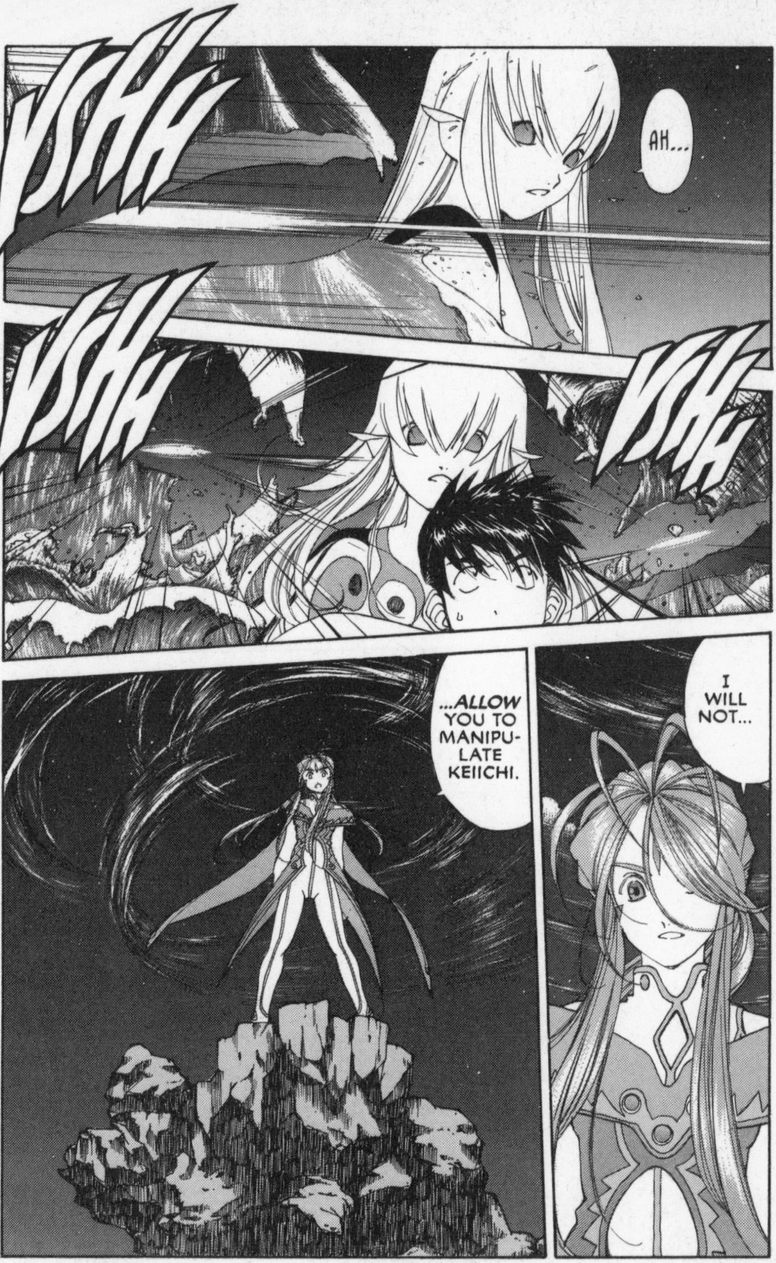
AH...
VSHH
VSHH
VSHH
I WILL NOT...
...ALLOW YOU TO MANIPULATE KEIICHI.

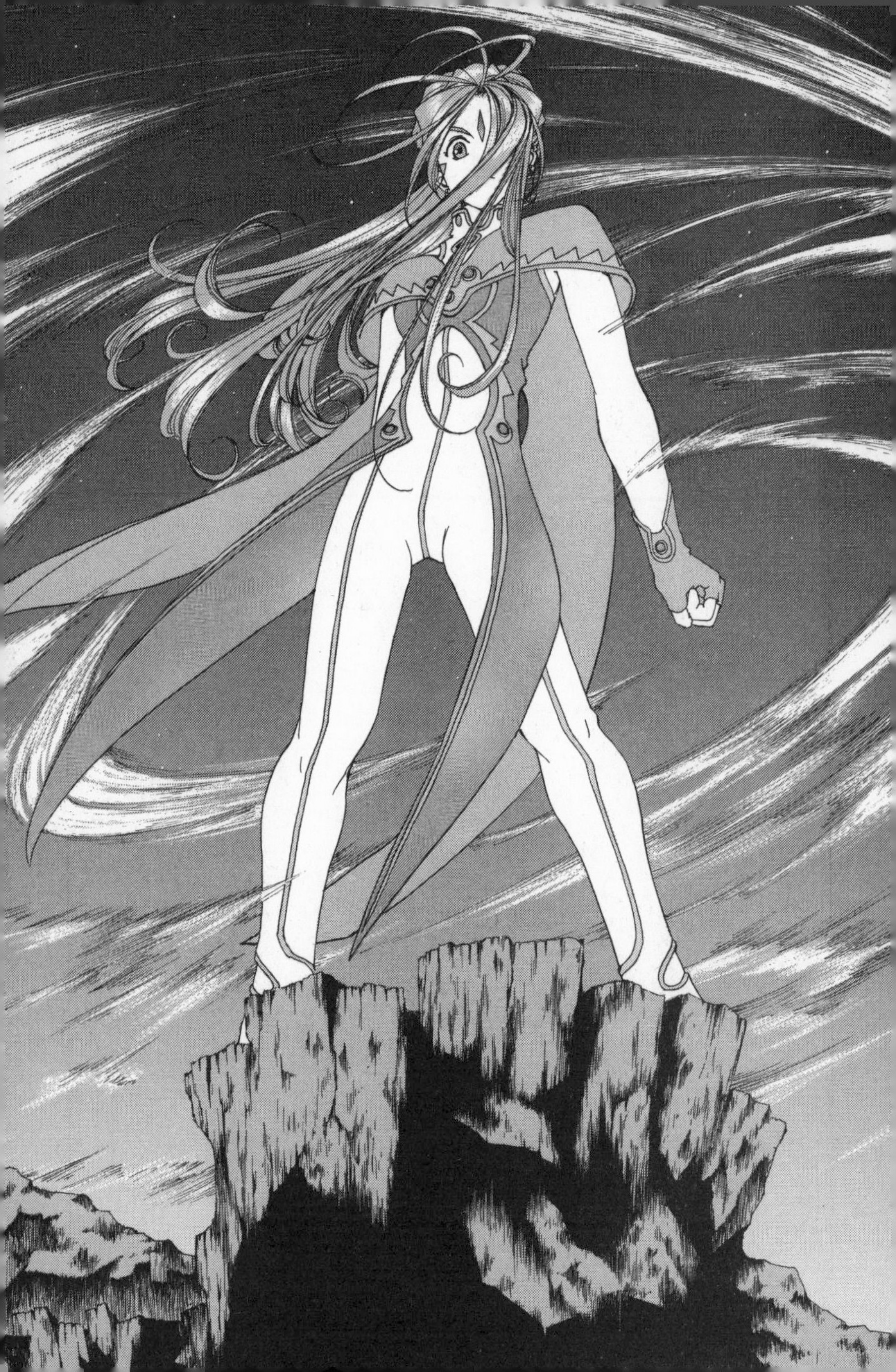

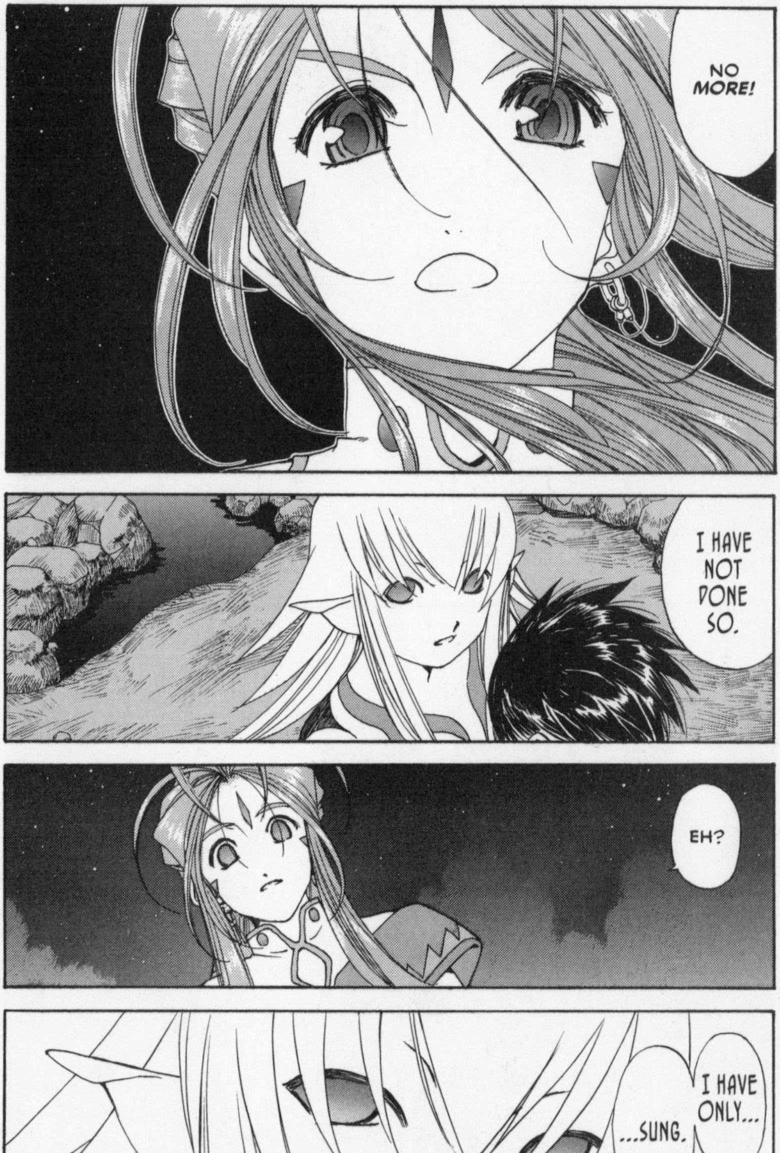
NO MORE!
I HAVE NOT DONE SO.
EH?
I HAVE ONLY...
...SUNG.

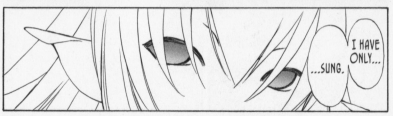

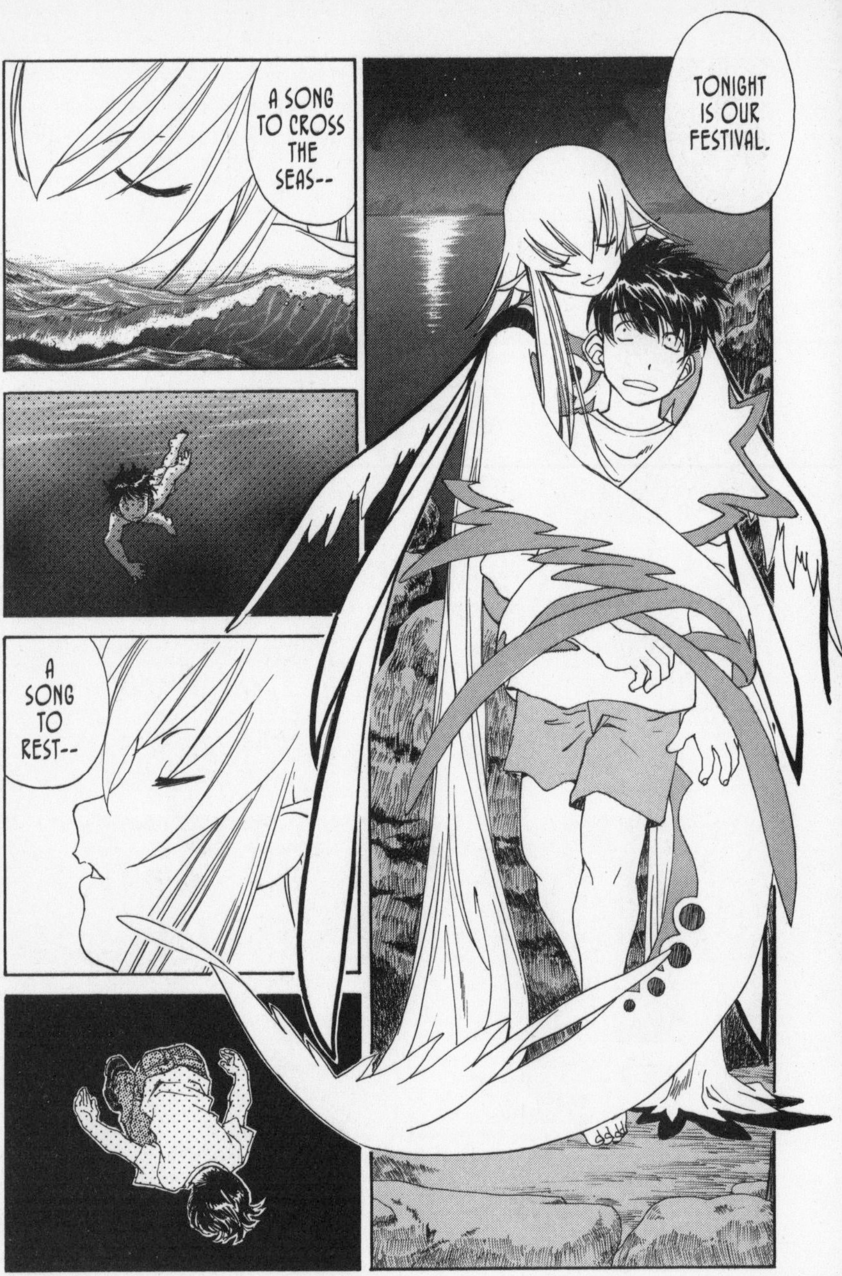
TONIGHT IS OUR FESTIVAL.
A SONG TO CROSS THE SEAS--
A SONG TO REST--

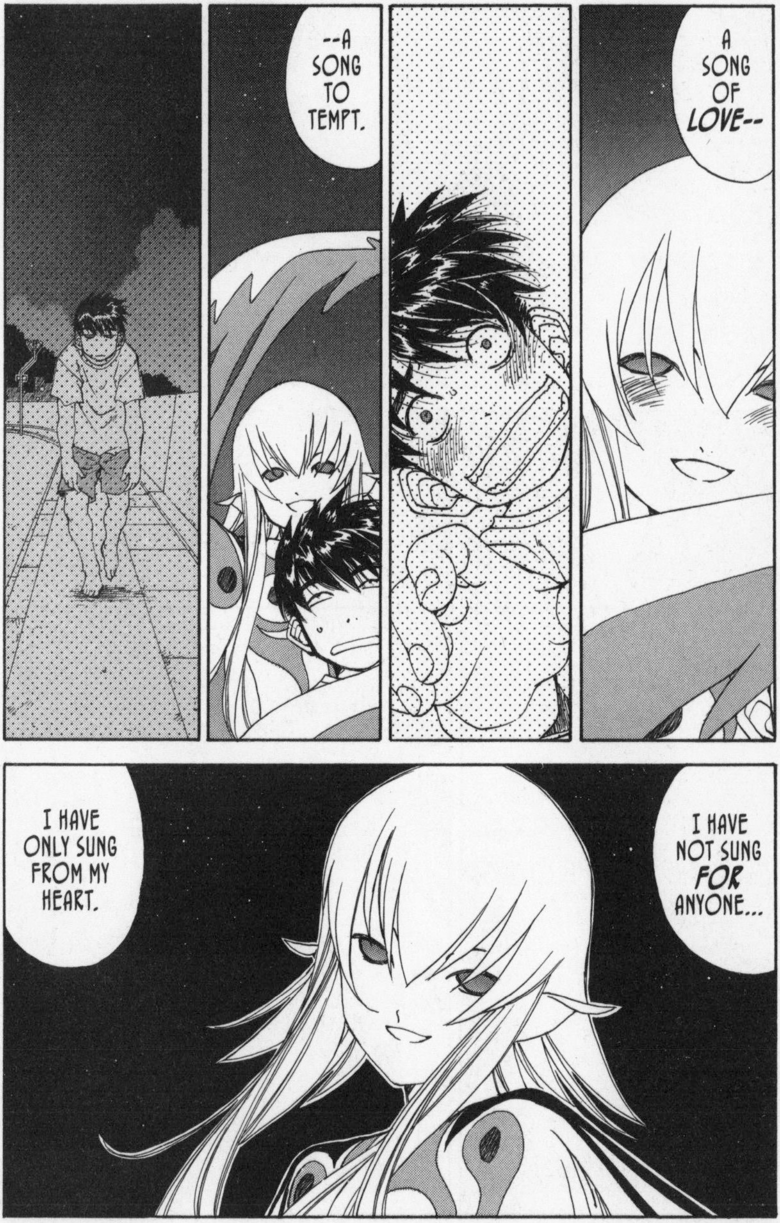
A SONG OF LOVE--
--A SONG TO TEMPT.
I HAVE NOT SUNG FOR ANYONE...
I HAVE ONLY SUNG FROM MY HEART.

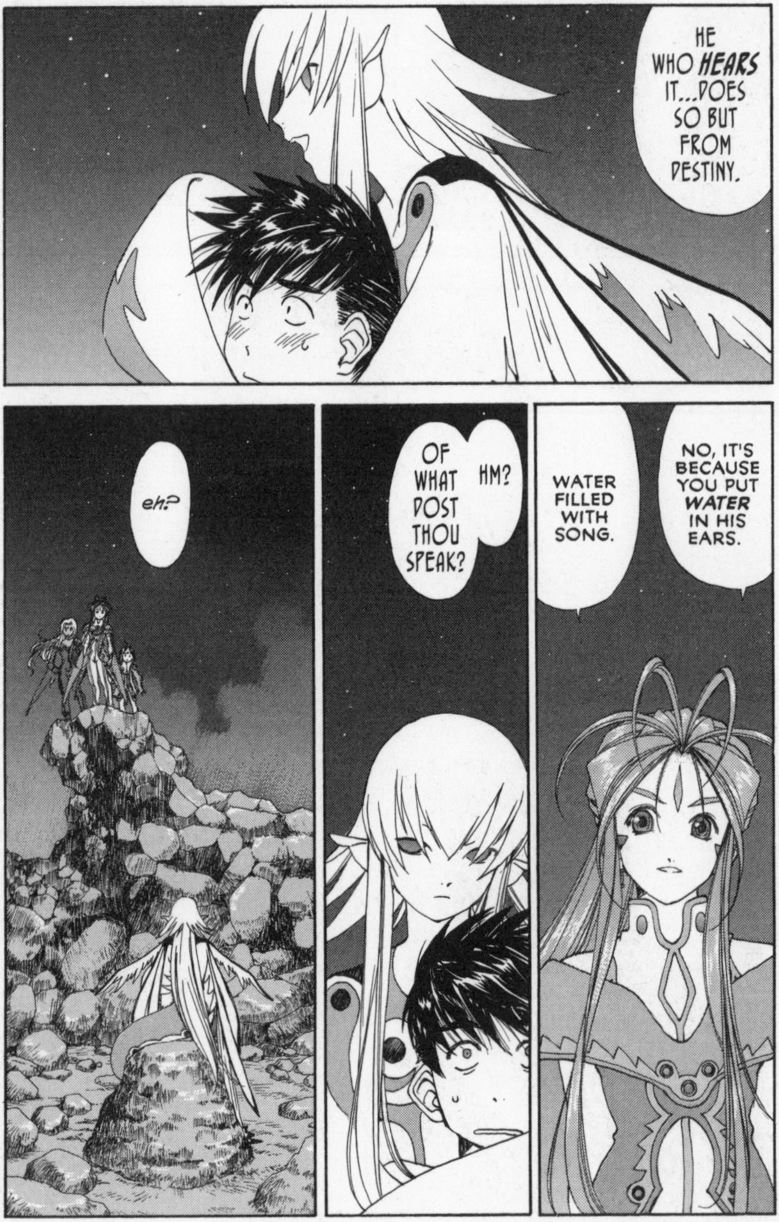
HE WHO HEARS IT...DOES SO BUT FROM DESTINY.
NO, IT'S BECAUSE YOU PUT WATER IN HIS EARS.
WATER FILLED WITH SONG.
HM?
OF WHAT DOST THOU SPEAK?
eh?

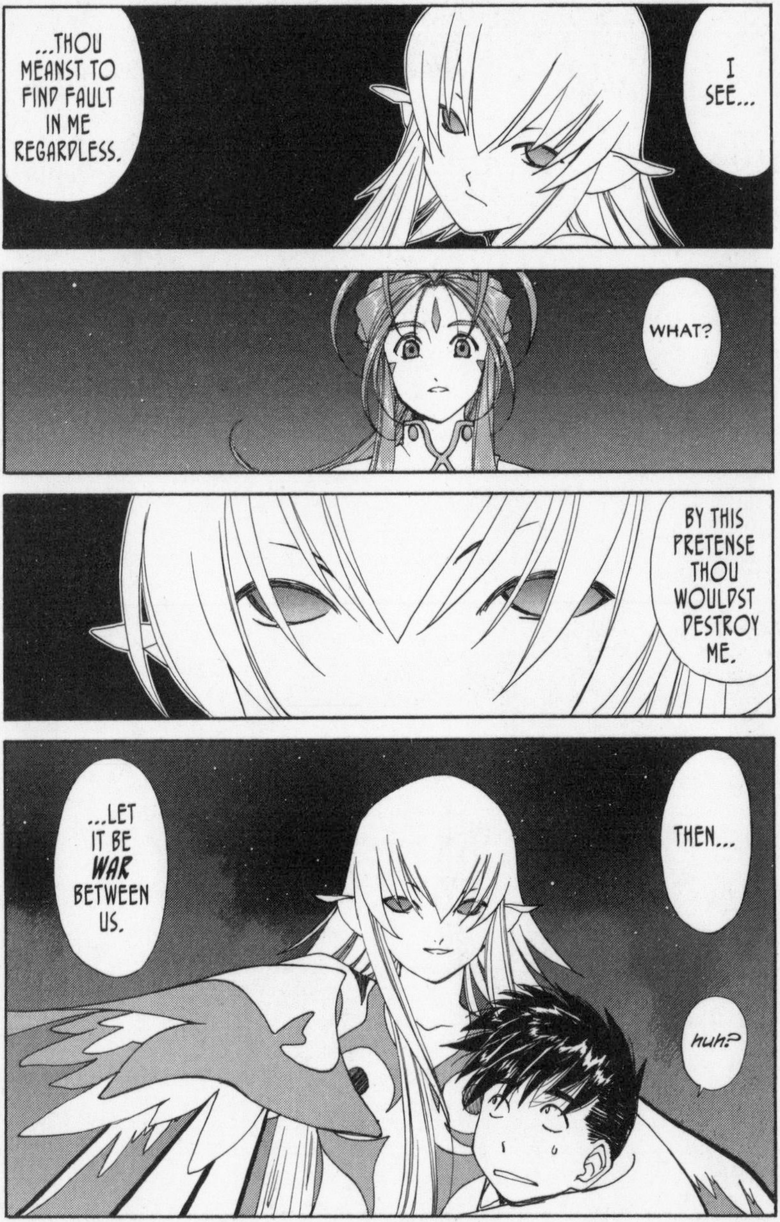
I SEE...
...THOU MEANST TO FIND FAULT IN ME REGARDLESS.
WHAT?
BY THIS PRETENSE THOU WOULDST DESTROY ME.
THEN...
...LET IT BE WAR BETWEEN US.
huh?

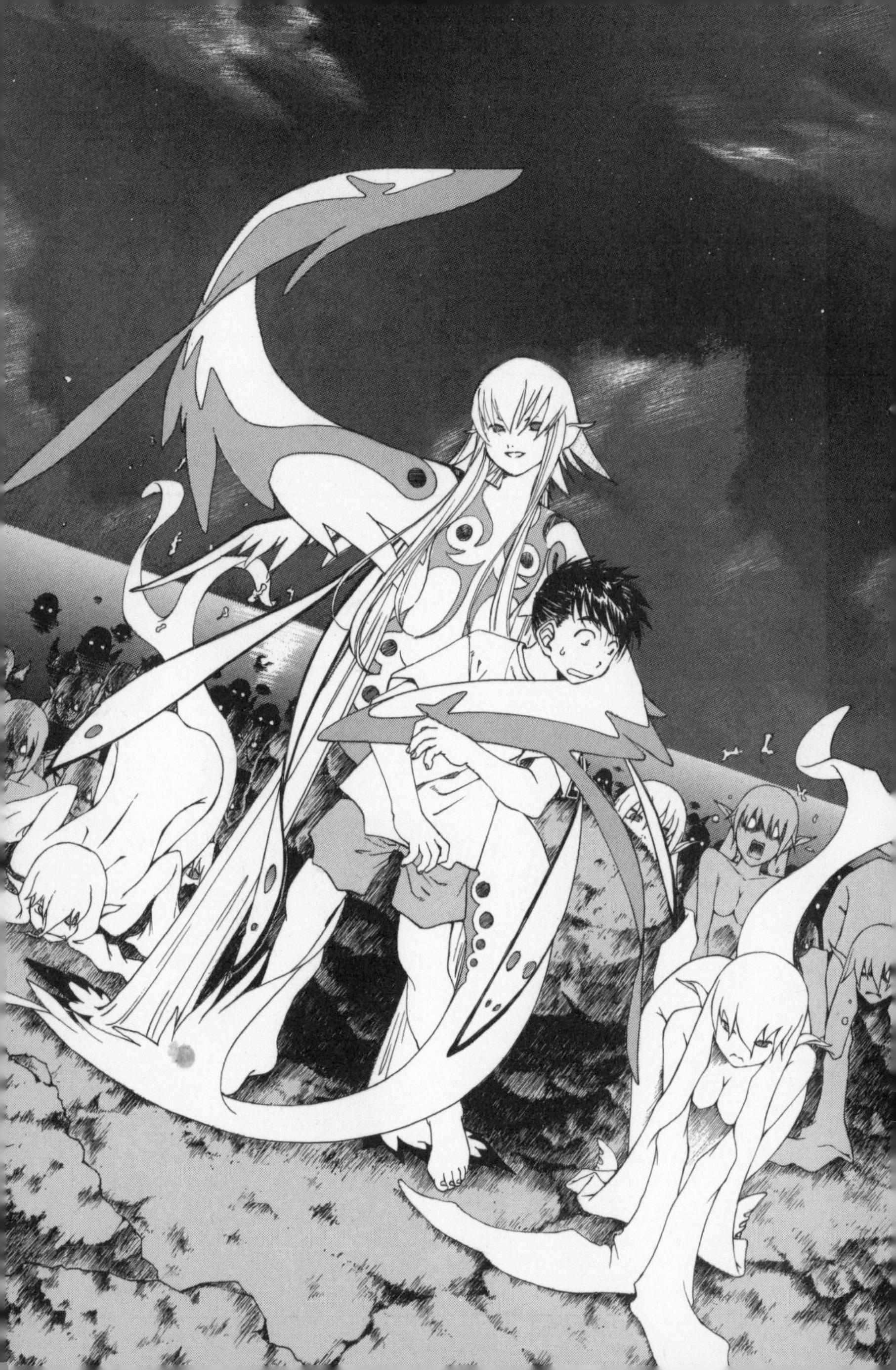

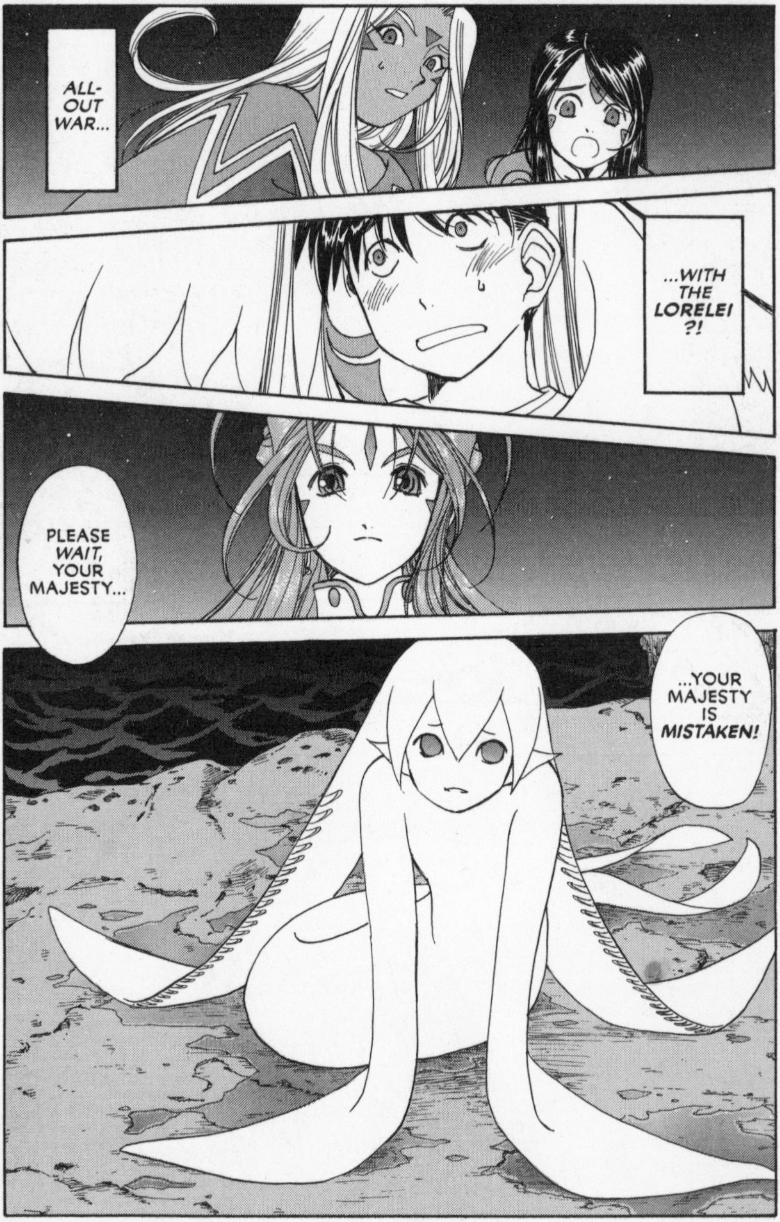
ALL-OUT WAR...
...WITH THE LORELEI?!
PLEASE *WAIT,* YOUR MAJESTY...
...YOUR MAJESTY IS *MISTAKEN!*

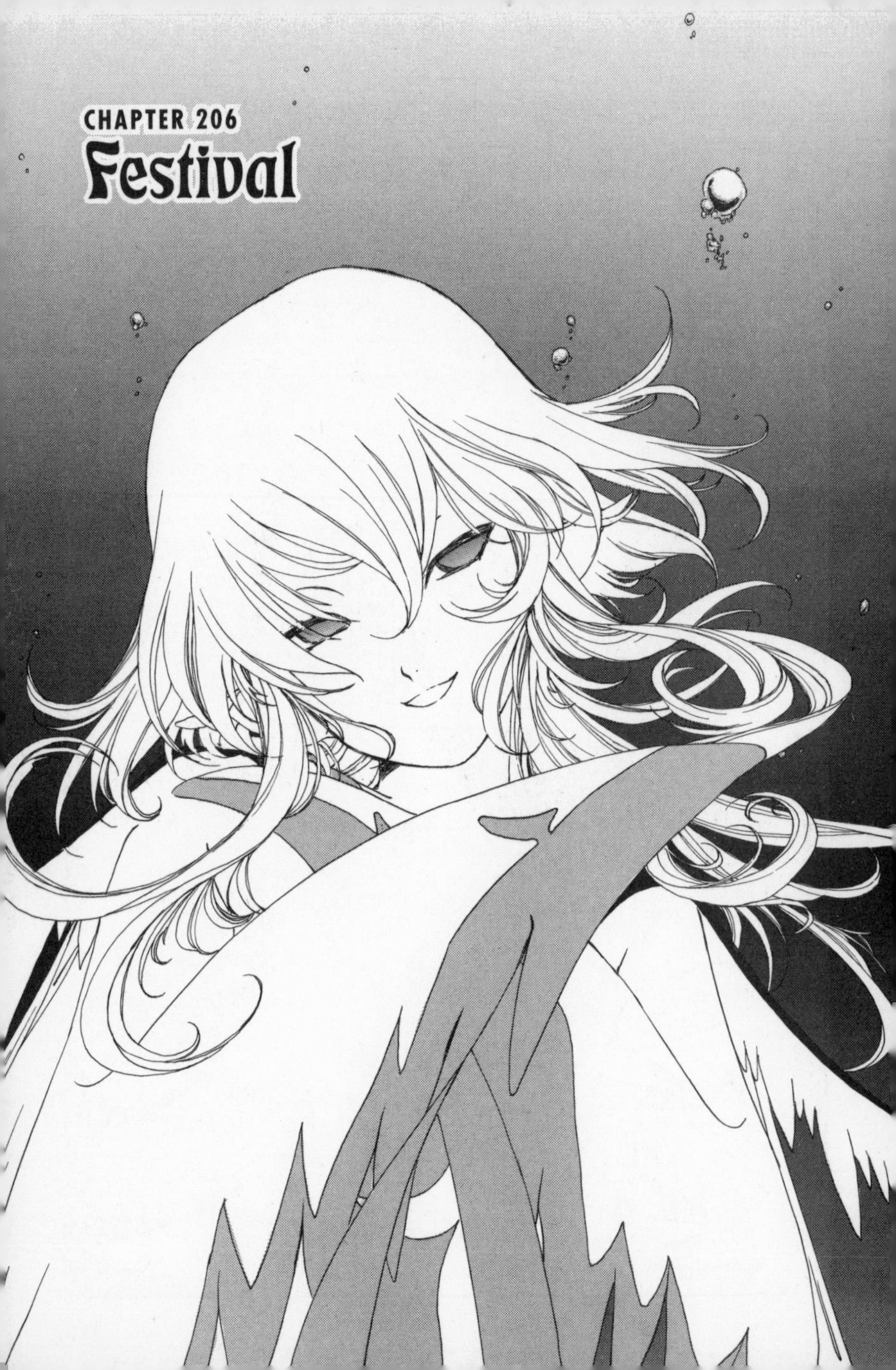
CHAPTER 206
Festival

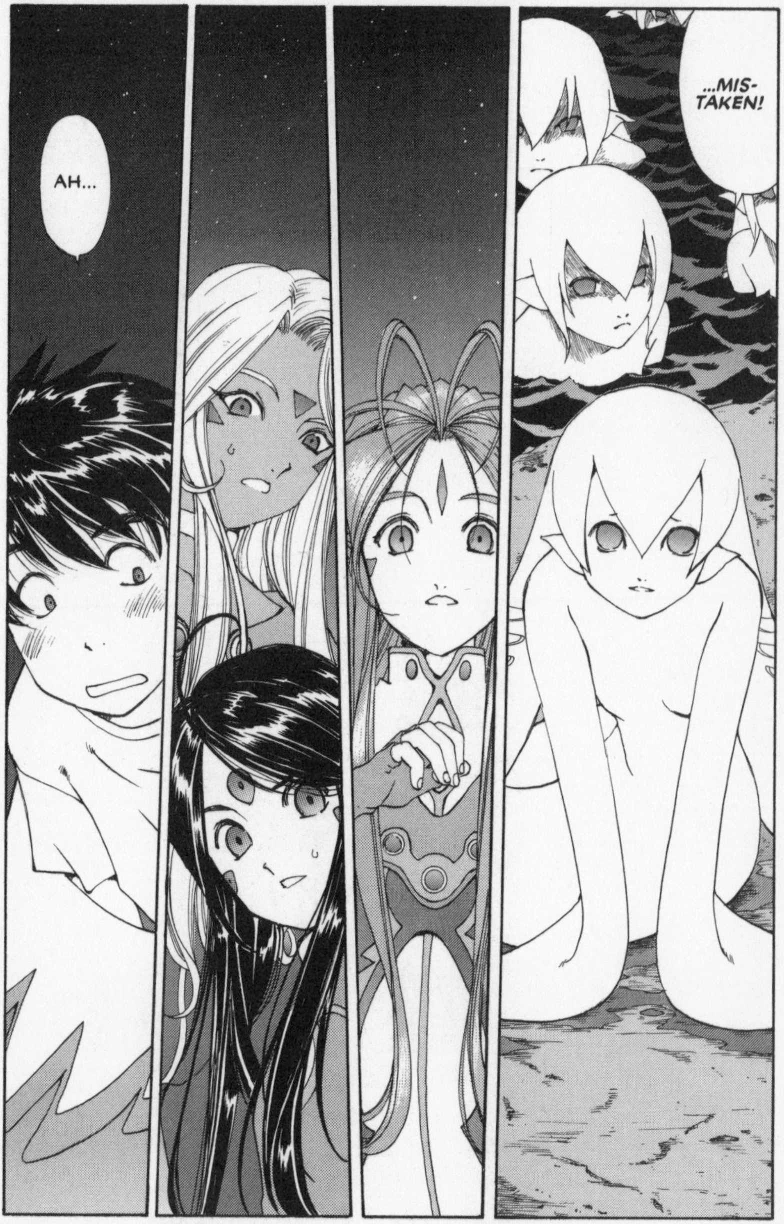
...MIS-
TAKEN!
AH...

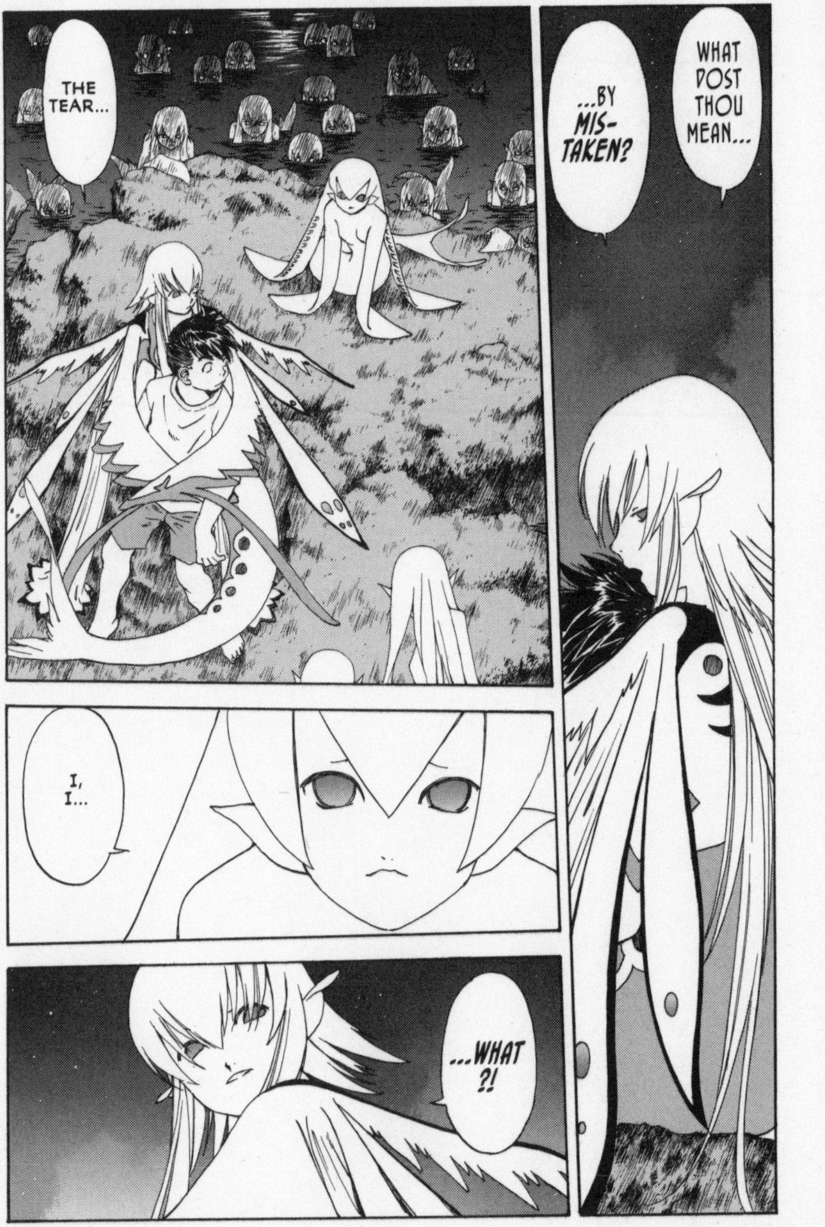
WHAT DOST THOU MEAN...
...BY MIS-TAKEN?
THE TEAR...
I, I...
...WHAT ?!

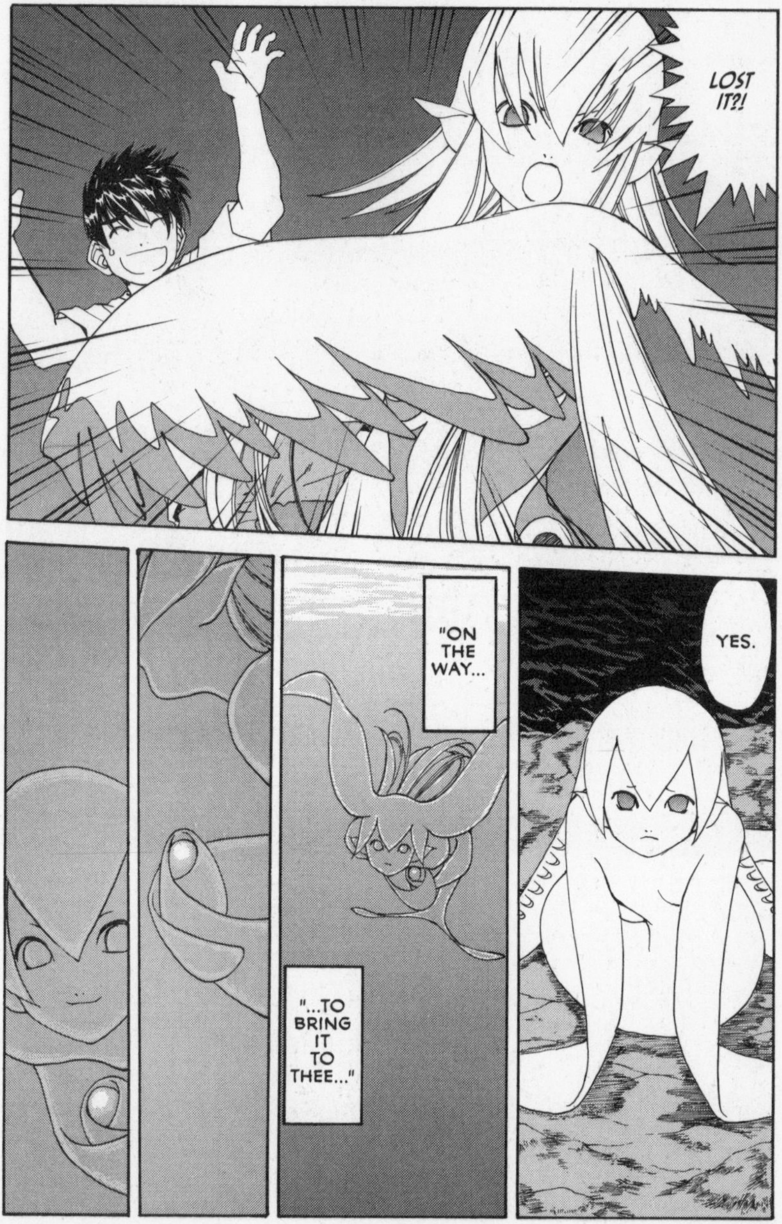
LOST IT?!
YES.
"ON THE WAY...
"...TO BRING IT TO THEE..."

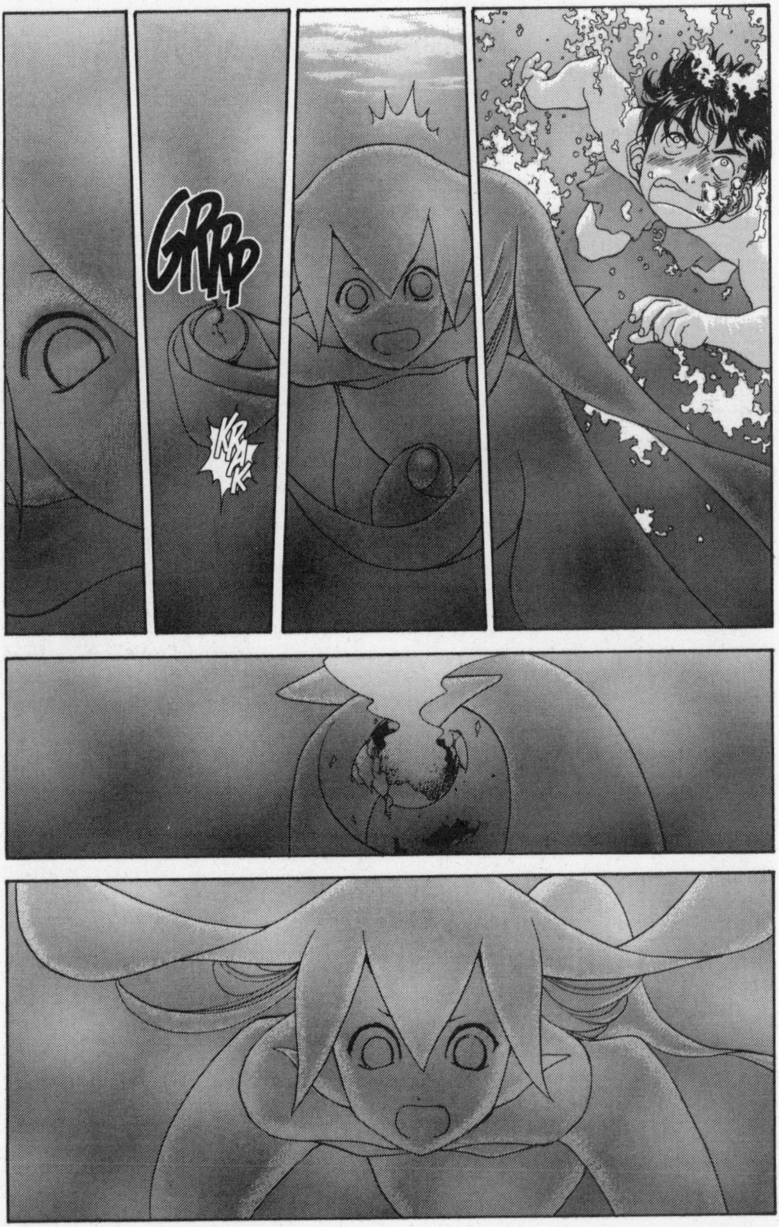
GRRD
KRAK

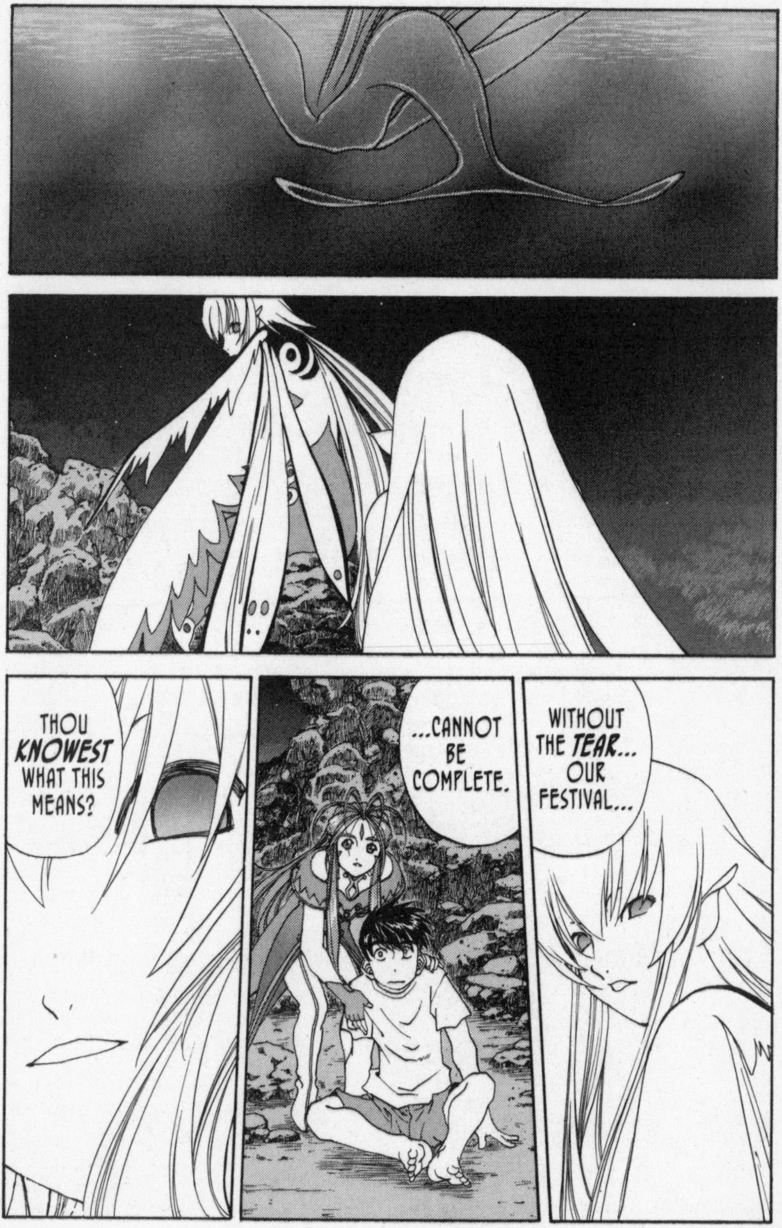
WITHOUT THE *TEAR*... OUR FESTIVAL...
...CANNOT BE COMPLETE.
THOU *KNOWEST* WHAT THIS MEANS?

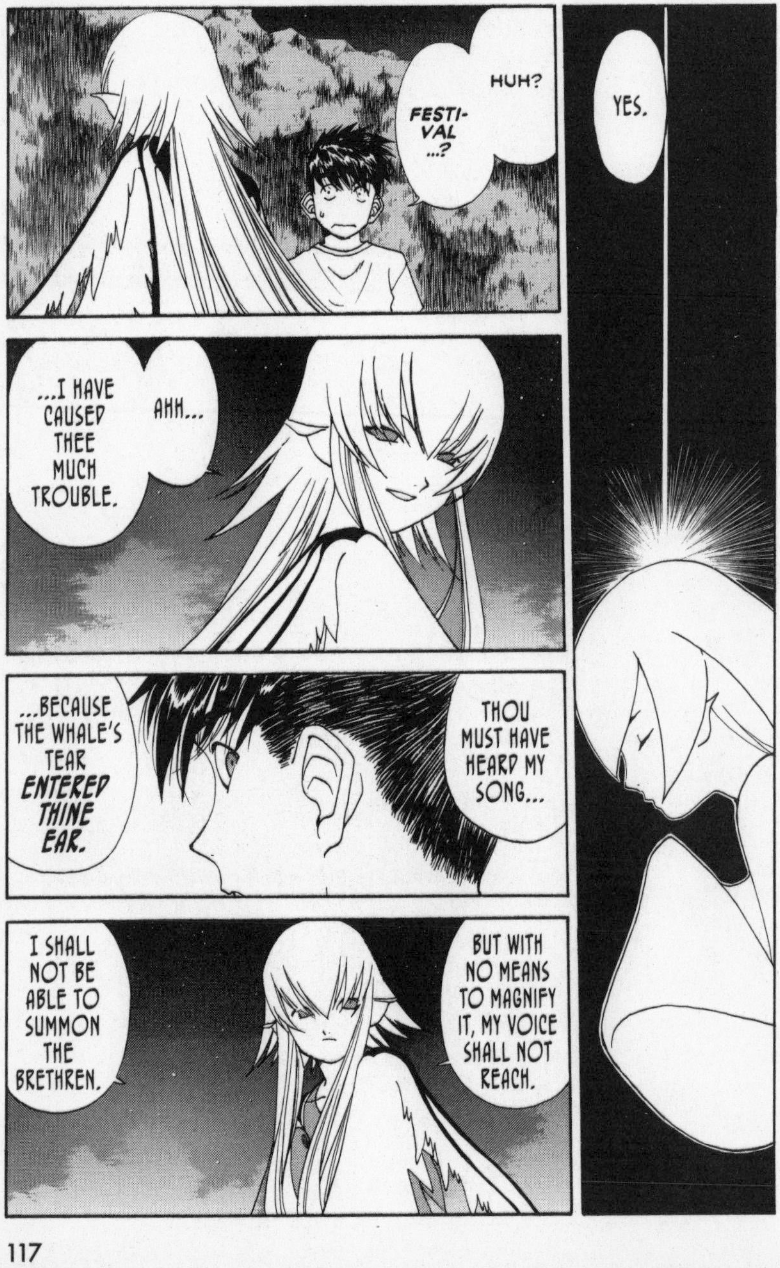
YES.
HUH? FESTI-VAL ...?
AHH...
...I HAVE CAUSED THEE MUCH TROUBLE.
THOU MUST HAVE HEARD MY SONG...
...BECAUSE THE WHALE'S TEAR *ENTERED THINE EAR.*
BUT WITH NO MEANS TO MAGNIFY IT, MY VOICE SHALL NOT REACH.
I SHALL NOT BE ABLE TO SUMMON THE BRETHREN.

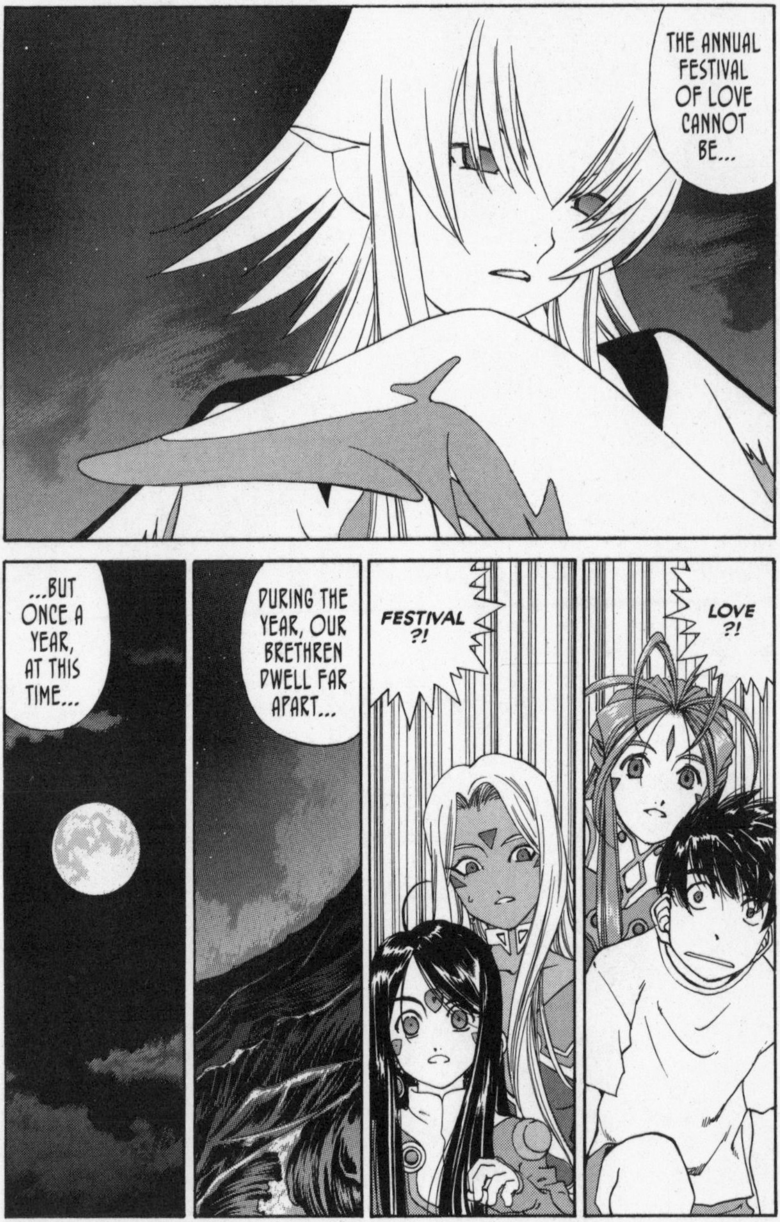
THE ANNUAL FESTIVAL OF LOVE CANNOT BE...
...BUT ONCE A YEAR, AT THIS TIME...
DURING THE YEAR, OUR BRETHREN DWELL FAR APART...
FESTIVAL ?!
LOVE ?!

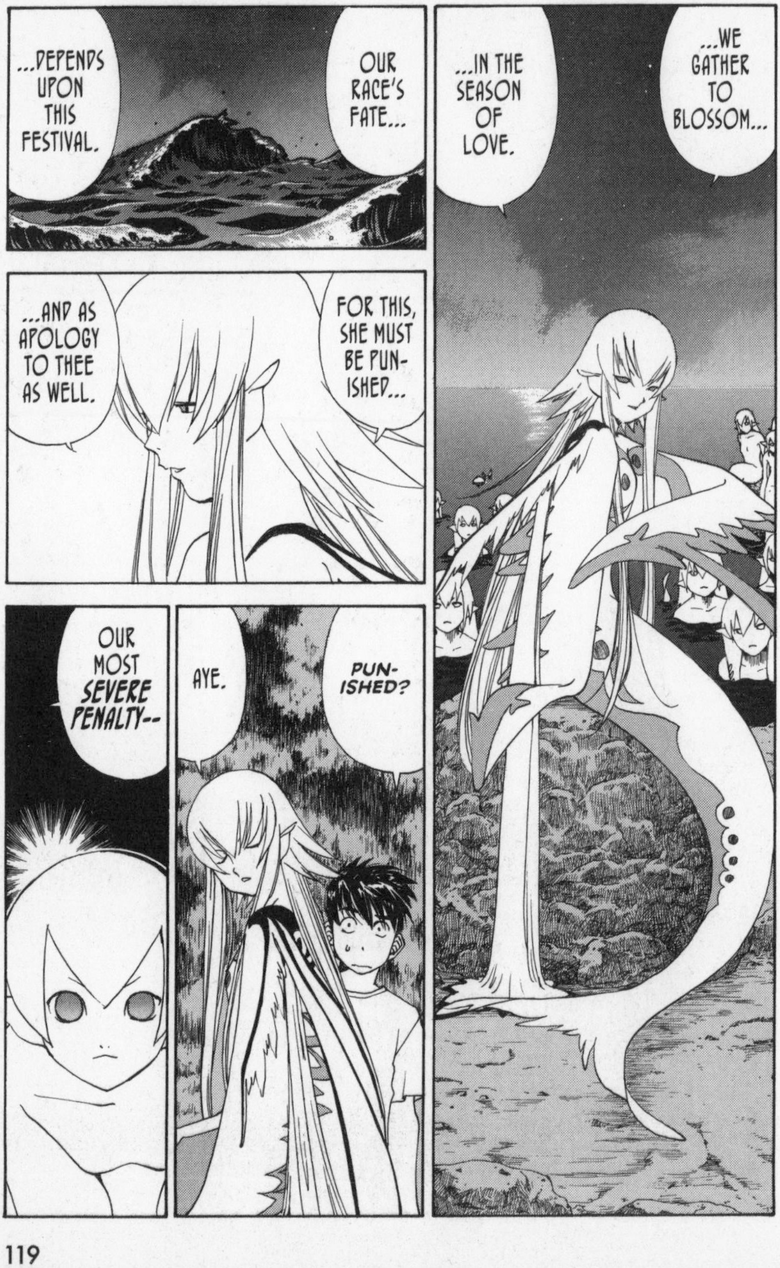
...WE GATHER TO BLOSSOM...
...IN THE SEASON OF LOVE.
OUR RACE'S FATE...
...DEPENDS UPON THIS FESTIVAL.
FOR THIS, SHE MUST BE PUN-ISHED...
...AND AS APOLOGY TO THEE AS WELL.
PUN-ISHED?
AYE.
OUR MOST SEVERE PENALTY--

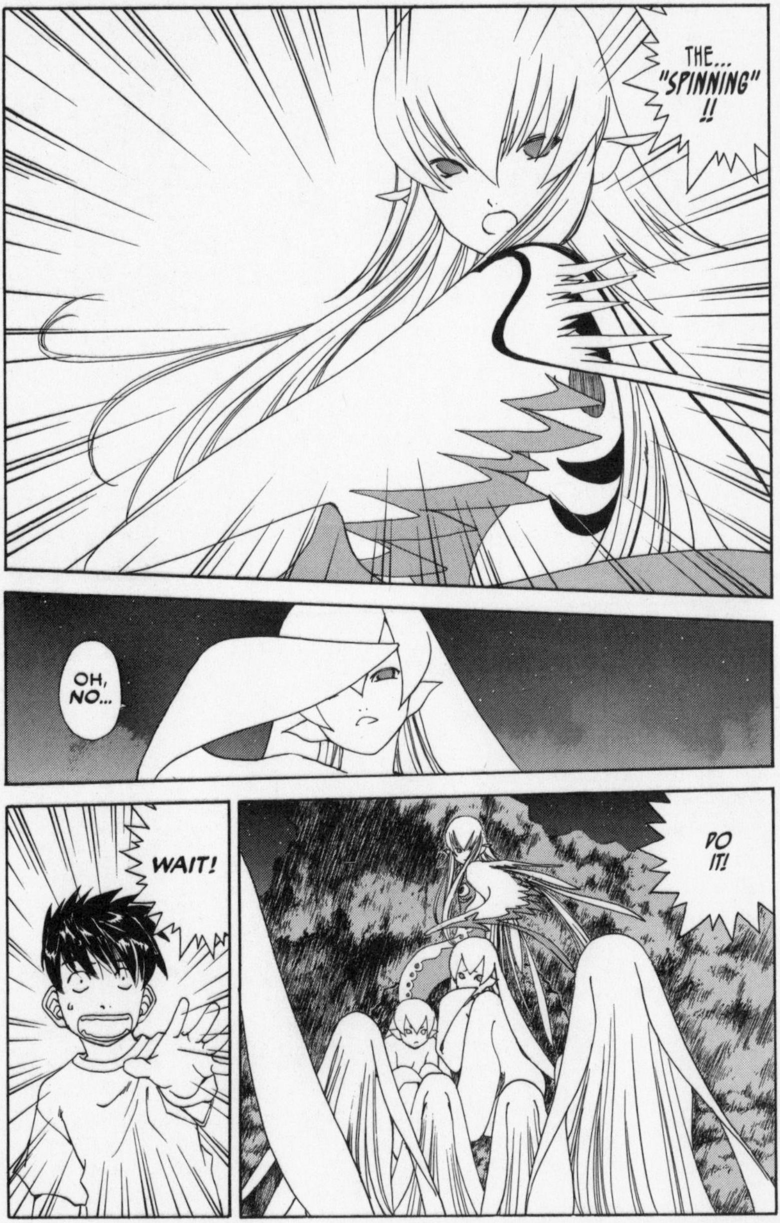
THE... "SPINNING" !!
OH, NO...
DO IT!
WAIT!

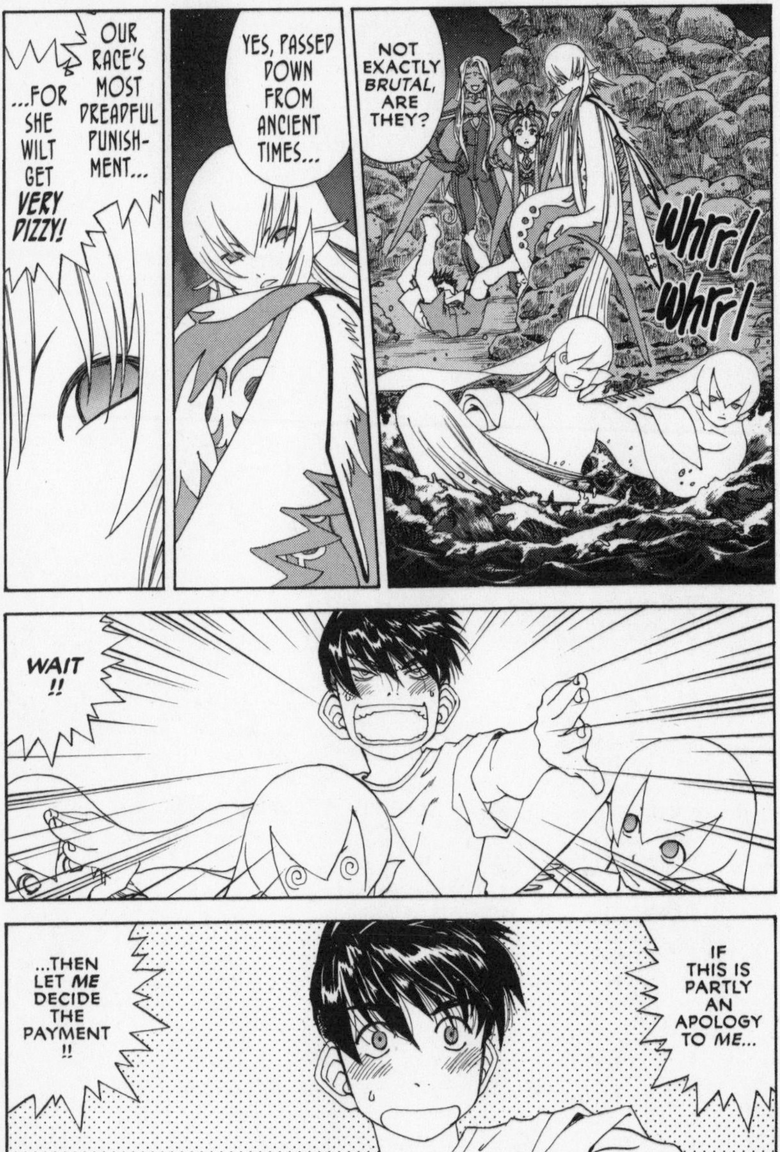
NOT EXACTLY *BRUTAL,* ARE THEY?
whrrl whrrl
YES, PASSED DOWN FROM ANCIENT TIMES...
OUR RACE'S MOST DREADFUL PUNISHMENT...
...FOR SHE WILT GET *VERY DIZZY!*
WAIT !!
IF THIS IS PARTLY AN APOLOGY TO *ME*...
...THEN LET *ME* DECIDE THE PAYMENT !!

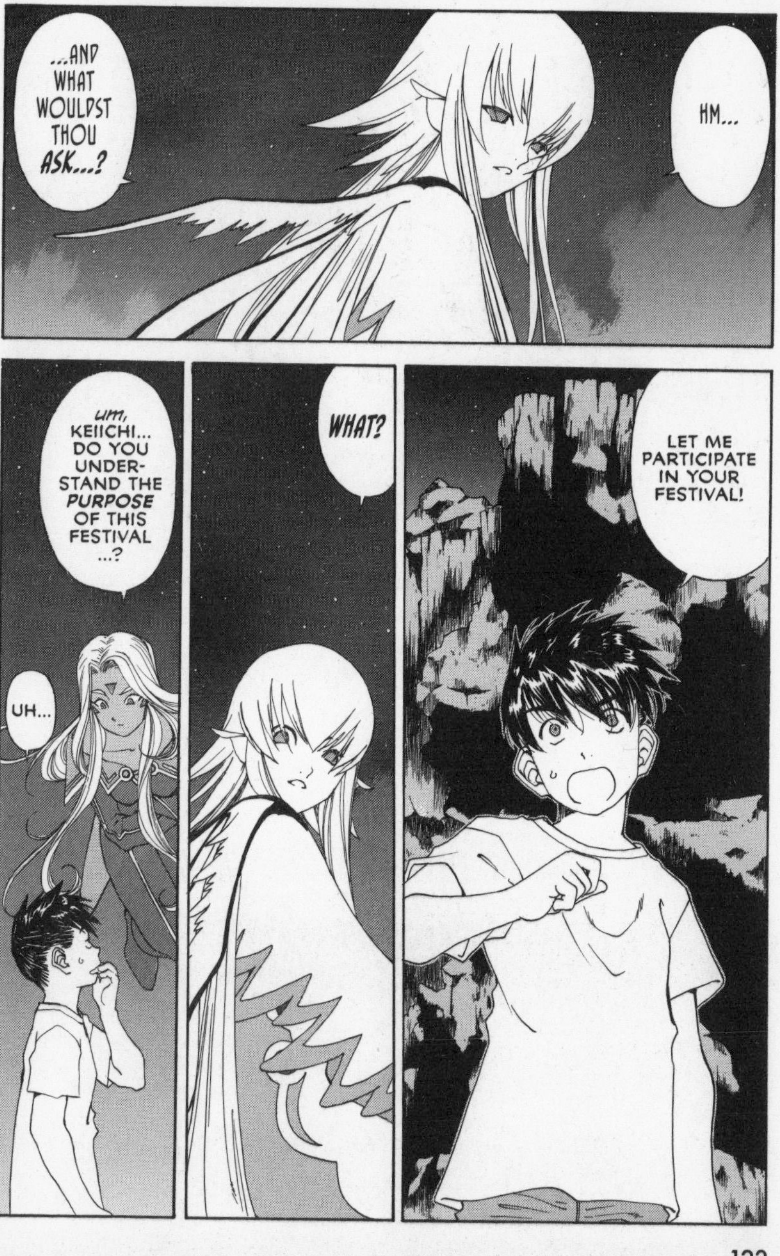
HM...
...AND WHAT WOULDST THOU ASK...?
LET ME PARTICIPATE IN YOUR FESTIVAL!
WHAT?
UM, KEIICHI... DO YOU UNDER-STAND THE PURPOSE OF THIS FESTIVAL ...?
UH...

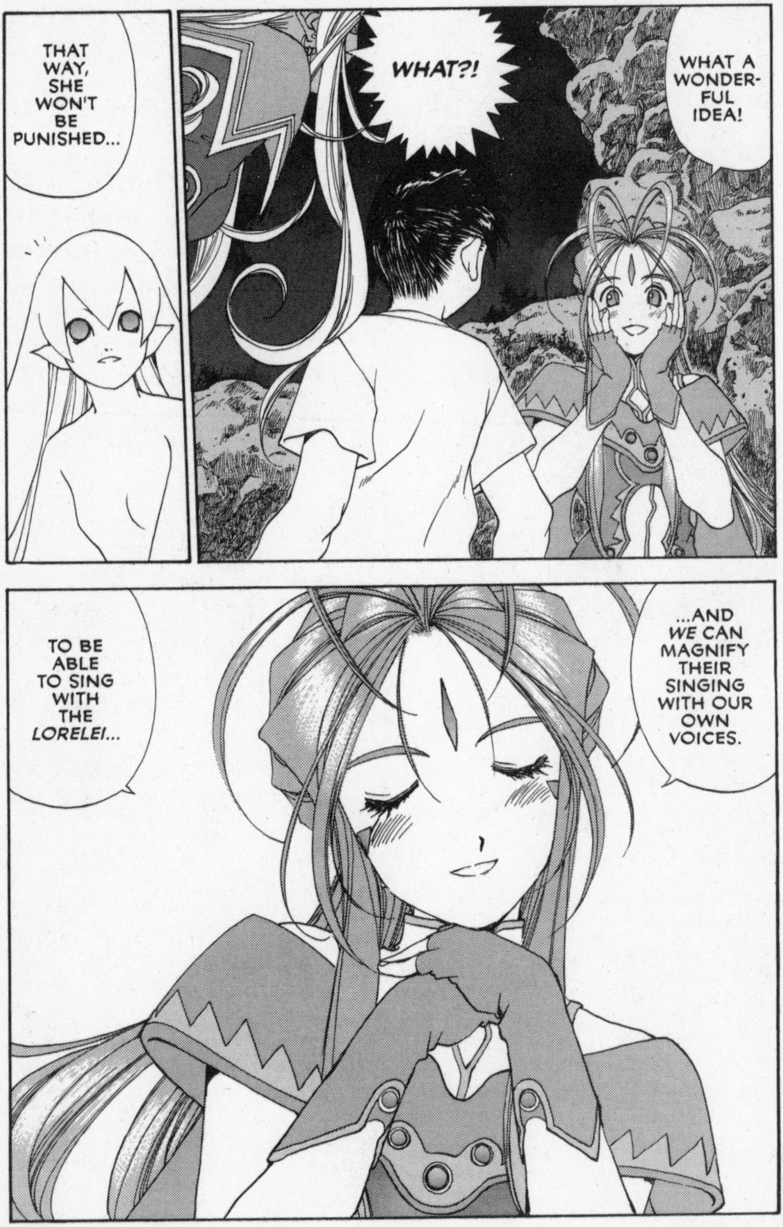
WHAT A WONDERFUL IDEA!
WHAT?!
THAT WAY, SHE WON'T BE PUNISHED...
...AND *WE* CAN MAGNIFY THEIR SINGING WITH OUR OWN VOICES.
TO BE ABLE TO SING WITH THE *LORELEI*...

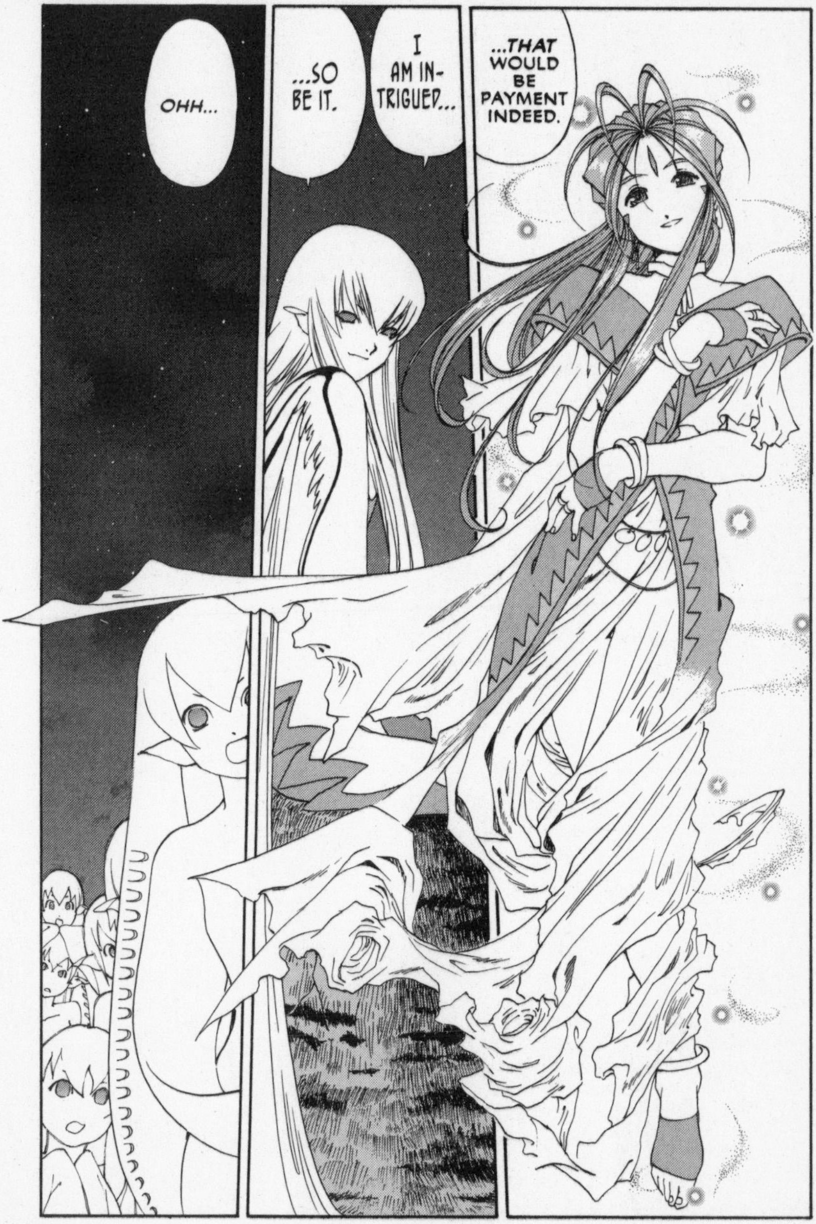

...THAT WOULD BE PAYMENT INDEED.
I AM IN-TRIGUED...
...SO BE IT.
OHH...

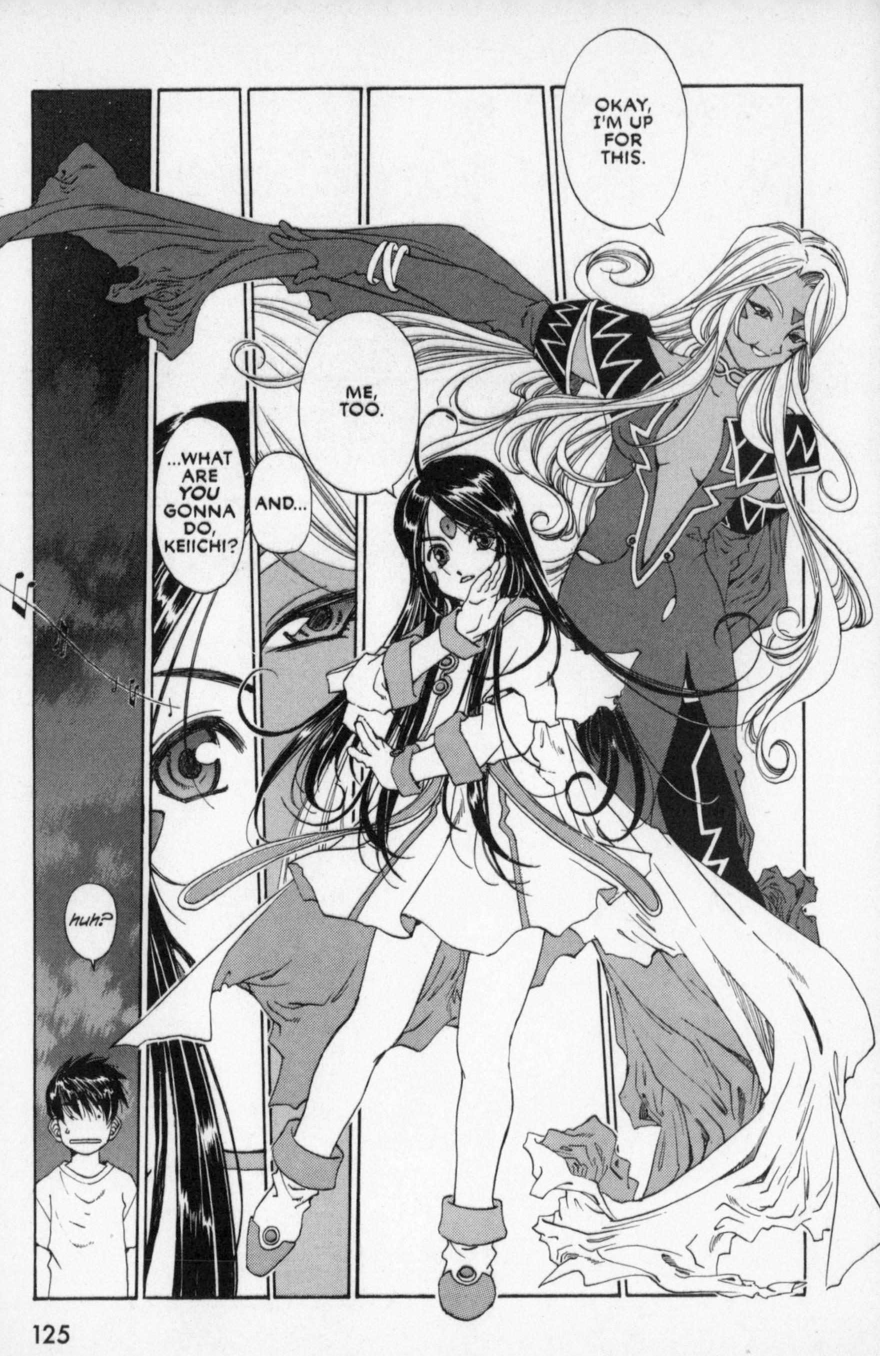
OKAY, I'M UP FOR THIS.
ME, TOO.
AND...
...WHAT ARE *YOU* GONNA DO, KEIICHI?
huh?

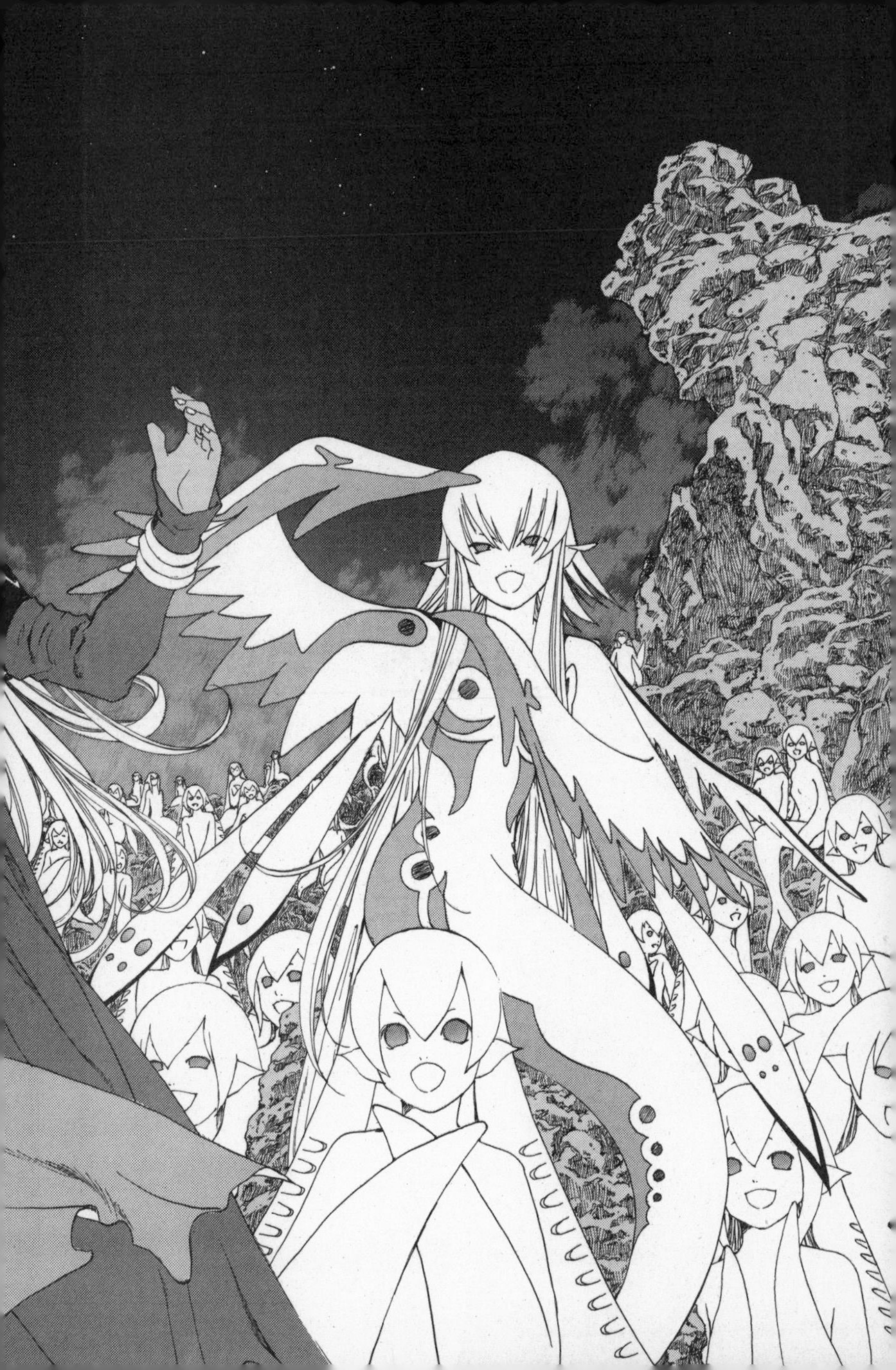

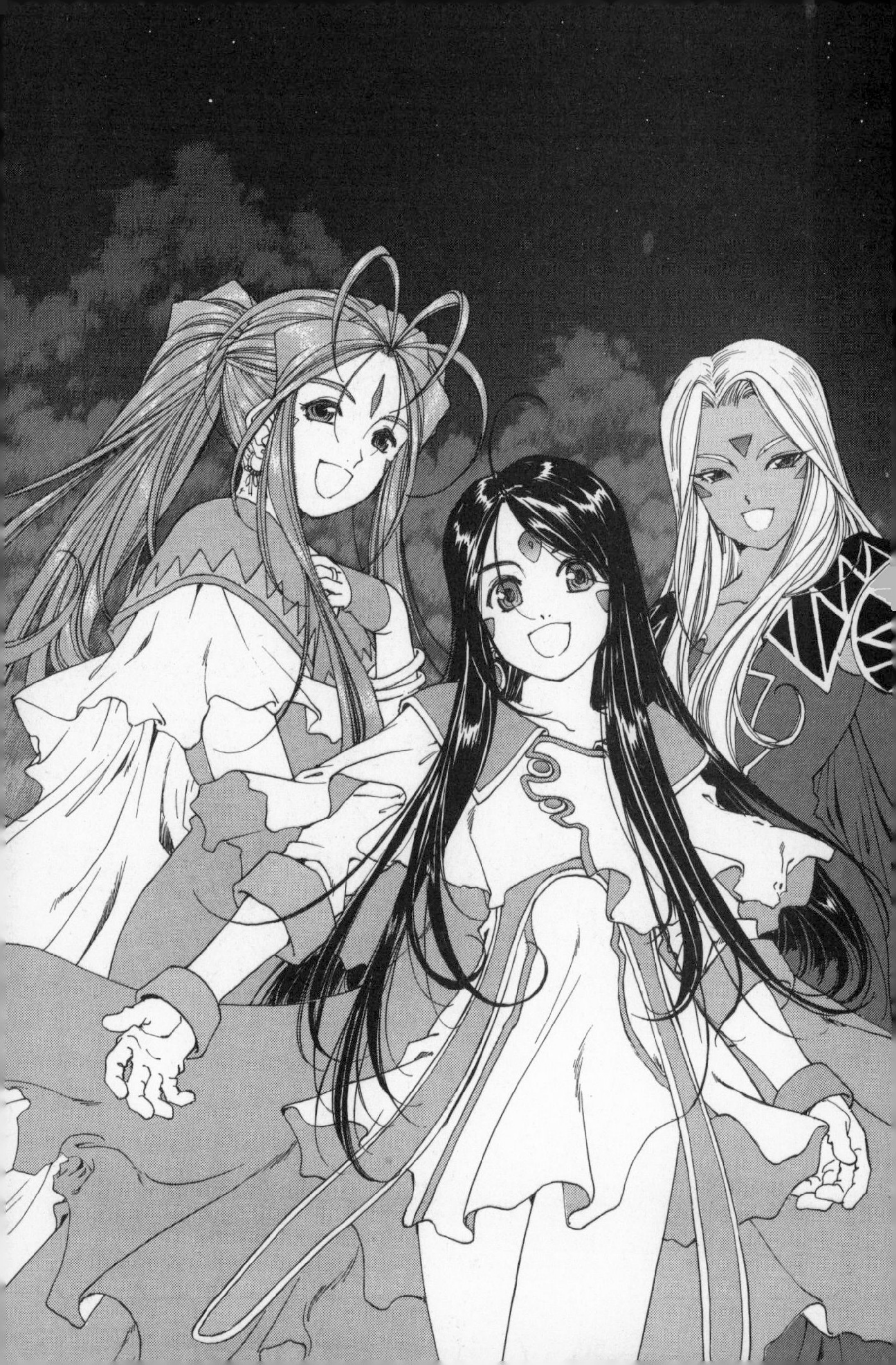

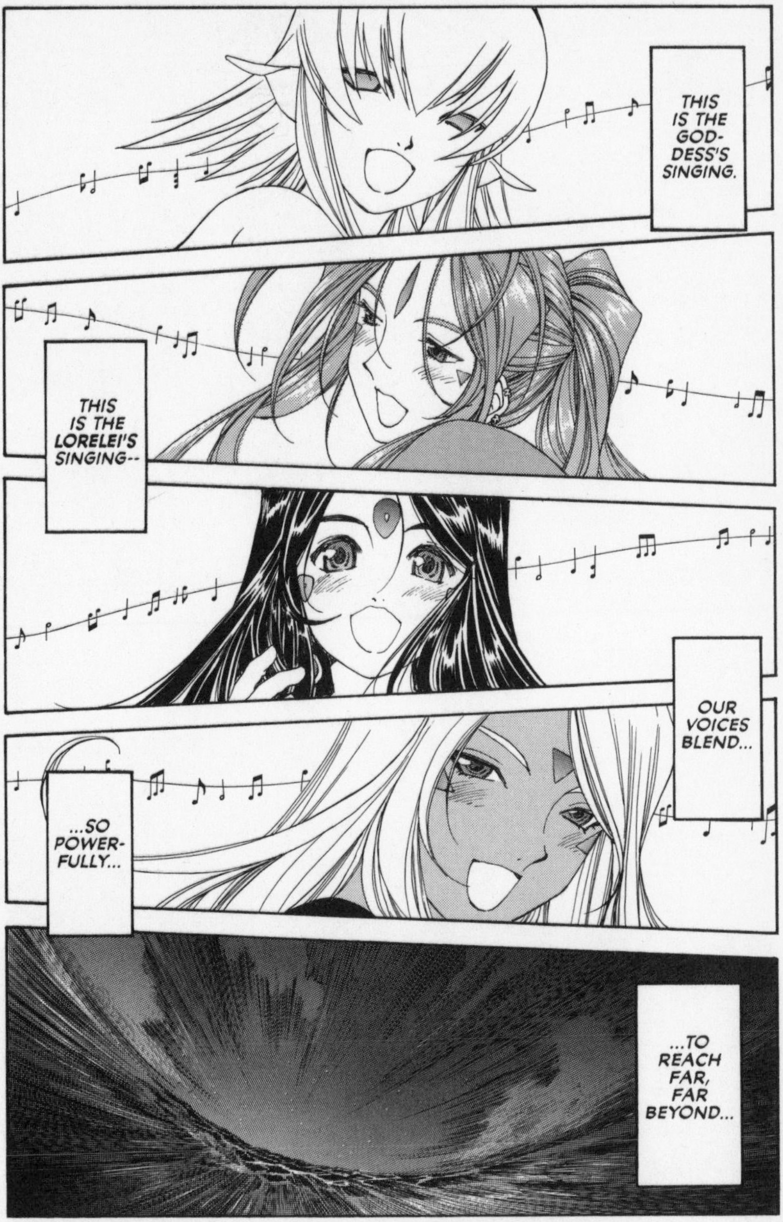
THIS IS THE GOD-DESS'S SINGING.
THIS IS THE LORELEI'S SINGING--
OUR VOICES BLEND...
...SO POWER-FULLY...
...TO REACH FAR, FAR BEYOND...

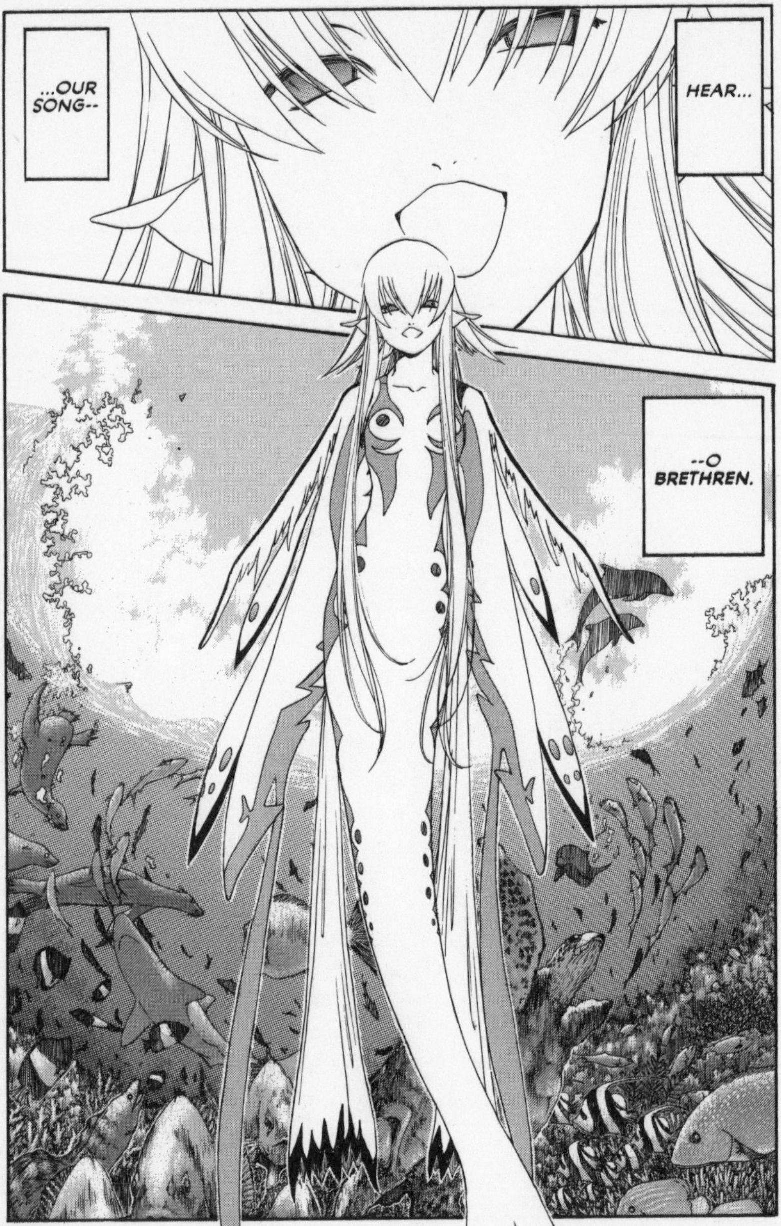
HEAR...
...OUR SONG--
--O BRETHREN.

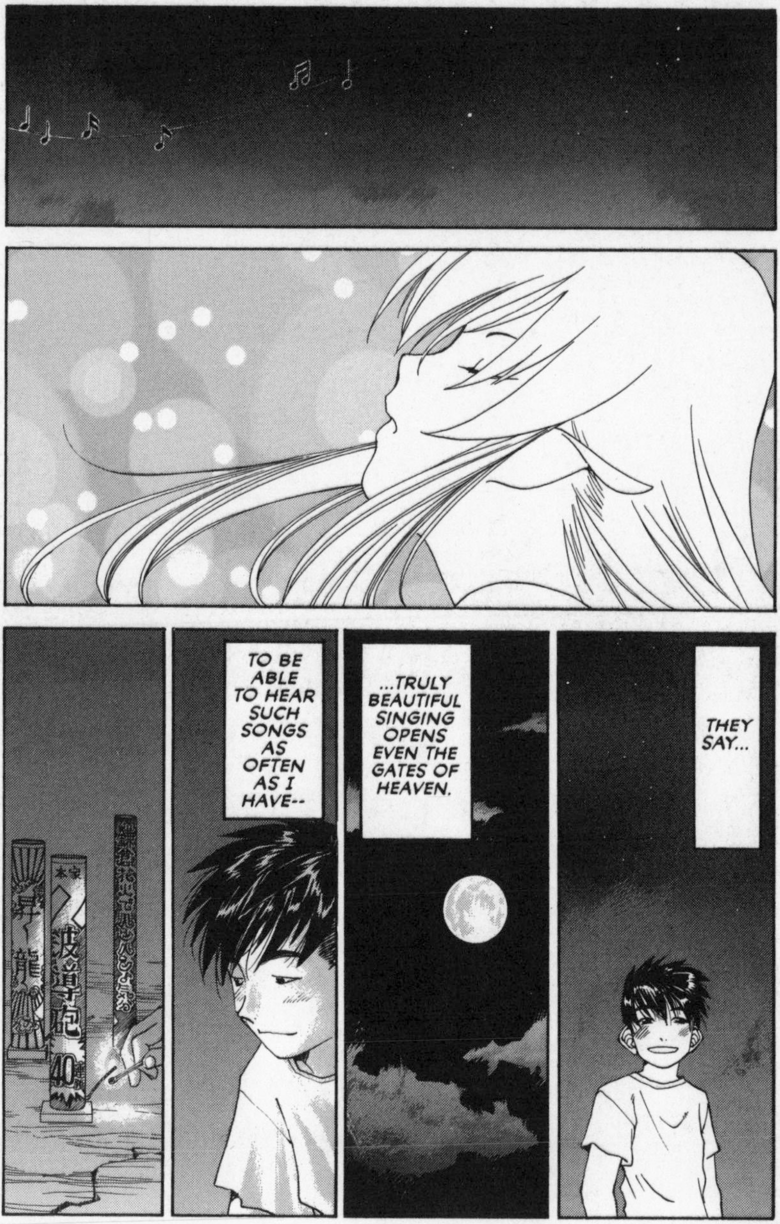
THEY SAY...
...TRULY BEAUTIFUL SINGING OPENS EVEN THE GATES OF HEAVEN.
TO BE ABLE TO HEAR SUCH SONGS AS OFTEN AS I HAVE--

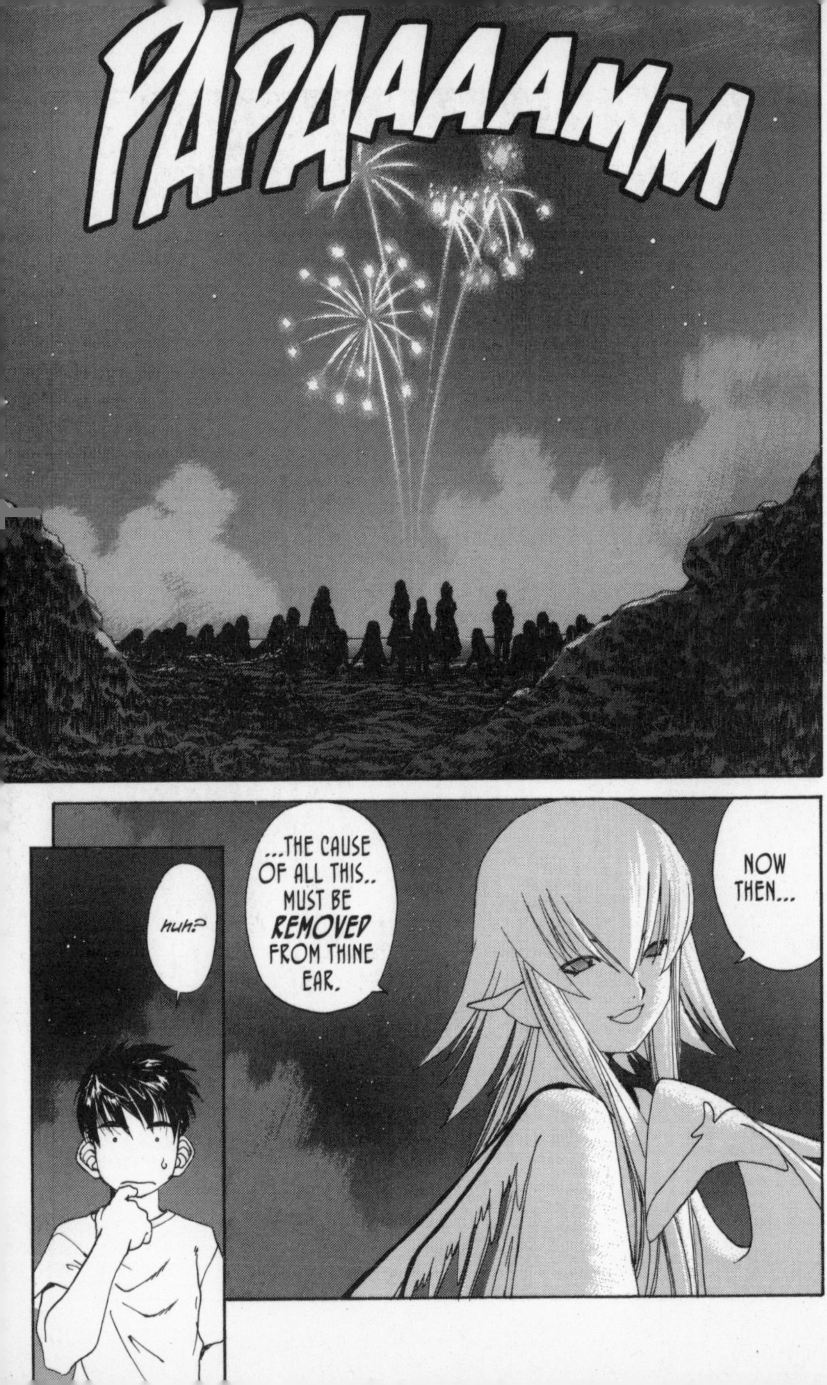
PAPAAAAMM
NOW THEN...
...THE CAUSE OF ALL THIS.. MUST BE REMOVED FROM THINE EAR.
huh?

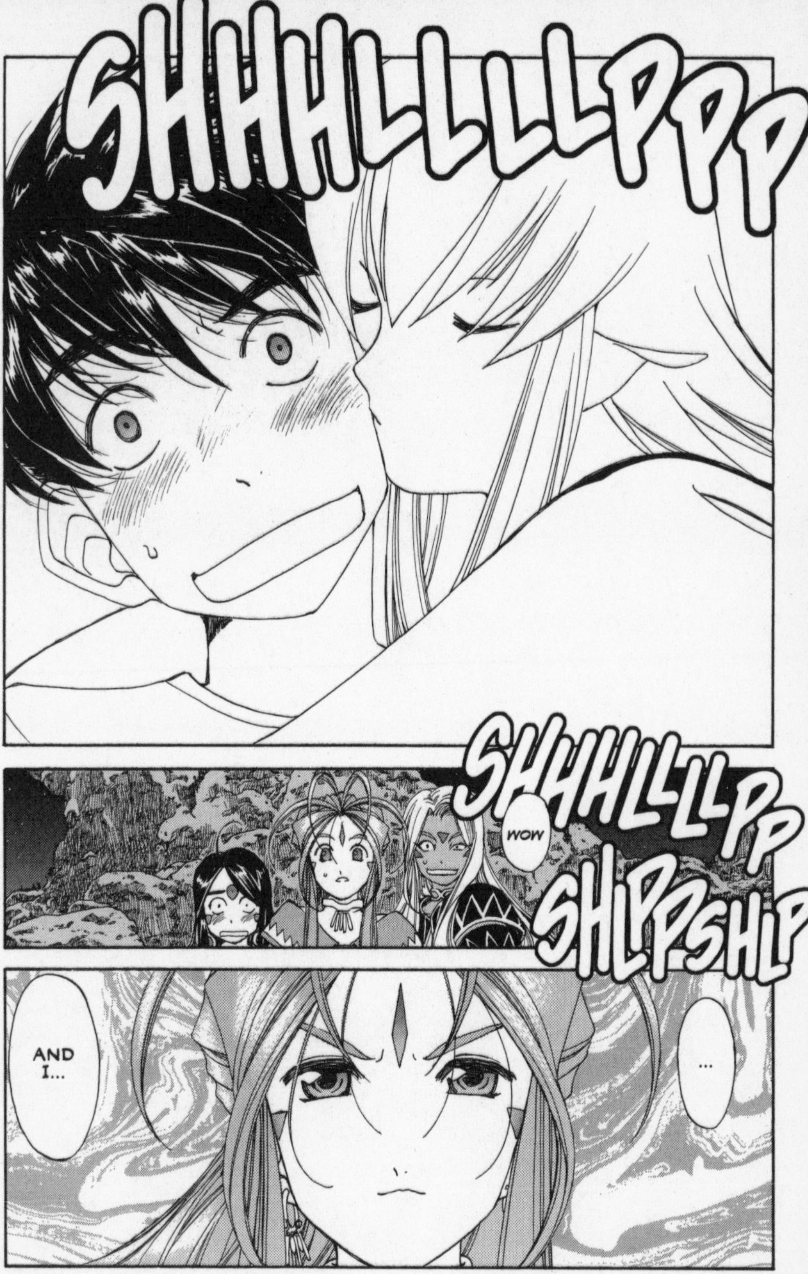
SHHHLLLLPPP
SHHHLLLPP
SHLPSHLP
WOW
...
AND I...

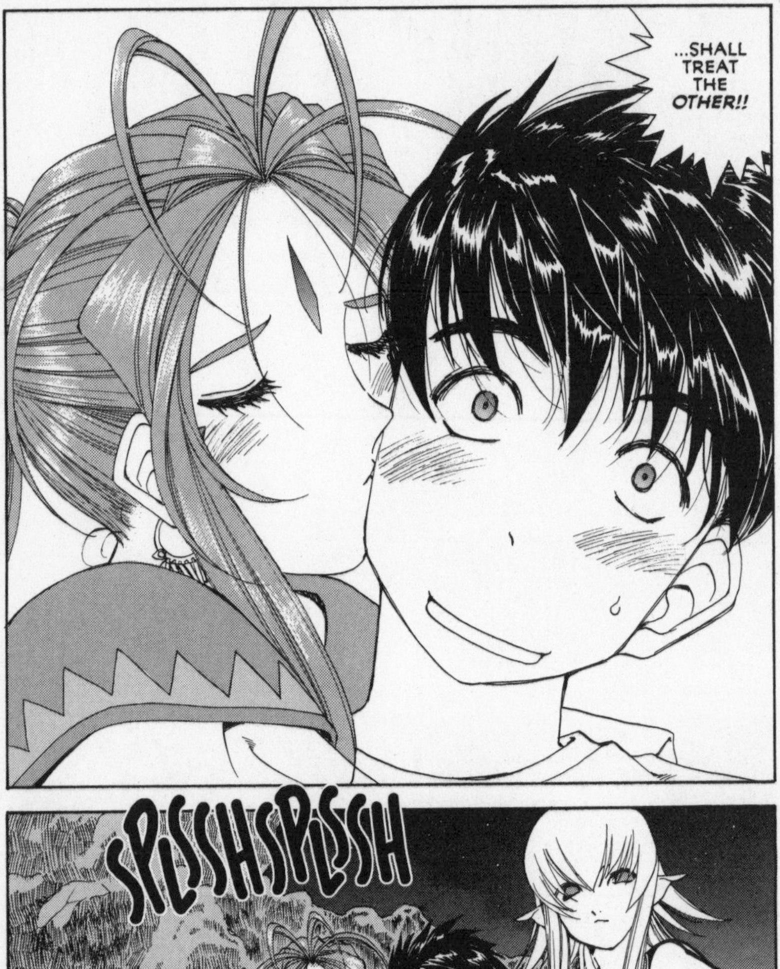
...SHALL TREAT THE *OTHER!!*
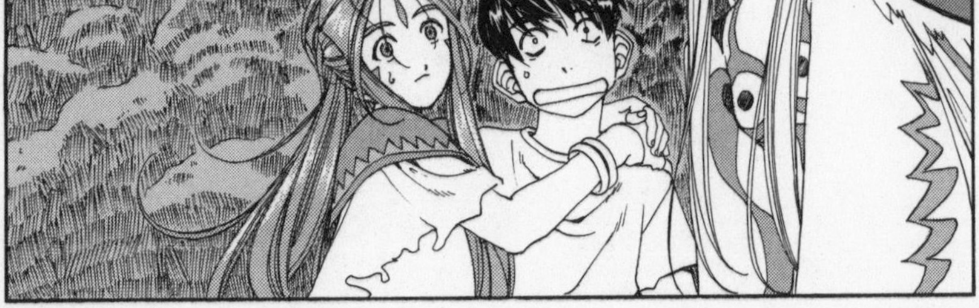
SPLSSHSPLSSH

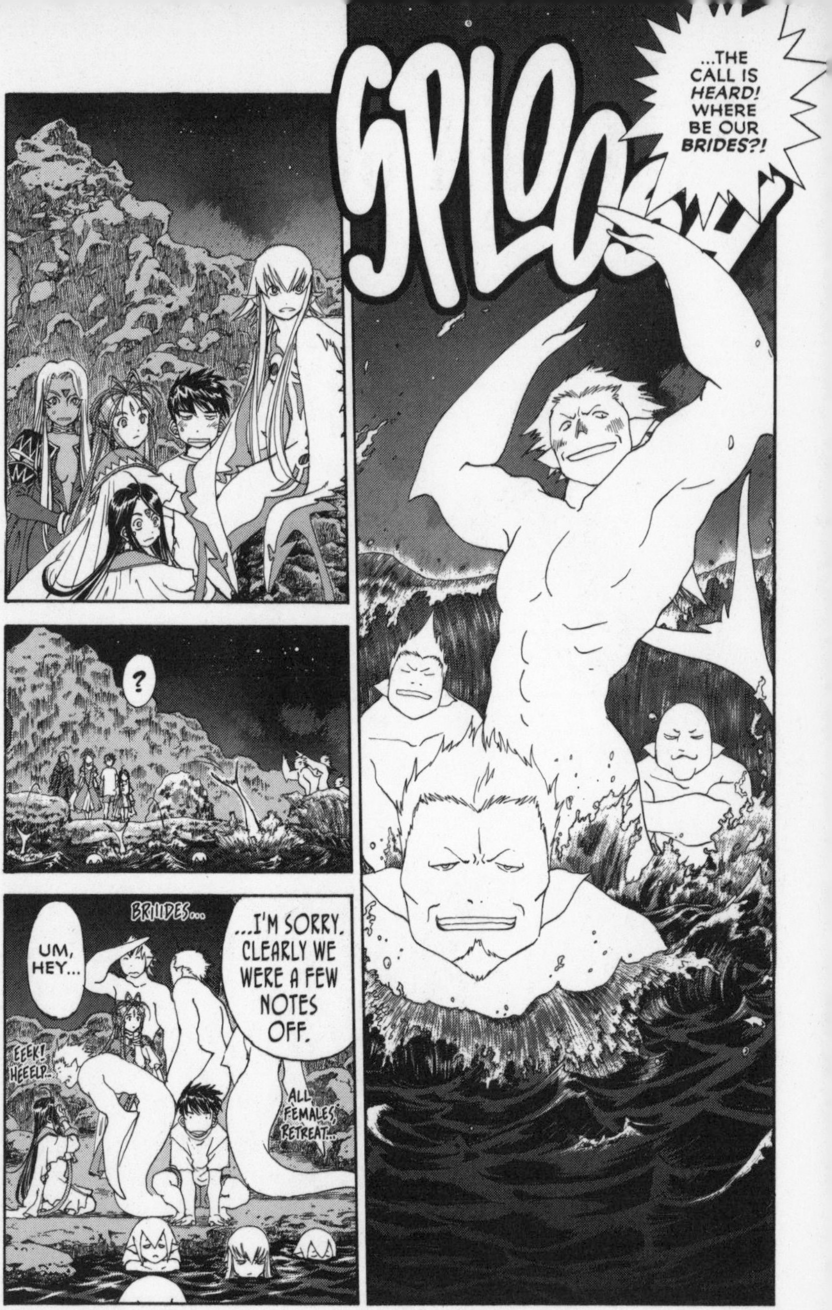
SPLOOSH
...THE CALL IS HEARD! WHERE BE OUR BRIDES?!
?
BRIIDES...
...I'M SORRY. CLEARLY WE WERE A FEW NOTES OFF.
UM, HEY...
EEEK! HEEELP...
ALL FEMALES, RETREAT...

OH MY GODDESS!
PEORTH

EDITOR
Carl Gustav Horn

DESIGNER
Scott Cook

PUBLISHER
Mike Richardson

English-language version
produced by Dark Horse Comics

OH MY GODDESS! Vol. 32

Published by Dark Horse Manga
A division of Dark Horse Comics, Inc.
10956 SE Main Street
Milwaukie, OR 97222
darkhorse.com

To find a comics shop in your area,
call the Comic Shop Locator Service
toll-free at 1-888-266-4226

First edition: May 2009
ISBN 978-1-59582-303-8

1 3 5 7 9 10 8 6 4 2

Printed in Canada

letters to the
ENCHANTRESS

10956 SE Main Street, Milwaukie, Oregon 97222
omg@darkhorse.com • darkhorse.com

NOTE: Full addresses and e-mail addresses will not be printed, unless you ask! All fan artwork, letters, and e-mails submitted become the property of Dark Horse Comics.

No doubt you're wondering what was up with Gate ending so many of her sentences with "you know?" This is to reflect her corresponding mannerism in Japanese of ending sentences with "*na no,*" which can be very cute or very irritating, depending on your point of view. This sort of thing is still somewhat fashionable among otaku-oriented manga. While otaku certainly aren't *OMG!*'s only readers, they have always supported it (what other manga would have had a cameo by Hideaki Anno five years **before** *Neon Genesis Evangelion*, you know?). I believe the trend kicked off about a decade ago with *Di Gi Charat,* in which most of the female leads had the affectation. The most prominent such figure today—in fact, she's an internet meme—is Suiseiseki from *Rozen Maiden,* who ends every sentence with "*desu.*" I liked the way Kohta Hirano (a super-otaku himself) mocked the trend in Vol. 5 of *Hellsing,* where the hero's guardian angel, who is literally the actor Bruce Willis, ends every sentence with the *moe*-sounding suffix "-Willis."

I've said enough-Willis! The rest of this volume's *Letters to the Enchantress* is in the command of the man who has to lay it out every time, designer Scott Cook!

Horn-sama!

It's me, the man upstairs! And I am not talking about the Almighty One! It's me, Scott, your designer on *OMG!* Recently, online, I stumbled across a fan piece of Haruhi Suzumiya done by my second-favorite manga-ka of all time (the first being Rumiko Takahashi), *Blade of the Immortal*'s one and only Hiroaki Samura! The way he depicted Haruhi in his own style inspired me to create some fan art of my own, and whom better to draw than the devilishly clever, stunning-at-all-times goddess extraordinaire Urd! Urd is my favorite character in the *OMG!* universe; just don't trust that smile! You know she is always up to something!

Oh My Goddess! is one of my favorite projects to work on here at Dark Horse. I particularly enjoy seeing all the fan art that comes in as well as reading all the letters. I just *wish* there were more! Maybe I should try giving Tamiya a call . . . that seemed to work well for Keiichi. ^_^

Only sometimes almighty,
Designer Scott

Note: The fireworks in 130.6 say "Jolly Jolly Kamakura Fireworks," "original Wave Motion Gun-40 Shots" (this is a *Yamato/Star Blazers* reference) and "Rising Dragon."

—CGH

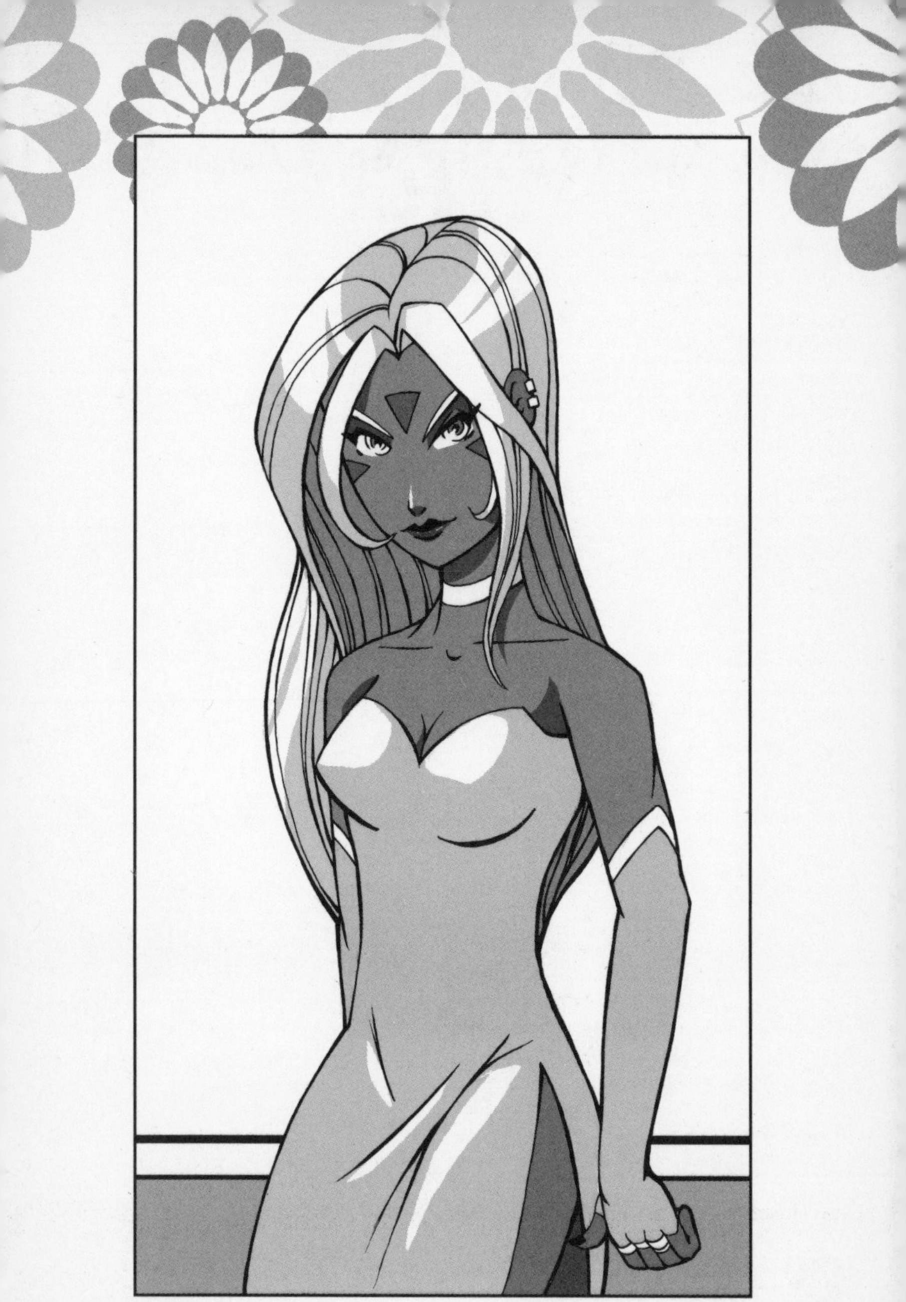

Kosuke Fujishima's Oh My Goddess!

Dark Horse is proud to re-present *Oh My Goddess!* in the much-requested, affordable, Japanese-reading, right-to-left format, complete with color sections, informative bonus notes, and your letters!

$10.95 each!

AVAILABLE AT YOUR LOCAL COMICS SHOP OR BOOKSTORE
*To find a comics shop in your area, call 1-888-266-4226

For more information or to order direct:
• On the web: darkhorse.com • E-mail: mailorder@darkhorse.com
• Phone: 1-800-862-0052 Mon.–Fri. 9 AM to 5 PM Pacific Time.

Kosuke Fujishima's

Oh My Goddess!

Can't wait on the Goddesses? Change directions!

Just gotten into the new unflopped editions of *Oh My Goddess!*, and found you can't wait to see what happens next? Have no fear! The first **20 volumes** of *Oh My Goddess!* are available ***right now*** in Western-style editions! Released between 1994 and 2005, our *OMG!* Western-style volumes feature premium paper, and pages 40% larger than those of the unflopped editions! If you've already got some of the unflopped volumes and want to know which Western-style ones to get to catch up, check out http://www.darkhorse.com/Zones/Manga for a complete breakdown of how the editions compare!

Vol. 1: Wrong Number
ISBN 1-56971-669-2 / $13.95

Vol. 2: Leader of the Pack
ISBN 1-56971-764-8 / $13.95

Vol. 3: Final Exam
ISBN 1-56971-765-6 / $13.95

Vol. 4: Love Potion No. 9
ISBN 1-56971-252-2 / $14.95

Vol. 5: Sympathy for the Devil
ISBN 1-56971-329-4 / $13.95

Vol. 6: Terrible Master Urd
ISBN 1-56971-369-3 / $14.95

Vol. 7: The Queen of Vengeance
ISBN 1-56971-431-2 / $13.95

Vol. 8: Mara Strikes Back!
ISBN 1-56971-449-5 / $14.95

Vol. 9: Ninja Master
ISBN 1-56971-474-6 / $13.95

Vol. 10: Miss Keiichi
ISBN 1-56971-522-X / $16.95

Vol. 11: The Devil in Miss Urd
ISBN 1-56971-540-8 / $14.95

Vol. 12: The Fourth Goddess
ISBN 1-56971-551-3 / $18.95

Vol. 13: Childhood's End
ISBN 1-56971-685-4/ $15.95

Vol. 14: Queen Sayoko
ISBN 1-56971-766-4 / $16.95

Vol. 15: Hand in Hand
ISBN 1-56971-921-7 / $17.95

Vol. 16: Mystery Child
ISBN 1-56971-950-0 / $18.95

Vol. 17: Traveler
ISBN 1-56971-986-1 / $17.95

Vol. 18: The Phantom Racer
ISBN 1-59307-217-1 / $17.95

Vol. 19/20: Sora Unchained
ISBN 1-59307-316-X / $18.95

Adventures of the Mini-Goddesses
ISBN 1-56971-421-5 / $9.95

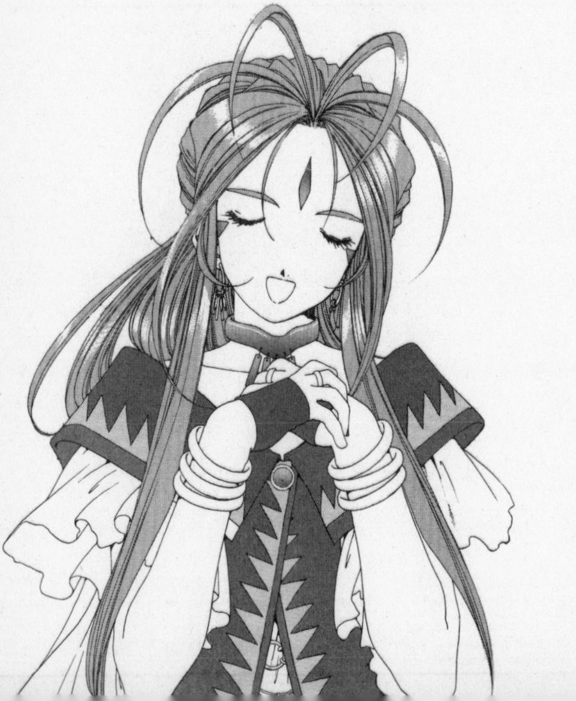

AVAILABLE AT YOUR LOCAL COMICS SHOP OR BOOKSTORE
*To find a comics shop in your area, call 1-888-266-4226

For more information or to order direct:
- On the web: darkhorse.com
- E-mail: mailorder@darkhorse.com
- Phone: 1-800-862-0052 Mon.-Fri. 9 A.M. to 5 P.M. Pacific Time.

AN ALL-NEW NOVEL BASED ON THE HIT MANGA AND ANIME!

OH MY GODDESS!
— FIRST END —

WRITTEN BY
YUMI TOHMA

WITH ILLUSTRATIONS BY
KOSUKE FUJISHIMA AND HIDENORI MATSUBARA

Keiichi Morisato was a typical college student—a failure with women, he was struggling to get through his classes and in general living a pretty nondescript life. That is, until he dialed a wrong number and accidentally summoned the goddess Belldandy. Not believing Belldandy was a goddess and that she could grant his every wish, Keiichi wished for her to stay with him forever. As they say, be careful what you wish for! Now bound to Earth and at Keiichi's side for life, the lives of this goddess and human will never be the same again!

ISBN 978-1-59582-137-9 | $14.95

---

darkhorse.com

AVAILABLE AT YOUR LOCAL COMICS SHOP OR BOOKSTORE
To find a comics shop in your area, call 1.888.266.4226. For more information or to order direct: •On the web: darkhorse.com •E-mail: mailorder@darkhorse.com •Phone: 1.800.862.0052 Mon.–Fri. 9 AM to 5 PM Pacific Time.

Oh My Goddess!: First End © 2006, 2007 Yumi Tohma/Kosuke Fujishima. All rights reserved. First published in Japan in 2006 by Kodansha Ltd., Tokyo. Publication rights for this English edition arranged through Kodansha Ltd. Dark Horse Books® and the Dark Horse logo are registered trademarks of Dark Horse Comics, Inc. All rights reserved. (BL7056)

EDEN

It's an Endless World!

Volume 1
ISBN 978-1-59307-406-7

Volume 2
ISBN 978-1-59307-454-8

Volume 3
ISBN 978-1-59307-529-3

Volume 4
ISBN 978-1-59307-544-6

Volume 5
ISBN 978-1-59307-634-4

Volume 6
ISBN 978-1-59307-702-0

Volume 7
ISBN 978-1-59307-765-5

Volume 8
ISBN 978-1-59307-787-7

Volume 9
ISBN 978-1-59307-851-5

Volume 10
ISBN 978-1-59307-957-4

Volume 11
ISBN 978-1-59582-244-4

$12.95 each!

【ㄣᄉᄉᄉᄉᄉ—ᄆᄉᄉ】
translucent

Can you see right through her?

By Kazuhiro Okamoto

Shizuka is an introverted girl dealing with schoolwork, boys, and a medical condition that has begun to turn her invisible! She finds support with Mamoru, a boy who is falling for Shizuka despite her condition, and with Keiko, a woman who suffers from the same illness and has finally turned *completely* invisible! *Translucent's* exploration of what people see, what people think they see, and what people wish to see in themselves, and others, makes for an emotionally sensitive manga peppered with moments of surprising humor, heartbreak, and drama.

VOLUME 1
ISBN 978-1-59307-647-4

VOLUME 2
ISBN 978-1-59307-677-1

VOLUME 3
ISBN 978-1-59307-679-5

VOLUME 4
ISBN 978-1-59582-218-5

$9.95 Each!

Previews for *TRANSLUCENT* and other DARK HORSE MANGA titles can be found at darkhorse.com!

AVAILABLE AT YOUR LOCAL COMICS SHOP OR BOOKSTORE
To find a comics shop in your area, call 1-888-266-4226. For more information or
to order direct: • On the web: darkhorse.com • E-mail: mailorder@darkhorse.com
• Phone: 1-800-862-0052 Mon.–Fri. 9 AM to 5 PM Pacific Time.

DARK
HORSE
MANGA

STOP! This is the back of the book!

This manga collection is translated into English, but arranged in right-to-left reading format to maintain the artwork's visual orientation as originally drawn and published in Japan. If you've never read comics this way before, take a look at the diagram below to give yourself an idea of how to go about it. Basically, you'll be starting in the upper right-hand corner, and will read each word balloon and panel moving right-to-left. It may take a little getting used to, but you should get the hang of it very quickly. Have fun! If this is the millionth manga you've read this way, never mind. ^_^

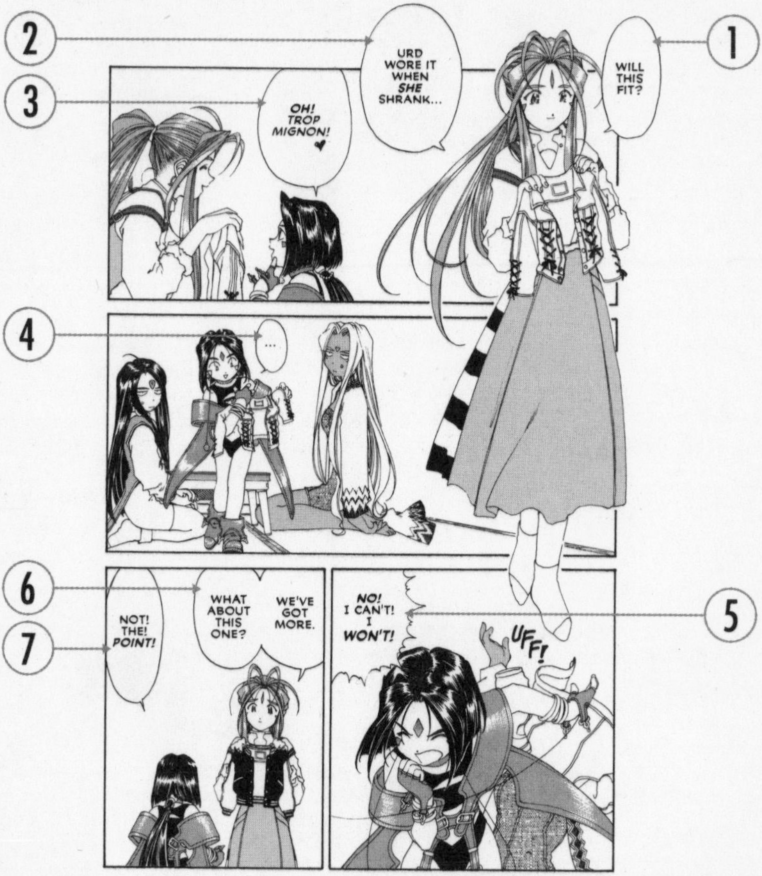
1
WILL THIS FIT?
2
URD WORE IT WHEN *SHE* SHRANK...
3
OH! TROP MIGNON! ♥
4
...
5
NO! I CAN'T! I *WON'T!*
UFF!
6
WE'VE GOT MORE.
WHAT ABOUT THIS ONE?
7
NOT! THE! *POINT!*